Motivational Analyses of Social Behavior

Building on Jack Brehm's Contributions to Psychology

Edited by

Rex A. Wright
University of Alabama at Birmingham
Jeff Greenberg
University of Arizona
Sharon S. Brehm
Indiana University–Bloomington

New York London

First published by
Lawrence Erlbaum Associates, Inc., Publishers
10 Industrial Avenue
Mahwah, New Jersey 07430

First issued in paperback 2012

This edition published 2012 by Psychology Press

Psychology Press
Taylor & Francis Group
711 Third Avenue
New York, NY 10017

Psychology Press
Taylor & Francis Group
27 Church Road
Hove, East Sussex BN3 2FA

Psychology Press is an imprint of Taylor & Francis, an informa group company

Cover design by Kathryn Houghtaling Lacey

Library of Congress Cataloging-in-Publication Data

Motivational Analyses of Social Behavior: Building on Jack Brehm's Contributions to Psychology, edited by Rex A. Wright, Jeff Greenberg and Sharon S. Brehm.
p. cm.
Includes bibliographical references and index.
ISBN: 0-8058-4266-7 (cloth: alk. paper).
ISBN: 978-0-415-65030-4 (Paperback)
Copyright information for this volume can be obtained by contacting the Library of Congress.

Contents

Preface

This book honors Jack Brehm's contributions to psychology. Jack is best known for his work on dissonance theory, reactance theory, and the intensity of motivation. These scientific contributions all revolve around a central theme of motivation and social behavior. And it is this theme that forms the major topic addressed by the substantive chapters of this book.

The idea of a festschrift for Jack has been floating about for some time. As best we can tell, it first was expressed over a decade ago when various of Jack's students and colleagues gathered in Lawrence, Kansas, to celebrate Jack's 60th birthday. The birthday event became known informally as "Jackfest" and was followed by a similar event ("Jackfest II") organized when Jack retired from his regular faculty position at the University of Kansas. Once the second "fest" was concluded, it was clear that a written festschrift would be forthcoming. The only uncertainties were when the volume would appear and who would contribute to it. We are delighted to have been able to participate as editors and authors, and we want to thank all the contributors for their fine contributions and eagerness to be involved in this project.

This volume reflects Jack's influence, personally as well as professionally. It begins with two personal chapters, one written by us and the other written by one of Jack's oldest friends in academia, Peter Schönbach. Our chapter provides a brief overview of Jack's academic life and accomplishments, and conveys something of what it has been like for us to know and work with Jack. Peter's chapter describes his own early experiences with

Jack, the development of their friendship, and the extension of their friendship across time.

The next section of the volume presents a collection of substantive chapters authored by people whose work Jack has strongly influenced. These chapters are ordered roughly in terms of their relevance to Brehm's best known contributions, with those most relevant to dissonance theory coming first, those most relevant to reactance theory coming next, and those most relevant to motivational intensity coming last. Approximately half of the substantive chapters were prepared by Jack's students, with the other half by professional colleagues. These chapters are current and significant contributions to the study of social motivation, and their worth is independent of any intention to honor Jack's contributions to psychology. Indeed, they honor Jack precisely by being of value in their own right. The volume concludes with a chapter by Jack that reflects on the field of social psychology, that discusses a new theory of social influence, and that offers ideas about the direction in which our understanding of human behavior could move. Following Jack's chapter is a listing of his PhD students.

There has been one very sad note to the otherwise gratifying experience of coediting this book. During the book's preparation, one of our coauthors, Shelley Duval, died unexpectedly and at a relatively young age. Shelley was a brilliant, gentle man as well as an important theorist and researcher in our field. We are honored to have his chapter with Paul Silvia included in this book; it displays many of his fine qualities. His loss is felt by many, both personally and professionally.

This book would not have been produced without the effort of people other than the editors and the chapter authors. We are especially indebted to Daniel Batson. Dan and his wife, Judy, have been two of Jack's closest friends since Jack moved to the University of Kansas in 1975. Sometimes at Jack's place, other times at Dan and Judy's, there has been a continuous stream of parties and dinners—with Jack or Judy doing the cooking, and Dan expressing his great appreciation. Every spring, for a number of years now, Jack, Judy, and some other Lawrence friends have taken off for the South Carolina beach to enjoy a week in the sun. In addition to being a close friend, Dan has been Jack's closest colleague in the Kansas Psychology Department. Along with other long-time Kansas faculty, they have sustained a legendary social psychology program that included in its early days such psychology luminaries as Roger Barker, Fritz Heider, and Beatrice Wright. Dan played a major role in organizing the conferences that gave rise to the idea of a festschrift, and he also generously allowed us to use biographical information from the introduction he gave when Jack received the Society of Experimental Social Psychology's Distinguished Scientist Award. We thank Dan for his support and encouragement throughout the preparation of this volume.

Others to whom we wish to express our appreciation include Judson Mills, Robert Zajonc, Debra Riegert, and Jason Planer. Jud and Bob responded kindly to questions we posed concerning past events at the Universities of Iowa and Minnesota. Debra and Jason were a joy to work with during the editorial process and are to be praised especially for their patience in dealing with a set of editors who did not always make the deadlines that they set for themselves.

I

ABOUT JACK

1

Biographical Sketch and Personal Perspectives

Rex A. Wright
University of Alabama at Birmingham

Jeff Greenberg
University of Arizona

Sharon S. Brehm
Indiana University Bloomington

The faculties of universities around the world include people who have made significant contributions to psychology. However, they contain few who have affected their field and those around them as profoundly as has Jack Brehm. Known internationally for his research and theorizing, Jack is also widely admired as a mentor, colleague, and human being of uncommon character. If Jung had known Jack, he likely would have declared him to be someone extraordinarily true to the archetype of the seeker of knowledge. As all who do know him soon realize, Jack marches to the sound of his own internal drummer. And what he marches toward is the goal of pure knowledge and understanding. Regardless of the social, cultural, or professional Zeitgeist, Jack has painstakingly studied what he has found to be interesting. The result has been a powerful body of work that will be utilized and built on for years to come.

In this chapter, we provide a brief biography of Jack and some personal glimpses of Jack as we have known him.

A BIOGRAPHICAL SKETCH

Jack W. Brehm was born January 16, 1928, to Carl and Charlotte Williams Brehm. He grew up in Des Moines, Iowa, not far from another Des Moines notable, Cloris Leachman. After high school, Jack served in the Navy for 2 years (1946–1948) and then attended Harvard College on the GI Bill (1948–1952). At Harvard, Jack took Social Psychology from Garner Lindzey and Group Dynamics from Howard Riecken. He also prepared an honors thesis under the supervision of Riecken and Robert Blake. Jack's mother was a welfare caseworker most of her life, and Jack intended to continue the helping tradition by becoming a clinical psychologist. However, he was advised by Blake to develop his research skills instead. In 1952, Jack traveled to the University of Minnesota to study with Leon Festinger, who at the time was developing his soon-to-be-famous theory of cognitive dissonance. Jack's PhD dissertation introduced the free-choice dissonance paradigm and was the first published experiment designed to test dissonance processes (Brehm, 1956).

During his career, Jack has been a member of the faculty at Yale University (1955–1958), Duke University (1958–1975), and the University of Kansas (1975–present). He has also held temporary appointments at the University of Washington (1963–1964, 1973–1974), the State University of New York at Stony Brook (1968–1969), Universität Mannheim (1978), Colorado College (1982), Princeton University (1986), and Universität Bielefeld (1994). While at Yale, Jack and Robert Cohen conducted seminal dissonance studies focusing on the role of choice and commitment in dissonance processes. After moving to Duke, Jack continued his research on dissonance and wrote extensively on the theory. His dissonance publications during the Duke years included a highly influential *Nebraska Symposium on Motivation* chapter (Brehm, 1962) and two classic books, one with Cohen (Brehm & Cohen, 1962) and another with Robert Wicklund (Wicklund & Brehm, 1976). Taken as a whole, Jack's work on dissonance has played a major role in the understanding and continuing investigation of dissonance processes for almost half a century.

At Duke, Jack conceived of and began testing another theory of motivation—psychological reactance. Jack's early reactance work at Duke led to numerous scientific publications, ranging from a classic article (Brehm & Cole, 1966) on the potential of a favor to diminish the tendency to help (which stands as the only article in the history of the *Journal of Personality and Social Psychology* to cite no references) to his monograph proposing and documenting the theory (Brehm, 1966). Later reactance work at the university led to additional publications, including a reactance theory update (Brehm, 1972) and a widely cited chapter with Camille Wortman that integrated reactance and learned helplessness processes (Wortman & Brehm, 1975). Like Festinger's dissonance theory, Jack's reactance theory has had an extraordinary impact, both in the United States and beyond. It has been studied extensively not only in social psychology, but also in other disciplines such as political science and marketing, and has been applied in countless contexts ranging from clinical psychology to business.

Since moving to the University of Kansas, Jack has continued to contribute to the dissonance and reactance literatures. For example, he and Sharon Brehm published their book evaluating reactance theory and comprehensively reviewing the research related to it (S. Brehm & J. Brehm, 1981). He also has written articles with Linda Simon, Jeff Greenberg, and others on topics such as trivialization as a mode of dissonance reduction (Simon, Greenberg, & Brehm, 1995) and the question of whether aversive behavioral consequences are necessary for dissonance to be aroused (Harmon-Jones, Brehm, Greenberg, Simon, & Nelson, 1996).

However, the bulk of Jack's time at Kansas has been devoted to understanding processes even more basic than dissonance and reactance. One central interest has been in the determinants of motivational intensity, or effort expended at a point in time. Work on this topic began with an unpublished paper (Brehm, 1979) that outlined elements of a motivation intensity theory (referred to at different points in its evolution as a "theory of motivational suppression" and later as "energization theory"). Work on this topic continued through the 1980s and led to various publications, most notably a chapter in the *Annual Review of Psychology* with Elizabeth Self (Brehm & Self, 1989). Since their proposal, Jack's ideas about motivational intensity have received attention from a variety of academic quarters, particularly from psychophysiologists attempting to understand effort-related cardiovascular responses (Wright, 1996; Wright & Kirby, 2001).

A second main interest at Kansas has been only a step removed from motivational intensity; the determinants of *emotional* intensity, or affect experienced at a point in time. Jack's ideas on this topic are still relatively new. Nonetheless, they have generated a good deal of research, much of which was reported in an article that appeared in the *Personality and Social Psychology Review* (Brehm, 1999).

PERSONAL PERSPECTIVES

As is the case with all academics, Jack's influence has not been restricted to the impact of his published work. He has also influenced many people through his personal interactions with them—as a mentor, as a colleague, as an individual of great kindness and generosity. To convey some of what it's like to know and work with Jack, each of us offers below a summary of how he has contributed to our own development.

Sharon Brehm

Somehow in writing this commentary, I have the sense that I'm in a 19th-century novel, and the author's voice is booming over me: "And, dear reader, she married him." Yes, I did marry Jack, in the fall of 1968, having first met him in the spring of 1967 when I applied for a job as research assistant and worked for him that summer. We lived in New York from 1968 to 1969 and then moved back to North Carolina. After I completed my PhD at Duke in 1973, we went to Seattle for Jack's sabbatical and for my clinical psychology internship. During our one year of a commuter marriage, when I had a temporary appointment at Virginia Tech and Jack was back at Duke, we also suffered through the challenges of a dual-career job hunt. Fortunately, we found a welcoming group of colleagues at the University of Kansas and moved to Lawrence in 1975. Unfortunately, however, our marriage had started to fray around the edges; by 1978, it had unraveled entirely.

But that's not the end of the story. After having been an extraordinarily supportive husband and mentor when I was in graduate school, and having insisted that I should have a "real" tenure-track job even if that meant that he would have to leave Duke, Jack became an extraordinarily supportive ex-husband and continuing mentor. We wrote a book together *after* we were divorced. And we tried to set an example of an amicable divorce, joking that we were the first in our neighborhood to have one! It was OK, we reassured people, to invite us to the same parties.

And here I am now, in 2002, working with Rex and Jeff on a book in honor of Jack's contributions to social psychology. But that's typical—not of me, but of Jack. In his quiet, unobtrusive way, he maintains one of the largest networks of friends and colleagues that I've ever seen. So, although you don't hear from him all that often nor see him **so** frequently, he is there, just enough, to stay in touch. Whenever there's a project afoot, like this one, the network is easy to mobilize.

Across all his relationships, two of Jack's most distinct characteristics can be easily observed. First, there is his absolute fidelity to the value of intellectual (and, for that matter, artistic) accomplishments of the first rank. Jack is playful, amusing, and in no way pompous. But he is fundamentally an aristocrat of the mind. He believes that there is first-class work in this world and that we should all strive for that level of understanding (or performance). Coming in as a close second, the more you get to know him, the more you realize that he is also an absolute egalitarian in his reaction to people. He simply doesn't care what gender you are, what your family background is, how rich you might be, or the titles you have on your business card. All he wants to know is whether you've got anything interesting to talk about. These two characteristics have helped to make him a fine scientist, and they have ensured that he would become one of social psychology's greatest teachers.

Rex Wright

I studied with Jack at the University of Kansas shortly after he moved there from Duke. I had worked as an undergraduate at the University of Texas with two of Jack's students, Richard Archer and Robert Wicklund. So the step from Austin to Lawrence seemed natural.

My memories of graduate school are a tangle of the personal and the professional, largely because of Jack's style in dealing with students. People who work with Jack do not meet with him only in his office and only at daily, weekly, or monthly intervals. Rather, they generally step into the stream of Jack's life. Research discussions are as likely to take place at a café or on the road to some gathering as they are in Jack's office. And when discussions do occur in Jack's office, they frequently are spontaneous, beginning when a student drops by unannounced and ending when someone simply has to attend to something more pressing. To be sure, there are formal aspects to studying with Jack. But those aspects are embedded in a context of informality. Among other things, this leads students to view academics not as a career separable from one's personal life, but as a way of life.

I am among Jack's greatest admirers. Therefore, it may come as a surprise that the fit between Jack and me as mentor and student initially was not perfect. For one thing, I found it maddening that Jack would respond so frequently to my research ideas with a reflective, "Hmm. So why do you find that interesting?" As a green graduate student not too far removed in time from the Gulf of Mexico shrimp boats around which I was raised, I felt that the ideas were interesting, darn it, just because they were. It was only later that I came to understand that Jack was nudging me to think about psychological processes, and in theoretical terms.

In addition, I arrived at Kansas when Jack was developing his ideas about the intensity of motivation. Although I tried to approach Jack's emerging intensity theory with an open mind, I found it at first to be dry and uninspiring. Little did I know then that within a few years, I would become captivated by motivation intensity questions and would begin devoting ridiculous amounts of time and energy to answering them.

Jack and I got on famously once we (read "I") moved past these problems. He guided me through the minefields of graduate school, and has remained available as a friend and consultant. Over the years, we have shared dozens of dinners together, traveled on occasion, and spent countless hours discussing matters large and small. I don't seek Jack's advice as often now as I did in the early years; but I do still seek his advice. Even when I don't consult with Jack directly, I sometimes do so indirectly by asking myself what he would do if confronted with the situation in which I find myself. The answer usually provides good direction for my behavior.

Many people have speculated about Jack's "secrets," those things that allow him to be so successful as a teacher and appealing as a colleague and friend. High on my list of guesses are the following:

1. integrity,
2. a lack of pretentiousness,

3. an openness to human diversity,
4. an acceptance of human frailty,
5. a gift for disagreeing with people without putting them on the defensive,
6. a gift for identifying strengths in others, and, of course,
7. a formidable intellect.

Noticeably absent from the list are controlling motives that might come to mind, such as the desires to shape young minds, to persuade, and to lead. Jack does *not* attempt to control those around him, and this almost certainly is one of his secrets too.

It seems that our images of people are set early in our experience with them, and this holds true with respect to my image of Jack. No matter how much time passes or how much we change, I will always think of Jack, vintage about 1980. I envision him walking into Fraser Hall on a winter day wearing his cotton turtleneck shirt, his brown, button-up sweater, his faded "high water" jeans, and his puffy, blue, down jacket, having just crawled from his mud-covered Jeep Cherokee parked in the lot immediately east of the building. The image is not traditional for an academic, and it is fitting that it is not. Jack has never had an interest in conveying a scholarly image; he has been too busy being scholarly. In the end, that may be his most important secret of all.

Jeff Greenberg

I also studied with Jack at the University of Kansas beginning in 1978 and, like Rex, came to Lawrence directly from Texas. I arrived in Lawrence with a master's degree in social psychology from Southern Methodist University and a lot of youthful enthusiasm for research. I remember the first time I met Jack. I came to his office where he was smoking his pipe, for the first time experiencing that pleasant smell that became a reliable sign of Jack's presence in Fraser Hall—as soon as one entered the building, even when his office was on the sixth floor! I recall being very amused that conversations with Jack entailed brief sentences separated by extensive silences sometimes lasting 10 minutes (as did his seminars). And he was entirely comfortable with such silences, an admirable quality indeed. You see, Jack actually thinks carefully before he speaks, an extremely rare practice in America. Imagine if we could all emulate this consistently! But this was only one aspect of Jack that I came to admire and sought to emulate.

I was duly impressed with Jack but had planned to focus on attribution research with Mike Storms. However, I quickly learned that Mike had discontinued his research on that topic. I began talking with Dan Batson and worked a bit with him on his groundbreaking altruism research. Although I knew this was important work, I felt a need to pursue my own developing interests in attribution, self-esteem, and prejudice. I had begun collaborating on research on these topics with Tom Pyszczynski, and he suggested that I consider Jack as an advisor because Jack was especially supportive of graduate students pursuing their own ideas. And so he was. I learned that Jack was working on difficult (impossible?) research on motivational suppression theory, and while I joined in on that endeavor, Jack was also quite supportive of the research directions I had begun cultivating with Tom and another graduate student who worked with Jack, Sheldon Solomon.

From that point on, Jack became my spiritual advisor in social psychology, and like Tom and Sheldon, I found myself wanting to be like Jack—pensive, scholarly, focused on theoretically meaningful work. I recall barging into Jack's office, which seemed open to me 24/7, raving about some stupid article I had just read in *Journal of Personality and Social Psychology*, and how I wanted to design a study to support the obvious alternative explanation the authors had inexplicably overlooked. Jack listened to me and then said, "Do you want to do reactive research, pursuing a minor point poorly made by someone else, or do work of theoretical import?" Well, knowing the job market was tight, sometimes I just wanted a publication, but his point sunk in for me over time.

All that was great, but what really convinced me to want to be like Jack was my first (and many subsequent) visits to his magnificent house, complete with great views and stereo, in a hilltop forest outside of Lawrence. Jack not only showed me how to be a scholar, but what a good life one could have in doing so as well. More important, I learned from these visits the value, regardless of one's status or age, of being open to new ideas and experiences and of dealing with students with generosity and respect. As just one example of his open-mindedness, I recall trying to convince Jack that Bob Marley's music was really special. Although skeptical, he was willing to listen, and soon after became a Marley fan. It's too bad that by this time, Jack's hair had thinned too much for dreadlocks! And, as to his generosity, what better example than Jack giving his graduate students free reign of his extensive liquor cabinet!

I have not aspired to acquire as spectacular a house or as impressive a liquor cabinet as his, but I have tried to follow Jack's example of providing students with a fertile intellectual atmosphere that allows them to grow in their own chosen directions, while treating them with respect, warmth, and generosity. In the process, like Jack, I have forged lifelong friendships, and, hopefully, have helped pass this mentoring style on to a new generation.

A LARGER POINT OF VIEW

Of course, we are but three of the many people who have been influenced through knowing Jack as mentor, colleague, or friend, and often all three simultaneously. The list of Jack's graduate students is extensive and includes some extremely productive and influential scholars (see back of this volume). A formal listing of academic associates who have expressed a profound admiration for, and in many cases an intellectual debt to, Jack would be even more impressive. In this context, special mention must be made of Edward E. Jones, a longtime friend and colleague of Jack's. During their years together at Duke, Ned and Jack were the perfect academic partners—distinct in their research interests and totally congenial personally. With never a false step, they created one of the very best social psychology graduate programs in the country—and the excitement and camaraderie of those days at Duke will always remain as a standard for what academic life can, and should, be.

Currently, Jack is Professor Emeritus in the Department of Psychology at the University of Kansas. He lives in the airy, glass-and-wood home that he and Sharon built some 25 years ago on a wooded hillside in Baldwin County, Kansas. Jack's nonprofessional interests include cooking, electronics, and travel. Abiding comforts are classical music, Tanqueray gin, and an occasional cigar. Except in severe Kansas snowstorms, Jack continues to commute to his office at the University in his all-wheel-drive Subaru.

In this brief first chapter, we have attempted to convey the professional and personal qualities that have made Jack such a potent force in psychology. The rest of this volume undoubtedly makes this case far more convincingly, as the chapters reveal Jack's ongoing impact on the scholarly study of motivation and social behavior.

REFERENCES

Brehm, J. W. (1956). Post-decision changes in the desirability of alternatives. *Journal of Abnormal and Social Psychology, 52*, 384–389.

Brehm, J. W. (1962). Motivational effects of cognitive dissonance. In M. R. Jones (Ed.), *Nebraska Symposium on Motivation* (Vol. X, pp. 51–77). Lincoln, University of Nebraska Press.

Brehm, J. W. (1966). *A theory of psychological reactance*. New York: Academic Press.

Brehm, J. W. (1972). *Responses to loss of freedom: A theory of psychological reactance*. Morristown, NJ: General Learning Press.

Brehm, J. W. (1979). *Perceived difficulty and energization*. Unpublished manuscript, University of Kansas.

Brehm, J. W. (1999). The intensity of emotion. *Personality and Social Psychology Review, 3*, 2–22.

Brehm, J. W., & Cohen, A. R. (1962). *Explorations in cognitive dissonance*. New York: Wiley.

Brehm, J. W., & Cole, A. (1966). Effect of a favor which reduces freedom. *Journal of Personality and Social Psychology, 3,* 420–426.

Brehm, J. W., & Self, E. (1989). The intensity of motivation. In M. R. Rosenzweig & L. W. Porter (Eds.), *Annual Review of Psychology* (pp. 109–131). Palo Alto: Annual Reviews, Inc.

Brehm, S. S., & Brehm, J. W. (1981). *Psychological reactance: A theory of freedom and control.* New York: Academic Press.

Harmon-Jones, E., Brehm, J. W., Greenberg, J., Simon, L., & Nelson, D. E. (1996). Evidence that the production of aversive consequences is not necessary to create cognitive dissonance. *Journal of Personality and Social Psychology, 70,* 5–16.

Simon, L., Greenberg, J., & Brehm, J. W. (1995). Trivialization: The forgotten mode of dissonance reduction. *Journal of Personality and Social Psychology, 68,* 247–260.

Wicklund, R. A., & Brehm, J. W. (1976). *Perspectives on cognitive dissonance.* Hillsdale, NJ: Lawrence Erlbaum Associates.

Wortman, C. B., & Brehm, J. W. (1975). Responses to uncontrollable outcomes: An integration of reactance theory and the learned helplessness model. In L. Berkowitz (Ed.), *Advances in experimental social psychology* (Vol. 8). New York: Academic Press.

Wright, R. A. (1996). Brehm's theory of motivation as a model of effort and cardiovascular response. In P. M. Gollwitzer & J. A. Bargh (Eds.), *The psychology of action: Linking cognition and motivation to behavior* (pp. 424–453). New York: Guilford.

Wright, R. A., & Kirby, L. D. (2001). Effort determination of cardiovascular response: An integrative analysis with applications in social psychology. In M. P. Zanna (Ed.), *Advances in experimental social psychology* (Vol. 33, pp. 255–307). San Diego, CA: Academic Press.

2

Early Friendship Lasting

Peter Schönbach
Ruhr-Universität, Bochum

It was a day in September 1953 that Peter, the import from Germany, first met Jack Brehm. Stan Schachter had taken pity on me when he came to know me as a junior assistant in the Frankfurt team that was in charge of the German part in Schachter's enormous 7-nation study on deviation and rejection. One day Stan said to me: "Peter, you don't learn a damn thing here, why don't you come to America?" I replied: "Oh, I should love to, if you can make it possible," and he did. Stan Schachter and Leon Festinger saw to it that I was offered a position as a graduate student at the University of Minnesota, and a research assistantship at the Laboratory for Research in Social Relations.

My life at the University of Minnesota started when Professor John G. Darley, Executive Secretary of the Laboratory for Research in Social Relations, kindly told me, after a brief interview, "Now, Peter, you just walk over to Ford Hall; there you will find a desk to stick your feet under." The largest room of the Lab contained several desks for the research assistants and Leon Festinger's secretary, Maxine. In my round of introduction, I arrived at the desk of Danuta Ehrlich, who had survived World War II in the Warsaw ghetto; I learned of Danuta's experience then and there. I was also asked, in a seemingly joking manner, by one of several research assistants who had gathered around us if I had come to teach some Nazi ideology. Just 8 years after the War and the Holocaust, I was indeed prepared for such a challenge. So, I said something along the lines of: "The short answer is 'No', but let me add: Please take your time to find out for yourself.

In the meantime, you may consider the fact that Horkheimer and Adorno accepted me as a junior coworker at the Institut für Sozialforschung in Frankfurt, which they reestablished after their return from the United States." There was no more probing after that. Somebody said to no one in particular, "well, let's go and have some coffee at the Union." As I did not know how inclusive that "us" was meant to be, I hesitated. It was Jack Brehm who nodded to me and asked me if I would come along, and, of course, I did with relief and pleasure. At that moment I felt that we would become friends, and so it turned out to be.

Within a few days I felt much at home and accepted in the Laboratory. Danuta and I worked very well together on two of the earliest studies on dissonance theory (Ehrlich et al., 1957; Festinger, 1957, pp. 162–176). Even though we have seen each other only rarely in the time since, we have, to this day, maintained a friendly line of communication, exchanging letters at least once a year. Jack and his first wife Lee were very helpful and hospitable during the 2 years that we shared at the University of Minnesota and the Laboratory. We never worked together on a particular project, but we did, of course, frequently talk shop and spend time together relaxing.

In 1955, Jack got his PhD, and the Brehms went to New Haven, where Jack took his first appointment as Assistant Professor at Yale. I got my PhD in 1956. On my way back to Germany, I stayed for a few days with Jack and Lee. I guess my biggest contribution to their merriment was my report on an experience in a New Haven liquor store. I had gone there to buy a fine bottle as my contribution to the celebration of our reunion. When I put forth my request, the clerk looked at me sharply and asked if I was over 18 years old. With my 28 years and a PhD (if recently acquired), I was simply aghast, but this impression sufficed. The clerk handed over the bottle without further ado.

Several years passed. Jack became prominent, together with Bob Cohen, for their "Explorations in Cognitive Dissonance" and earned a full professorship at Duke University. After a 3-year stint in market research, I was offered a position at the Institut für Sozialforschung in Frankfurt, which allowed me to return to social research and some teaching. In 1963, Ned Jones, then also at Duke University, was due to follow an invitation to the Center for Advanced Studies at Stanford. Jack suggested me as a replacement, and the Department offered me a position as Visiting Associate Professor for 10 months.

I had a marvelous academic year at Duke, with many scientific and social experiences, starting with the Brehm's good care in helping me getting settled in Durham in a two-room apartment and buying the necessary household utensils. The Brehms stayed at the core of a quickly widening circle of friendship and hospitality. Kurt Back sold me an old little Fiat for $100 and bought it back for $100 when I returned to Frankfurt in the summer of 1964. Like Jack and Lee, Mike and Lise Wallach also provided a haven for me (floating Peter), and so did Norman and Ronnie Guttman, just to name a few.

At that time, Jack had turned his scientific attention to the phenomena of reactance, and we often discussed problems posed to a theory of reactance and corresponding empirical research. As much as I was impressed by many aspects of that theory and the unfolding research that it engendered, I could not agree with the view (see now Brehm & Brehm, 1981, chap. 14) that favored a restrictive notion of control motivation as reactive and outcome-specific, and would not accept the notion of a general control motivation, as proposed by White (1959) and others. Jack and I repeatedly had a civilized controversy on that issue, but here I abstain from going into details.

During her Christmas vacation of 1963–1964, my wife Ruth—then a teacher of German and History at a Gymnasium in Frankfurt—came for a visit of 2 weeks. That was a special highlight, not only for Ruth and me, but for Jack and Lee too. Another highlight, shortly before my departure in June 1964, was a week with the Brehms on and around Topeka Beach. All these experiences and many others are fondly remembered. But I also bitterly remember, as Jack undoubtedly does too, one of the darkest days in our lives. On the evening of November 22, 1963, Jack, Lee, and I sat together at their home in helpless mourning, trying to grasp the fact and meaning of President Kennedy's assassination.

The summer of 1967 furnished Ruth and me with an opportunity to reciprocate in some small measure for the Brehms' marvelous hospitality. They had announced their intention to come to Europe, and we invited them to come with us on a tour through some parts of Central Europe. We started late in July, spending several days in Frankfurt and vicinity, with a loop to and on the Rhine river. Then we went into Bavaria, with main stops in Rothenburg and Munich. From there we went to Salzburg and the Salzkammergut, with tickets for Mozart's Entführung aus dem Serail, part of the Salzburg Festival. Our way back to Frankfurt led us to St. Gallen, Konstanz, the Black Forest, and Heidelberg. On August 15, we said goodby to Jack and Lee at the Frankfurt Airport.

Several years passed before Jack and I met again, after a number of changes in our lifes. We both had moved. Jack moved with his second wife, Sharon, to the University of Kansas at Lawrence. Ruth and I moved (in 1969) to Bochum, where I was to take over the newly established chair of social psychology in the Psychology Department of the Ruhr-Universität. In 1976 I had a sabbatical and went on a tour of several universities in the United States. Needless to say, Lawrence, Kansas was high on my list of places to visit, and I was kindly received there by Jack, Sharon, and their dogs.

In 1986 I had another chance for a stop-over in Lawrence, but Jack was in New York at that time. Fortunately, he had become a traveler of renown. In the 1980s and 1990s he frequently came to Europe, including Germany. So we met on several occasions, especially when he spent a few months at the University of Bielefeld, supported by a Senior Research Award of the Alexander-von-Humboldt Stiftung. Our professional discussions then centered mostly on the intensity of emotions, and again Jack responded with gentle civility to some doubts I raised concerning the relationships between deterrence, intensity, and energization value of emotions.

It was, of course, not all work, but some play too, such as visits to Münster and to the old little town of Hattingen near Bochum. Most recently, in July 2001, Ruth and I had once more the great pleasure of having Jack with us for a couple of days. This time we stayed in our vacation resort in the Black Forest, providing him with both an excursion to the Schliffkopf, with its 360° view, as well as some much-needed rest on his European tour of visits with many challenges and stimulations.

Dear reader, please accept this sketch of a transatlantic friendship, easily sustained over decades despite few personal encounters since 1964. I am happy to add that since the turn of the century it has been miraculously enriched by the ease and swiftness of email communication.

REFERENCES

Brehm, S. S., & Brehm, J. W. (1981). *Psychological reactance: A theory of freedom and control*. New York: Academic Press.

Ehrlich, D., Guttman, I., Schönbach, P., & Mills, J. (1957). Postdecision exposure to relevant information. *Journal of Abnormal and Social Psychology, 54*, 98–102.

Festinger, L. (1957). *A theory of cognitive dissonance*. Evanston, IL: Row, Peterson & Co.

Schachter, S., Nuttin, J., De Monchaux, C., Maucorps, P. H., Osmer, D., Duijker, H., Rommetveit, R., & Israel, J. (1954). Cross-cultural experiments on threat and rejection. *Human Relations, 7*, 403–439.

White, R. W. (1959). Motivation reconsidered: The concept of competence. *Psychological Review, 66*, 297–333.

II

INFLUENCES

3

Dissonance Theory: History and Progress

Joel Cooper
Princeton University

The very first letter that I received in the mail when I became an assistant professor of psychology contained exactly one word:

"So?"

It was signed by Jack W. Brehm.

The letter reinforced what I already knew. Jack Brehm was a man of few words, but those words meant a lot. I quickly completed the manuscript that he and I were working on, ironically the only dissonance article that we ever wrote together.

In 1956, Jack published a short, six-page paper in the *Journal of Abnormal & Social Psychology,* then the flagship journal for social psychological research. It presented data on a new theory of choice behavior. In the space of fewer than 100 words, the paper defined cognitive elements, explained the dissonant or consonant relationship among cognitions and the motivation to reduce dissonance. This paper, presenting a single study from the author's PhD dissertation under the supervision of Leon Festinger, was the public birthplace of cognitive dissonance theory (Brehm, 1956). It showed that choices have consequences and that those consequences can be predicted from the magnitude of dissonance that is created by the choice. The more similar in attractiveness the choice alternatives are, the more dissonance that is created, and the more people are motivated to pull apart their postdecisional evaluation of the choice alternatives. Simple. Succinct. To this day, I wonder if Jack and his mentor knew that they had fired an opening salvo on behalf of a theory that would rock the social psychological world. It would challenge existing wisdom, not only in the area of choice behavior, but would also challenge the supremacy of the prevailing zeitgeist that pervaded most of psychology—reinforcement theory. Cognitive dissonance theory, presented so elegantly and succinctly in the 1956 paper, would ultimately become part of the established wisdom of social psychology, with myriad research studies spread over the journals to prove, disprove, reprove, and ultimately improve it. Could they have foreseen that it would still be an active part of the psychological literature almost 50 years later, in the first decade of the 21st century?

In this chapter, I briefly examine some of the early controversies provoked by dissonance theory, trace its transformation through the decades, and present a synthesis of some of the major prevailing views of dissonance today.

DISSONANCE PROVOKES CONTROVERSIES: THE ARTIFACT CRITIQUE

From the distance of 50 years, it may be hard to understand how cognitive dissonance theory could have provoked the heated controversies that it did. The theory itself was reasonably parsimonious, all stemming from the basic proposition that cognitive dissonance arose from inconsistency among cognitive elements, that it was experienced as psychological discomfort, and that people were motivated to seek its reduction. It shared many principles in common with various forms of balance principles (e.g., Heider 1944; Newcomb, 1956) and social comparison theory (Festinger, 1954), neither of which generated the controversies that dissonance generated. The studies were straightforwardly derived from the theory. Why, then was it controversial?

One reason for controversy was that it made predictions that similar theories could not make. As Brehm and Cohen (1962) pointed out in their now-classic volume, the form of balance envisioned by dissonance had a magnitude. People could have more of it or less of it. In prior forms of balance theories, relationships could be balanced or not, but magnitudes could not be specified. By indexing dissonance to the ratio of dissonant to consonant cognitive elements, Festinger and his students were specifying a magnitude. Thus, Brehm (1956) could make predictions about postdecisional dissonance being more intense when a choice was made between two alternatives that were close in initial attractiveness than when the alternatives were widely discrepant in initial attractiveness. Previous balance theories could not. Brehm and Cohen (1959) could predict that choice alternatives high in cognitive overlap would not result in dissonance, even if their attractiveness was quite similar prior to the choice. Previous balance theories could not.

Festinger and Carlsmith (1959) were even more provocative when they presented their first study in what was then called "forced compliance." Volunteers participated in a study that required them to perform a dull and boring task. They were then asked if they would be willing to play the role of confederate and tell the next student that the task was exciting and interesting. Clearly, such a situation presents a set of imbalanced cognitions; thus, several theories could conclude that there would be attitude change in the direction of the counterattitudinal position. Specifically, people who make statements contrary to their attitudes may come to believe those attitudes. The key ingredient in Festinger and Carlsmith's study was the magnitude of monetary incentive offered to students to play the role of confederate. The well-known result is that, as predicted by dissonance theory, people who were paid less money for their counterattitudinal role playing experienced more dissonance and changed their attitudes more than did people paid a much larger sum. The large incentive was considered to be an important cognition consistent with the behavior and thus served to decrease the magnitude of dissonance.

The hallmark of forced compliance, like Brehm's (1956) choice-of-alternatives study, was how simply and elegantly it was derived from the theory. Also like Brehm's study, Festinger and Carlsmith's predictions exceeded those that could be made by existing balance theories. However, Festinger and Carlsmith's study went even further by producing a result that seemed to fly in the face of fundamental principles of reinforcement: People paid more for a behavior were less influenced by that behavior than were people paid less. Smaller incentives produced greater liking for the position than did higher incentives. For many years, social psychologists had tried to apply what had been learned from animal models to human behavior. Persuasion researchers in particular had been actively applying principles of reinforcement to attitude change (e.g., Hovland, Janis, & Kelley, 1953). Now, using dissonance theory, Festinger and Carlsmith made a straightforward prediction that higher reinforcements, instantiated as magnitudes of money, would lead to less rather than more persuasion. And the data said they were right.

Aronson and Mills (1959) jumped into the developing drama as well. They predicted that the more people suffered in conjunction with trying to get into a group, the more they would like the group. Wasn't suffering a negative reinforcement? Shouldn't it lead to greater disliking? Again, the data supported the dissonance prediction. Not just *despite* the negative nature of the suffering, but *because* of the negative valence of the suffering, people came to like what they had suffered for.

Critics clamored to engage in the debate. Surely, they reasoned, these studies must have artifacts. The data are wrong, they said. Too many people dropped out of key conditions. There were alternative ways to view the manipulation that, when corrected, support reinforcement theory and not dissonance theory, they said. The suggestions were too numerous to detail here, but one example will provide the flavor of the discussion. Perhaps Festinger and Carlsmith had offered so much money in their high incentive condition that people became suspicious (Chapanis & Chapanis, 1964), or worried about how their integrity would appear to the experimenter (Janis & Gilmore, 1965; Rosenberg, 1965). However, Jack Brehm's colleague, Bob Cohen (Brehm & Cohen, 1962) had already addressed this question. In a very careful replication of Festinger and Carlsmith's experiment, he modified the huge gap between $1 and $20 to a graduated scale that began at $.50 and ended at $10.00. Cohen found a significant difference in attitude between students who had volunteered to say something they did not believe in for the incentive of $.50 and students who volunteered for $1. One dollar's payment was hardly going to make someone unduly suspicious or feel that he or she was being bribed. Nonetheless, as predicted by dissonance theory, there was significantly more attitude change in the face of a tiny incentive than there was following a larger, although still small, incentive. Other studies continued to support the theoretical predictions (Linder, Cooper, & Jones 1967). Dissonance theory survived the early criticisms. The criticisms, however, had done a service for the theory. First, they called attention to the iconoclast upstart of a theory that Festinger, Brehm, Aronson, Carlsmith, and Mills had laid before the public. The criticisms also forced dissonance theorists to become more precise in their derivations and more thoughtful about their manipulations. Dissonance research was stronger as it moved into the next phase of its history.

The Second Wave: The Data Are Right, But the Theory Is Wrong

The second family of criticisms changed the nature of the debate. Daryl Bem argued that the data were accurate but that they offered support for a more parsimonious theory; an attribution-based theory that he called self-perception (Bem, 1967, 1972). Bem argued that the data collected by dissonance theory accurately reflected how people arrive at their attitudes. However, in a clever theoretical twist, Bem argued that, rather than people being worried about inconsistency and feeling an internal motivation to reduce the dissonance, people merely observe their own behavior and the reinforcement contingencies that surround it. They then infer what their attitudes must be. People observing a person making a counterattitudinal statement for a meager reward will infer that the behavior reflected the individual's attitudes. People observing similar behavior in the context of a large inducement do not know what to infer. Clearly, the behavior was under the control of the monetary stimulus and had little implication for the person's attitude. Bem's clever twist was to challenge the notion that inconsistency among cognitions, and an internal motivation to reduce dissonance, was at all relevant to the final attitude assessment (see also Kelley, 1972). And Bem presented the results of several studies that showed that people who were simply given a description of participants' behavior in forced compliance research inferred the very same attitudes that involved participants had reported in the original experiments. There were no assumptions of inconsistency, no internal states of arousal, just inferences about behaviors.

A group of investigators at Duke University that included Jack Brehm and a second group at Yale showed that Bem's analysis was based on an unrealistic assumption about participants' knowledge at the time of the behavior (Jones, Linder, Kiesler, Zanna, & Brehm, 1968). Then, studies began to accumulate that showed that, consistent with Brehm's (1956) and Festinger's (1957) statements of psychological pressure and discomfort, dissonance was indeed accompanied by a state of psychological arousal. At least, these investigators showed that when dissonance occurred, it interfered with simple and complex learning in a way that was consistent with the presence of physiological arousal (Pallak & Pittman, 1972; Waterman & Katkin, 1968).

In the mid–1970s, Mark Zanna and I used a misattribution paradigm to confront Bem's assertion that dissonance was not a motivational state (Zanna & Cooper, 1974). We showed that people who engaged in counterattitudinal behavior but who could attribute their discomfort to the side effects of a pill they had just ingested, did not show the attitude change that usually accompanies counterattitudinal behavior. Apparently, participants who thought their discomfort was due to their counterattitudinal behavior changed their attitudes in order to reduce their discomfort. Just as Brehm (1956) and Festinger (1957) had theorized, cognitive dissonance produced a motivation for attitude change whose function was the reduction of the discomfort. If the discomfort was thought to have been brought on by the pill, then attitude change would be irrelevant for reducing the discomfort and, indeed, the counterattitudinal behavior resulted in no attitude change. Later, Robert Croyle and I introduced a methodology for measuring physiological arousal that occurred following counterattitudinal behavior (Croyle & Cooper, 1983). Using nonspecific skin conductance measures, we found that skin conductance was elevated whenever people made counterattitudinal statements under the conditions that usually lead to dissonance (e.g., low incentive and high choice). Both the misattribution findings and the arousal findings have been replicated many times in the literature (Axsom, 1989; Elkin & Leippe, 1986; Fazio, Zanna, & Cooper, 1979; Losch & Cacioppo, 1990). The nonmotivational alternatives to dissonance theory were fascinating developments that led to stimulating debate and the collection of an impressive spate of data. It prodded investigators to find evidence for the initial assumptions about the motivating force behind attitude change in the face of inconsistent cognitive elements. It is fair to say that, by the mid-1980s, nonmotivational theories were no longer serious contenders as explanations for the consequences of inconsistent behavior.

The Self-Improvement of Dissonance Theory

In a symposium held in New York City to commemorate the 25th anniversary of dissonance theory, Leon Festinger spoke eloquently of the need for theories to evolve and change. No set of assumptions and derivations can go unchallenged and unmodified as they meet decades worth of experiments and data. Not even dissonance theory. Festinger welcomed the challenges and changes that psychologists working within dissonance theory proposed. The challenges began with Elliot Aronson's alternative view that stressed the importance of the self. I begin, however, with a challenge for which I will take responsibility, and then discuss two theories that emphasized the role of the self.

The New Look: A Cure for the "But-Onlys"

Cooper and Fazio (1984) reviewed the experimental results that had accrued during the first quarter-century of work on dissonance, much of it summarized nicely by Wicklund and Brehm (1976) a few years earlier. It seemed to us that the simple, elegant notion that inconsistent cognitive elements lead to the arousal of dissonance had already been qualified in a number of interesting ways. Brehm and Cohen (1962) had pointed out that inconsistency leads to dissonance, but only if people are committed to their cognitions (see also, Davis & Jones, 1960). Inconsistency also requires choice. If people engage in behavior that is inconsistent with their attitudes, it leads to dissonance, but only if they perceive that they had freely chosen to engage in that behavior (Brehm & Cohen, 1962; Cooper, 1971; Davis & Jones, 1960; Linder, Cooper, & Jones, 1967). Indeed, many investigators now use the term *induced compliance* rather than forced compliance to emphasize the importance of choosing to engage in attitude-inconsistent behavior.

Fazio and I also noted that inconsistency did not lead to dissonance arousal if it did not produce some consequence that the actor found to be unwanted, unpleasant, or aversive. For example, Cooper and Worchel (1970) reconsidered Festinger and Carlsmith's (1959) original induced compliance experiment. What would have happened if people had made statements contrary to their beliefs about how boring the experimental task was, but no one heard? Would such behavior, inconsistent as it was with the actor's attitudes, produce dissonance? Or, imagine that the waiting subject had heard but was neither convinced nor affected by the actor's stated opinion that the task was interesting. Would it create dissonance? Cooper and Worchel repeated the Festinger and Carlsmith procedure, but systematically varied whether the alleged waiting subject was convinced or not. The results were clear. When the waiting subject pretended to be convinced by the participant's remarks, the results replicated those found by Festinger and Carlsmith: Participants who agreed to praise the dull task for just a small incentive came to believe that the task was actually fun. Participants who made the speech for a large incentive did not. However, when the waiting subject pretended that he did not believe the participant, then the participant did not experience attitude change, regardless of the magnitude of incentive. Dissonance follows from counterattitudinal behavior, but only when it is followed by aversive consequences.

We also noted that people experience dissonance when counterattitudinal behavior is freely chosen and results in aversive consequences, but only when the consequences could have been foreseen at the time of the commitment. In several experiments (Cooper, 1971; Cooper & Brehm, 1971; Goethals & Cooper, 1975; Goethals, Cooper, & Naficy, 1979), freely chosen counterattitudinal behavior whose aversive consequences were not foreseeable at the time of the commitment did not lead to dissonance-produced attitude change.

Fazio and I proposed the new look model as the most parsimonious explanation for several decades of research whose results offered strong support for dissonance theory, but only under special and specifiable conditions. We proposed that dissonance was a motivational state that occurs when people feel responsible for bringing about an aversive or unwanted consequence. Brehm and Cohen (1962) had foreshadowed this finding decades earlier when they discussed the postdecisional consequences of behavior. As they viewed it, a choice to behave in a counterattitudinal way necessarily invoked what they called a "negative consequence" (p. 202), made more potent by commitment and volition. However, Cooper and Fazio's statement went further by disconnecting the notion of inconsistency from the valence of the consequence. People can act inconsistently and experience no unpleasant consequence (Cooper & Worchel, 1970) and, conversely, people can bring about an aversive consequence without it stemming from inconsistent behavior. For Cooper and Fazio (1984), then, inconsistency among cognitions was not necessary for the arousal of dissonance. Responsibly bringing about an aversive event was the necessary and sufficient condition for dissonance arousal.

Scher and Cooper (1989) put the full proposition to the test. Participants were asked to write an essay about significantly raising college tuition fees at their university. Half were asked to take the counterattitudinal position that tuition fees should be raised; the other half took the proattitudinal position that fees should not be raised. Participants knew that their essays would be shown to the Board of Trustees, therefore setting up the possibility that their essays would have policy consequences. They were also told that, in the experience of the researchers, essays written by students sometimes convince an audience, such as the people sitting on Boards of Trustees, but sometimes have ironic consequences of boomeranging—that is, of convincing the Board to take a position opposite to what they have read in the essay. Whether it has a positive or a boomerang effect depends on such factors as the order in which people read it, the kinds of arguments that are used, and so forth. Following their essay writing, half of the participants were told that there was a good chance that the essays would actually convince the Trustees to believe what was argued in the essay and the other half were told that the essay would probably boomerang.

When attitudes toward tuition increases were measured, the results supported the new look prediction. Participants were more likely to change their opinion in the direction of supporting higher tuition fees if their essay was likely to bring about the potential aversive consequence of convincing the Board to support higher fees. This was true regardless of whether students wrote in favor of higher tuition or against higher tuition. An aversive consequence occurred in the proattitudinal condition when students believed the essay would boomerang. It occurred in the counterattitudinal condition when students believed it would have a straightforward persuasion effect. It did not matter whether the essays were pro or counterattitudinal. The necessary and sufficient condition for dissonance was that the essay produced a foreseeable, unwanted consequence.

It seems a long way from Festinger's initial theory to say that inconsistency is not necessary for dissonance. However, even in the early theorizing about dissonance, the word inconsistency was often alternated with the phrase "unpleasant event" (e.g., Brehm & Cohen, 1962, p. 202). Behaving in an inconsistent manner usually has the result of bringing about something that is unpleasant, negative, or aversive. Convincing someone to believe that a dull experiment will be interesting, convincing a Board of Trustees to believe in raising tuition, convincing a high school student to smoke marijuana (Nel, Helmreich, & Aronson, 1969) all are examples of inconsistency that simultaneously bring about unpleasant events. So, too, is choosing one consumer item over another similarly attractive alternative, thereby giving up all of the attractive features of the latter alternative. Rather than being the cause of dissonance, Cooper and Fazio argued that inconsistency is a useful stand-in for the factor that is the real cause of the dissonance—that is, responsibly bringing about an unwanted event.

Implicating the Self: A Self-Consistency View of Dissonance

Elliot Aronson (1968, 1999) took a different approach to modifying dissonance theory. Unlike Cooper and Fazio's view, Aronson reaffirmed the position that inconsistency is the primary cause of dissonance, but only an inconsistency of a particular type. In order for inconsistency to arouse dissonance, it must implicate the self-concept. At its center, he argued that dissonance was a theory about the self. People strive for consistent views of themselves. If people feel reasonably positive about themselves, they see themselves as competent and moral human beings. Anything that challenges that view will result in dissonance. Cognitive inconsistency results in dissonance because good, competent, and moral people do not usually act in ways that run contrary to their beliefs. They do not convince other students that a dull task is interesting, they do not extol the virtues of marijuana to high school youngsters, they do not write essays about raising college tuition fees if they believe that the fees should not be raised. When people find that they have acted in ways that compromise their sense of competence or moral integrity, they are motivated to change their attitudes. If you have written an essay arguing for increased college fees, then your view of yourself as a moral and competent person will be compromised, unless you convince yourself that you actually believe that position.

One implication of the self-consistency position is that people who do not chronically think of themselves as competent would not be as likely to change their attitudes following counterattitudinal behavior. That is, people with lower self-esteem should experience little dissonance after behaving in a counterattitudinal fashion. Self-esteem establishes an expectancy about how a person is likely to behave. When people violate that expectancy, dissonance is created. Several pieces of evidence converge to support this viewpoint. Aronson and Mettee (1968) manipulated what people thought about themselves. Those whose self-esteem had been lowered were less bothered by an attitude-discrepant act than were people whose self-esteem had been raised. Similarly, Glass (1964), Maracek and Mettee (1972), and Gibbons, Eggleston, and Benthin (1997) also found that dissonance arousal was lower for people with low self-esteem.

Aronson and Carlsmith (1962) directly manipulated what people expected of themselves on a particular task. They led people to believe that they were either highly competent or highly incompetent at a social perception task. They found that people were bothered by any behavior that was at variance with what they had come to expect of themselves. Those who felt they were incompetent at social perception were more bothered by success than by failure. Those who had a positive sense of their ability were more bothered by their failure. In short, Aronson's view is that behavior that calls into question one's competence and morality, such as advocating something you do not believe in, creates cognitive dissonance, provided you expect positive outcomes for yourself—that is, that you have a positive sense of self-esteem.

Self-Affirmation

Claude Steele and his colleagues (e.g., Steele, 1988; Steele & Liu, 1983; Steele, Spencer, & Lynch, 1993) have also linked the experience of dissonance to a person's self-esteem. Like the self-consistency position, the self-affirmation view of dissonance holds that people are primarily motivated to affirm the competence and morality of their self-view. However, self-affirmation makes a drastically different prediction when it comes to the role of self-esteem. Steele et al. (1993) argued that people with low self-esteem are the ones who feel particularly threatened when they engage in counterattitudinal behavior. Their self-view is already fragile, and acting in a counterattitudinal fashion further compromises their sense of competence. On the other hand, a solid sense of self-esteem can serve as a resource—a buffer against the feeling of incompetence. Steele, Spencer, and Lynch (1993) found that when people with high self-esteem engage in counterattitudinal behavior, they change their attitudes less than do people with low self-esteem. This, of course, is opposite to the prediction made by the self-consistency view.

TOWARD A RESOLUTION: THE SELF-STANDARDS MODEL OF DISSONANCE

At least four models of dissonance have been active contenders to be the most accurate and complete explanation of the process that underlies dissonance effects. Two of the theories implicate the self as integral parts of the dissonance formula, but each makes different predictions about the way that the strength of self-esteem projects onto the magnitude of dissonance. The new look model of dissonance and the original model offered by Brehm (1956) and by Festinger (1957) make no such presuppositions for the self. The importance of behavioral consequences for the arousal of dissonance plays the most prominent role in the new look model, but is also consistent with the predictions made by self-affirmation and self-consistency. According to Harmon-Jones, Brehm, Greenberg, Simon, and Nelson (1996), behavioral consequences play no such role in the original cognitive inconsistency model.

Jeff Stone and I recently proposed a self-standards model (SSM) of dissonance that pulls together much of the research on prior models (Stone & Cooper, 2001; see also Stone, 1999; Cooper, 1999). I focus on the SSM in this chapter because it integrates many of the strands that, when taken together, may more fully explain the cognitive processing that underlies the arousal of dissonance. According to the self-standards model, whether or not the self is involved in the arousal of dissonance depends on the standard of judgment that is accessible following a counterattitudinal act.

We begin our analysis with behavior. A person acts. How shall he or she interpret the act? Does it reflect well on the self? Was it foolish or competent? Did it lead to a wanted or an unwanted outcome? We contend that people typically ask such questions about their behavior, but are especially likely to do so when the act is at variance with their private attitudes. How shall actors make sense of such behavior?

These questions cannot be answered in a vacuum. Is the act a good or bad one; did it lead to something wanted or unwanted? These are questions that can only be answered when compared to some standard of judgment. The dilemma is that there are many standards of judgment that can be used. Actors might compare their behavior to a personal standard of morality. If they do so, they may ask questions like, Am I the kind of person who usually does such a thing? Do I typically act in a way that compromises my morality? If the actor is a person who thinks quite highly of him or herself, the compromised behavior may lead to the kind of discrepancy with one's personal expectations that self-consistency theorists believe leads to the arousal of dissonance.

But perhaps the actor thinks of a different standard of comparison. Perhaps he or she asks the question, "Would most people act in such a way that they would convince someone to believe something that is not true?" If this is the standard of comparison, then questions about how the actor usually behaves, or about whether he or she is typically a good person, or about his or her level of self-esteem and self-competence, are not at all relevant. The question is phrased in normative terms: How would most people evaluate my behavior? Would most people evaluate my behavior as foolish or immoral? Would most people view the consequences of my action as unwanted?

Some people chronically use personal standards to evaluate their behavior. In most circumstances, they will typically refer to their own history, expectations, and resources to evaluate their behavior. Others may chronically avoid such personal evaluations for behavior. For most of us, however, it is the situation that determines the standards of judgment that become accessible following a potentially dissonance producing act. If people are primed to think about their personal standards, they will use those standards for evaluating their behavior. If they are primed to think about normative standards—that is, what most people would do or think—then they will use those normative standards to evaluate their behavior. If personal standards are accessible, then the self will play a major role. If normative standards are accessible, then the self will play no role.

The self-standards model also speaks to the difference between the self-affirmation and self-consistency models of dissonance. Recall that each of those models bases dissonance reduction on protecting one's view of oneself as moral and competent, but each model makes a different prediction about the direction of the relationship between self-esteem and dissonance. The SSM holds that the relationship between self-esteem and attitude change can be positive (as per self-consistency) or negative (as per self-affirmation), depending on the relevance of the personal attributes that are accessible in memory. We think the relationship works like this: The more the person thinks of attributes that are relevant to the attitude-discrepant behavior, the more the process will take the form predicted by self-consistency. In such cases, the self will function as an expectancy. A person with high self-esteem will reason, "I am the kind of person who usually does good things, says what she thinks, never dupes another person." Therefore, this person's decision to, let us say, convince another student that a dull experiment will be exciting is discrepant with her attributes of honesty and morality. It will create a high degree of dissonance. On the other hand, if people with high self-esteem can think of attributes that are orthogonal to the attributes that were potentially compromised by their attitude-discrepant behavior, then their positive feelings about themselves serve as a buffer against the need to change their attitudes. Such a person may reason, "I may have convinced someone to believe something that is not true, but I should remember that I have other attributes that make me loveable. For example, I am creative; I am a wonderful chef; I play tennis extremely well." Bringing these positive attributes to mind lessens the impact of the attitude discrepant behavior (J. Aronson, Blanton, & Cooper, 1995; Blanton, Cooper, Skurnik, & J. Aronson, 1997; Galinsky, Stone, & Cooper, 2000).

A Test of the Model

Stone and Cooper (2003) put some of the predictions of the SSM to an empirical test. Research participants at the University of Arizona (whose level of self-esteem was known from a prior assessment) were asked to write an essay on what they believed was a topic currently being debated by the university administration. The University officials, they were told, were proposing to cut the amount of funds spent on facilities for the handicapped. Then, using the timeless procedure recommended by Brehm and Cohen (1962), the participants were told that research has shown that the best way to understand the arguments about an issue is to have people write strong and forceful essays favoring only one side. In the high choice condition, participants were allowed to choose the side they wanted to write on but were told that the research really needed people to write strong, forceful arguments in favor of the decrease. In the no-choice control condition, participants were simply instructed to write strong and forceful arguments in favor of the decrease.

This typical induced-compliance experiment now contained a twist. After writing their attitude-discrepant essays, but before filling out the dependent measure that would assess their attitudes, participants were asked to take part in a study on language and cognition. They were presented with blocks of scrambled words and were told to make complete sentences out of the words. The sentences formed the priming manipulation (Bargh, Chen, & Burrows, 1996).

What would constitute a *relevant prime*? Students in this condition advocated that the university take action that was uncompassionate and unhelpful to the handicapped. Therefore, the sentences that primed relevant categories included, "I am a compassionate person," and "Helping people is important." In the *irrelevant prime* condition, the sentences made accessible positive self-attributes that had not been implicated by the counterattitudinal essay. Sentences in this condition included, "I am a creative person," and, "I try to be imaginative." Creativity and imagination are positive attributes, but they have little to do with the compassion and helpfulness that were implicated by the essay. In addition to the relevant and irrelevant prime conditions, other participants were primed with *neutral* attributes as a control—features of self that people do not usually rate as terribly important to their self-esteem such as "I try to be quiet."

Participants then had their attitudes toward handicapped funding measured by a questionnaire that the experimenter had purportedly "forgotten" to administer earlier. The results are shown in Fig. 3.1. In the low-choice conditions, there is only a small and nonsignificant amount of attitude change that does not vary as a function of self-esteem. On the other hand, when choice is high and dissonance is therefore activated, we see the pattern predicted by the SSM. Starting with the bars on the right-hand side of the figure, when positive but irrelevant attributes were primed and were therefore accessible as the standard of judgment for behavior, people with low self-esteem showed more attitude change than did people with high self-esteem. These conditions are consistent with the self-affirmation view, because participants with high self-esteem could use their standing

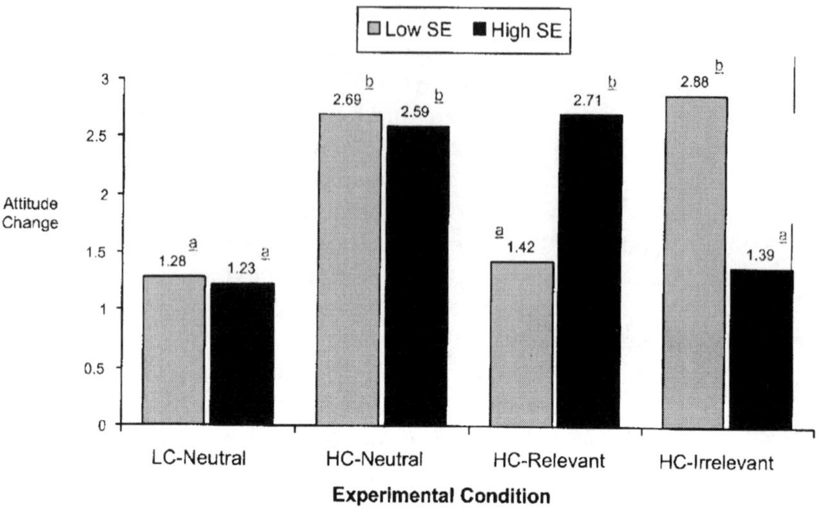

FIG. 3.1. A test of the Self-Standards Model: Attitude change as a function of self-esteem, choice, and primed self-standard. Means with different superscripts differ significantly at $p < .05$.

on the irrelevant traits to buffer their sense of self and lessen their need to resolve their dissonance through attitude change. Those with low self-esteem had no such luxury.

The next set of bars of the graph depicts the results of people whose primed attributes were relevant to their behavior. As predicted, they show quite a different picture. Again, as SSM had predicted, self-esteem seemed to function as an expectancy. The higher participants' standing on the relevant traits, the more they expected that they would act compassionately and helpfully. The fact that they had written an essay that compromised their view as helpful, compassionate people resulted in higher dissonance and greater attitude change.

And then there are the participants who wrote their essays under high-choice conditions but who did not have important self-attributes primed. These participants were affected by their essays, experienced dissonance, and changed their attitudes, regardless of their level of self-esteem. We suggest that these participants compared their behavior not to an ideographic personal standard but rather to the normative standard of judgment. To assess the meaning of their behavior, they compared their actions to what they believed most people would have thought of their behavior. Would most people have considered their actions to be good or bad, proper or improper? Were the consequences desirable or aversive? They concluded that people in general do not go about trying to convince the authorities to implement unhelpful and uncompassionate policies. Thus, consistent with the new look and original models of dissonance, they experienced dissonance, changed their attitudes—and their level of self-esteem had nothing to do with it.

"So?" The Art of Going Forward

I have presented the self-standard model in this tribute to Jack Brehm because I think it is consistent with his influence on me and on the field of social psychology. Jack viewed dissonance theory, as he viewed so many of the theoretical advances for which he is responsible, as part of a wider network of motivational phenomena that affect people as they interact with their social environment. He has always emphasized expanding theory, rather than restricting it, synthesizing approaches whenever possible. In the self-standards model, Stone and I hope to cast dissonance in a more inclusive, synthesizing framework. A good squabble that pits one version of dissonance theory against another can be productive and profitable. We learn much crucial information in the course of resolving the squabble. But, we have now learned enough about the role of the self in dissonance to synthesize the theories and ask the more difficult questions about the cognitive processing that sometimes, but not always, implicates the self in the arousal of dissonance. The SSM is one such model that seeks a synthesis and that incorporates several different views under one motivational umbrella.

It should come as no surprise that there are issues left unresolved. The SSM helps us understand why the self is sometimes involved in dissonance and sometimes not. It posits that all dissonance emanates from the same judgment: How shall I interpret the behavior I have chosen, and against what standard of judgment shall I make this interpretation? Dissonance is activated by an assessment of whether I have done something unwanted or aversive. However, the question of what is aversive has been expanded. It can be aversive because it violates my sense of what I expect of myself, or it can be aversive because it violates my normative judgment of what most people consider to be unwanted or immoral.

But the theory needs to become more inclusive yet. There are still data that do not fit easily into this expanded framework, some of them collected by Jack and his colleagues on dissonance in the absence of aversive consequences (Harmon-Jones, et al., 1996). What theoretical synthesis will incorporate these findings? And is there a more comprehensive theory of motivation that might incorporate dissonance and other motivational phenomena? For example, Harmon-Jones and his colleagues (e.g. Harmon-Jones, this volume; Harmon-Jones & Harmon-Jones, 2002) have proposed an action orientation model that views dissonance resolution as a way to implement decisions and orient the individual to the requirements for action. In this approach, dissonance is connected both to distal motivational variables on the one hand and to specific brain activation on the other. Perhaps this model will also bear empirical fruit and continue the search for understanding the breadth and depth of dissonance phenomena. At the very least, these are the types of broad questions that Jack Brehm has always encouraged us to examine.

It would be an error to say that Jack Brehm merely influenced dissonance theory. He *introduced* dissonance to the pages of our journals. He guided much of the experimental work on dissonance through its early years as evidenced by his two comprehensive volumes of theoretical syntheses and experimental evidence (Brehm & Cohen, 1962; Wicklund & Brehm, 1976) and continued to offer advice and guidance even as his focus shifted to other motivational theories represented by the various chapters in this book. Despite the nearly 50 years of research generated by the theory of cognitive dissonance, there are more questions to answer, more phenomena to synthesize under its theoretical rubric. If we take Jack's question to me in his 1969 letter to mean, "Let's get on with the task ahead," then I am sure that Jack will ask himself as he asks the rest of us,

"So? Let's get on with it."

REFERENCES

Aronson, E. (1968). Dissonance theory: Progress and problems. In R. Abelson, E. Aronson, W. McGuire, T. Newcomb, M. Rosenberg, & P. Tannenbaum (Eds.), *Theories of cognitive consistency: A sourcebook* (pp. 5–27). Chicago, IL: Rand McNally.

Aronson, E. (1999). Dissonance, hypocrisy, and the self-concept. In E. Harmon-Jones & J. Mills (Eds.), *Cognitive dissonance: Progress on a pivotal theory in social psychology* (pp. 103–126). Washington, DC: American Psychological Association.

Aronson, E., & Carlsmith, J. M. (1962). Performance expectancy as a determinant of actual performance. *Journal of Abnormal and Social Psychology, 65,* 178–182.

Aronson, E., & Mettee, D. R. (1968). Dishonest behavior as a function of differential levels of induced self-esteem. *Journal of Personality and Social Psychology, 9,* 121–127.

Aronson, E., & Mills, J. M. (1959). The effect of severity of initiation on liking for a group. *Journal of Abnormal and Social Psychology, 59,* 177–181.

Aronson, J., Blanton, H. S., & Cooper, J. (1995). From dissonance to disidentification: Selectivity in the self-affirmation process. *Journal of Personality and Social Psychology, 68,* 986–996.

Axsom, D. (1989). Cognitive dissonance and behavior change in psychotherapy. *Journal of Experimental Social Psychology, 25,* 234–252.

Bargh, J. A., Chen, M., & Burrows, L. (1996). Automaticity of social behavior: Direct effects of trait construct and stereotype activation on action. *Journal of Personality and Social Psychology, 71,* 230–244.

Bem, D. J. (1967). Self-perception: An alternative interpretation of cognitive dissonance phenomena. *Psychological Review, 74,* 183–200.

Bem, D. J. (1972). Self-perception theory. In L. Berkowitz (Ed.), *Advances in experimental social psychology*. New York: Academic Press.

Blanton, H. S., Cooper, J., Skurnik, I., & Aronson, J. (1997). When bad things happen to good feedback: Exacerbating the need for self-justification with self-affirmations. *Personality and Social Psychology Bulletin, 23,* 684–692.

Brehm, J. W. (1956). Postdecision changes in the desirability of alternatives. *Journal of Abnormal and Social Psychology, 52,* 384–389.

Brehm, J. W., & Cohen, A. R. (1959). Re-evaluation of choice alternatives as a function of their number and qualitative similarity. *Journal of Abnormal and Social Psychology, 58,* 373–378.

Brehm, J. W., & Cohen, A. R. (1962). *Explorations in cognitive dissonance*. New York: Wiley.

Chapanis, N. P., & Chapanis, A. (1964). Cognitive dissonance. *Psychological Bulletin, 61,* 1–22.

Cooper, J. (1971). Personal responsibility and dissonance: The role of foreseen consequences. *Journal of Personality and Social Psychology, 18,* 354–363.

Cooper, J. (1999). Unwanted consequences and the self: In search of the motivation for dissonance reduction. In I. E. Harmon-Jones & J. Mills (Eds.), *Cognitive dissonance 40 years later: Revival with revisions and controversies* (pp. 149–174). Washington, DC: American Psychological Association.

Cooper, J., & Brehm, J. W. (1971). Prechoice awareness of relative deprivation as a determinant of cognitive dissonance. *Journal of Experimental Social Psychology, 7,* 571–581.

Cooper, J., & Fazio, R. H. (1984). A new look at dissonance theory. In L. Berkowitz (Ed.), *Advances in experimental social psychology* (Vol. 17, pp. 229–262). Hillsdale, NJ: Lawrence Erlbaum Associates.

Cooper, J., & Worchel, S. (1970). Role of undesired consequences in arousing cognitive dissonance. *Journal of Personality and Social Psychology, 16,* 199–206.

Croyle, R. A., & Cooper, J. (1983). Dissonance arousal: Physiological evidence. *Journal of Personality and Social Psychology, 45,* 782–791.

Davis, K. E., & Jones, E. E. (1960). Changes in interpersonal perception as a means of reducing cognitive dissonance. *Journal of Abnormal and Social Psychology, 61,* 402–410.

Elkin, R. A., & Leippe, M. R. (1986). Physiological arousal, dissonance and attitude change: Evidence for a dissonance-arousal link and a "don't remind me" effect. *Journal of Personality and Social Psychology, 51,* 55–65.

Fazio, R. H., Zanna, M. P., & Cooper, J. (1979). On the relationship of data to theory. A reply to Ronis & Greenwald. *Journal of Experimental Social Psychology, 15,* 70–76.

Festinger, L. (1954). A theory of social comparison processes. *Human Relations, 7,* 117–140.

Festinger, L. (1957). *A theory of cognitive dissonance*. Stanford, CA: Stanford University Press.

Festinger, L., & Carlsmith, J. M. (1959). Cognitive consequences of forced compliance. *Journal of Abnormal and Social Psychology, 58,* 203–210.

Galinsky, A. D., Stone, J., & Cooper, J. (2000). The reinstatement of dissonance and psychological discomfort following failed affirmations. *European Journal of Social Psychology, 30,* 123–147.

Gibbons, F. X., Eggleston, T. J., & Benthin, A. (1997). Cognitive reactions to smoking relapse: The reciprocal relation of dissonance and self-esteem. *Journal of Personality and Social Psychology, 72,* 184–195.

Glass, D. (1964). Changes in liking as a means of reducing cognitive discrepancies between self-esteem and aggression. *Journal of Personality, 32,* 531–549.

Goethals, G. R., & Cooper, J. (1975). When dissonance is reduced: The timing of self-justificatory attitude change. *Journal of Personality and Social Psychology, 32,* 361–367.

Goethals, G. R., Cooper, J., & Naficy, A. (1979). Role of foreseen, foreseeable and unforeseeable behavioral consequences in the arousal of cognitive dissonance. *Journal of Personality and Social Psychology, 37,* 1179–1185.

Harmon-Jones, E., Brehm, J. W., Greenberg, J., Simon, L., & Nelson, D. E. (1996). Is the production of aversive consequences necessary to create cognitive dissonance? *Journal of Personality and Social Psychology, 70,* 5–16.

Harmon-Jones, E., & Harmon-Jones, C. (2002). Testing the action-based model of cognitive dissonance: The effect of action-orientation on post-decisional attitudes. *Personality and Social Psychology Bulletin, 28,* 711–723.

Heider, F. (1944). Social perception and phenomenal causality. *Psychological Review, 51,* 358–374.

Hovland, C. I., Janis, I. L., & Kelley, H. H. (1953). *Communication and persuasion.* New Haven, CT: Yale University Press.

Janis, I. L., & Gilmore, J. B. (1965). The influence of incentive conditions on the success of role playing in modifying attitudes. *Journal of Personality and Social Psychology, 1,* 17–27.

Jones, R. A., Linder, D. E., Kiesler, C. A., Zanna, M. P., & Brehm, J. W. (1968). Internal states or external stimuli: Observers' attitude judgments and the dissonance-theory—self-persuasion controversy. *Journal of Experimental Social Psychology, 4,* 247–269.

Kelley, H. H. (1972). Attribution in social interaction. In E. E. Jones, D. E. Kanouse, H. H. Kelley, R. E. Nisbett, S. Valins, & B. Weiner (Eds.), *Attribution: Perceiving the causes of behavior* (pp. 1–26). Morristown, NJ: General Learning Press.

Linder, D. E., Cooper, J., & Jones, E. E. (1967). Decision freedom as a determinant of the role of incentive magnitude in attitude change. *Journal of Personality and Social Psychology, 6,* 245–254.

Losch, M., & Cacioppo, J. T. (1990). Cognitive dissonance may enhance sympathetic tonus, but attitudes are changed to reduce negative affect rather than arousal. *Journal of Experimental Social Psychology, 26,* 289–304.

Maracek, J., & Mettee, D. (1972). Avoidance of continued success as a function of self-esteem, level of esteem certainty, and responsibility for success. *Journal of Personality and Social Psychology, 22,* 98–107.

Nel, E., Helmreich, R. A., & Aronson, E. (1969). Opinion change in the advocate as a function of the persuasibility of his audience: A clarification of the meaning of dissonance. *Journal of Personality and Social Psychology, 12,* 117–124.

Newcomb, T. M. (1956). The prediction of interpersonal attraction. *American Psychologist, 11,* 575–586.

Pallak, M., & Pittman, T. (1972). General motivational effects of dissonance arousal. *Journal of Personality and Social Psychology, 21,* 349–358.

Rosenberg, M. J. (1965). When dissonance fails: On eliminating evaluation apprehension from attitude measurement. *Journal of Personality and Social Psychology, 1,* 28–42.

Scher, S. J., & Cooper, J. (1989). Motivational basis of dissonance: The singular role of behavioral consequences. *Journal of Personality and Social Psychology, 56,* 899–906.

Steele, C. M. (1988). The psychology of self-affirmation: Sustaining the integrity of the self. In L. Berkowitz (Ed.), *Advances in experimental social psychology* (Vol. 21, pp. 261–302). Hillsdale, NJ: Lawrence Erlbaum Associates.

Steele, C. M., & Liu, T. J. (1983). Dissonance processes as self-affirmation. *Journal of Personality and Social Psychology, 45,* 5–19.

Steele, C. M., Spencer, S. J., & Lynch, M. (1993). Dissonance and affirmational resources: Resilience against self-image threats. *Journal of Personality and Social Psychology, 64,* 885–896.

Stone, J. (1999). What exactly have I done? The role of self-attribute accessibility in dissonance. In E. Harmon-Jones & J. Mills (Eds.), *Cognitive dissonance: Progress on a pivotal theory in social psychology* (pp. 175–200). Washington, DC: American Psychological Association.

Stone, J., & Cooper, J. (2001). A self-standards model of cognitive dissonance. *Journal of Experimental Social Psychology, 37,* 228–243.

Stone, J., & Cooper, J. (2003). The effect of self-attribute relevance on how self-esteem moderates attitude change in dissonance. *Journal of Experimental Social Psychology, 39,* 508–515.

Waterman, C. K., & Katkin, E. S. (1967). The energizing (dynamogenic) effect of cognitive dissonance on task performance. *Journal of Personality and Social Psychology, 6,* 126–131.

Wicklund, R. A., & Brehm, J. W. (1976). *Perspectives on cognitive dissonance.* New York: Wiley.

Zanna, M. P., & Cooper, J. (1974). Dissonance and the pill: An attribution approach to studying the arousal properties of dissonance. *Journal of Personality and Social Psychology, 29,* 703–709.

4

From Cognitive Dissonance to the Motivational Functions of Emotions

Eddie Harmon-Jones
University of Wisconsin–Madison

As an undergraduate at the University of Alabama at Birmingham, I began my research career with work on Brehm's theory of motivational intensity (Wright, Tunstall, Williams, Goodwin, & Harmon-Jones, 1995). With an interest in Brehm's motivational theory and his approach to science, I moved to the University of Kansas (KU) as a graduate student to continue working on the theory, and more importantly, to learn from Jack's approach to and love for behavioral science. However, I chose to work with Jack primarily because I was impressed with his lack of ego-involvement or competitiveness. When I was about to leave KU and go visit the University of Missouri (while visiting potential graduate programs), rather than say something competitive, he simply said, "Tell my good friend Russ Geen hello." Having known Jack for the last 12 years or so, I realize that that was simply him being the humble person he is, one who does not feel ego-threatened by excellence in others.

In my time at KU, Jack never criticized my interest in a diverse set of problems, all concerned with motivation and emotion. Moreover, he was always available to talk about any issues I had on my mind, despite the fact that those issues frequently were far removed from his own academic interests at the time. He listened patiently, nodding in his assuring Jack-like way, and then provided incisive and sagacious comments. Jack displays a wonderful curiosity about people and fascination with truth. He is ever the keen, dispassionate observer of human behavior, and practices testing hypotheses derived from broad, general theories with straightforward, "bare-bones" experiments. After I became intensely interested in terror management theory (and received many hours of feedback from Jack about my terror management experiments), I moved, with Jack's best wishes, to the University of Arizona to continue my graduate work with Jeff Greenberg.

Some of my first research with Jack involved cognitive dissonance theory (Harmon-Jones, Brehm, Greenberg, Simon, & Nelson, 1996). Jack had a long history of involvement with dissonance, because some of his first research had focused on the same theory (Brehm, 1956). In this chapter, I briefly review our collaborative work on dissonance and then present some more recent work that was inspired by our collaborative work and by Brehm and Cohen (1962). Then, I finish by describing some other research that has benefitted greatly from Jack's theories of motivational and emotional intensity.

AVERSIVE CONSEQUENCES REVISION OF DISSONANCE

In the early 1990s, Jack and I began collaborating on a series of experiments designed to test whether dissonance could be aroused in situations where individuals did not feel personally responsible for producing aversive consequences. Cooper and Fazio (1984) proposed that the discomfort experienced in dissonance experiments was not due to an inconsistency between the individual's cognitions. Instead, they argued that the discomfort was due to individuals feeling personally responsible for producing aversive consequences. They stated, "dissonance has precious little to do with the inconsistency among cognitions per se, but rather with the production of a consequence that is unwanted" (Cooper & Fazio, 1984, p. 234). Jack and I had discussed Cooper and Fazio's widely accepted revision and its supporting research, and we were not persuaded. We still believed that cognitive inconsistency, not aversive consequences, was necessary and sufficient to produce dissonance. The research on which the aversive consequences model was based had demonstrated that dissonance-related attitude change only occurred in situations in which aversive consequences were produced.

However, results obtained in paradigms other than the counterattitudinal action paradigm are not consistent with the aversive consequences model (e.g., Batson, 1975; Brock & Balloun, 1967; Burris, Harmon-Jones, & Tarpley, 1997; Stone, Aronson, Crain, Winslow, & Fried, 1994). It is difficult to reconcile any of these lines of dissonance research with a conception of dissonance theory in which the production of an aversive consequence is the only motivator of dissonance-related cognitive and behavioral changes.

Certainly, according to the original theory of cognitive dissonance, the production of aversive consequences would be expected to increase the amount of dissonance produced (see Harmon-Jones, 1999). However, the original theory would deny that the production of an aversive consequence is necessary to produce dissonance.

The research testing the aversive consequences model, however, did find that, in the induced-compliance paradigm, attitude change only occurred when the participants believed they caused an aversive consequence. Why might this have occurred? First of all, the lack of attitude change in the no-aversive consequences conditions is a null effect. Null effects are notoriously difficult to explain and subject to multiple alternative explanations. Attitude change may have been produced, but may have been too slight to be detected with the small sample sizes of these experiments. It is also possible that not enough dissonance was aroused in these experiments to produce attitude change without the additional power of an aversive consequence. For example, too much justification for the counterattitudinal behavior may have been provided, and the aversive consequences were necessary to arouse dissonance sufficient to produce attitude change. It is also possible that, in these experiments, dissonance was produced, but it was not detected or was reduced by a route other than by attitude change (see Harmon-Jones, 1999, for a more detailed discussion of these and other explanations).

Jack, myself, and our colleagues conducted experiments to assess whether dissonance-related attitude change can occur without the production of aversive consequences (Harmon-Jones et al., 1996). Under the guise of experiments on memory, participants were exposed to an attitudinal object. Participants were assured of privacy and anonymity, and were then given high or low choice to write a counterattitudinal statement about the object. They were asked to discard the statement in the trash after writing it, so that there was no chance of the statement causing an aversive consequence. This manipulation was based on Cooper and Fazio's (1984) statement that, "making a statement contrary to one's attitude while in solitude does not have the potential for bringing about an aversive event" (p. 232).

In one experiment (Harmon-Jones et al., 1996), participants were asked to read a boring passage. They were then given high or low choice to write that they found the boring passage interesting. Nonspecific skin conductance responses (NS-SCRs) were assessed during the 3 min between the writing of the statement and the assessment of the participants' attitudes toward the passage. Although no aversive consequences were produced, persons in the high-choice condition changed their attitudes to be more favorable toward the passage. In addition, NS-SCRs indicated that participants in this condition experienced more emotional arousal, suggesting that dissonance was evoked.

In another experiment, participants who liked chocolate were asked to eat a piece of chocolate and then given high or low choice to write a statement that they disliked the chocolate (Harmon-Jones, 2000a). This experiment was conducted because it had been suggested that reading the boring passage, in itself, was aversive and that participants in the high-choice condition could have believed they had high choice to read the passage as well as to write the statement. Because eating the chocolate was pleasant, rather than aversive, that alternative could not apply in this case. Participants in the high-choice condition changed their attitudes to dislike the chocolate. In addition, self-reported negative affect was increased following dissonance-producing behavior and was reduced following the attitude change.

The results obtained in these and other experiments demonstrate that dissonance-produced negative affect and dissonance-related attitude change can occur in situations where cognitive inconsistency is present but the production of aversive consequences is not present. These experiments supported the original conception of dissonance theory over the aversive consequence revision. But why does dissonance evoke this negative motivational state? Why is inconsistency aversive? Festinger proposed no answer to the question of what underlies dissonance motivation.

ACTION-BASED MODEL OF DISSONANCE

Although the research on the aversive consequences revision settled one theoretical controversy, it led to questions about the motivation underlying dissonance reduction. To address these questions, I developed an action-based model of cognitive dissonance that extends Brehm and Cohen's (1962) discussion of the importance of behavioral commitment to dissonance processes (Harmon-Jones, 1999, 2000-b). Brehm and Cohen (1962) proposed that the concept of behavioral commitment assists in specifying which relevant cognitions are dissonant and which are consonant. They also proposed that commitment increased the resistance to change of a cognition (or set of cognitions), which would affect the manner in which dissonance was reduced.

The action-based model begins with the assumption that perceptions and cognitions can serve as action tendencies. The model then proposes that dissonance between cognitions evokes an aversive state because the dissonance has the potential to interfere with effective and unconflicted action. Dissonance reduction, by bringing cognitions into consonance, serves the function of facilitating the execution of effective and unconflicted action (see also Jones & Gerard, 1967). The action-based model accepts the ideas of Brehm and Cohen (1962) but assumes that commitment can occur without overt behavior. That is, organisms can regard cognitions that may not involve a behavioral commitment as "true" and would experience dissonance if information were presented that was inconsistent with these cognitions. As an example, consider a person's knowledge of the law of gravity. Information that violates the law of gravity would probably arouse dissonance in most people. Therefore, according to the action-based model, a commitment occurs when an individual regards a behavior, belief, attitude, or value as a meaningful truth. The psychological commitment to the cognition then guides information processing, which serves the ultimate function of producing and guiding behavior.

After a decision (commitment) is made, the processing that occurs should assist with the execution of the decision. The tendency to view the chosen alternative more favorably and the rejected alternative more negatively after a decision is made (i.e., spreading the alternatives) should help the individual to follow through and act on the decision in a more effective manner.

State Action Orientation and Spreading of Alternatives

An action-oriented state is a state that often occurs following a decision (Gollwitzer, 1990; Heckhausen, 1986; Kuhl, 1984). When a person is in an action-oriented state, implementation of decisions is enhanced. Harmon-Jones and Harmon-Jones (2002) integrated these ideas with the action-based model of dissonance theory to propose that this action-oriented state that follows decision making is equivalent to the state in which dissonance motivation operates and dissonance reduction occurs. They hypothesized that experimentally manipulating the degree of action orientation experienced following a decision should affect the degree of dissonance reduction.

I first proposed the action-based model to Jack in 1994. He disagreed with my adaptive, functionalist view of dissonance processes and he described some situations that he believed countered the idea. However, I persisted with the action-based model, and I'm not sure whether I've convinced Jack yet.

To test some predictions derived from the model, Harmon-Jones and Harmon-Jones (2002) conducted an experiment in which participants were asked to make either an easy decision or a difficult decision (i.e., which physical exercise to perform later in the session). Participants were asked to fill out a mindset questionnaire after the decision. The neutral mindset asked participants to list seven things they did in a typical day, whereas the action-oriented mindset questionnaire asked participants to list seven things they could do to perform well on the exercise they had chosen. Participants were then asked to reevaluate the exercises. Results indicated that participants in the difficult-decision, action-oriented condition spread the alternatives more than did participants in the other conditions.

In a second experiment testing the action-based model, Harmon-Jones and Harmon-Jones (2002) replicated the results of the first experiment using a different manipulation of action orientation. In this experiment, action orientation was induced by asking participants to think of an important decision that they had made and to list the steps they intended to use to successfully follow through with their decision. The participants in the action-orientation condition engaged in more spreading of alternatives following a difficult decision than did participants in the comparison conditions. This study replicated the results of the previous study, but provided stronger support for the action-based model because it used an action-orientation induction unrelated to the decision in the experiment.

Action Orientation, Frontal Brain Activity, and Spreading of Alternatives

The previous experiments provided support for the action-based model of dissonance and cannot be easily interpreted by other revisions of dissonance theory (see Harmon-Jones & Harmon-Jones, 2002). In addition to conducting these experiments, my colleagues and I have conducted other research aimed at testing predictions, derived from the action-based model, regarding the involvement of the frontal cortices in dissonance reduction.

Over the last 20 years, there has been an impressive convergence of research findings obtained from a variety of methodological approaches that have suggested that the left and right frontal cortical regions have different motivational and emotional functions, with the left frontal region being involved in approach-related processes, and the right frontal region being involved in withdrawal-related processes. For instance, Robinson and colleagues (e.g., Robinson & Downhill, 1995) observed that it is damage specifically to the left frontal lobe that causes depressive symptoms. They found that for persons with left hemisphere brain damage, the closer the lesion is to the frontal pole, the greater the depressive symptoms. In contrast, persons with damage to the right frontal hemisphere are more likely to respond with mania.

The left frontal cortical region has been described as an important center for intention, self-regulation, and planning (Kosslyn & Koenig, 1995; Petrides & Milner, 1982). These functions have often been described as properties of the will, a hypothetical construct important in guiding approach-related behavior. Persons with damage to this region are apathetic, experience less interest and pleasure, and have difficulty initiating actions.

Research using measures of electroencephalographic activity (EEG) has shown that increased left-frontal cortical activation relates to dispositional tendencies toward approach motivation (Harmon-Jones & Allen, 1997, 1998) and repression (Tomarken & Davidson, 1994), and that decreased left-frontal activity relates to depression (Henriques & Davidson, 1991). It is interesting to note that repression has been linked to an increased likelihood of reducing dissonance via attitude change (Olson & Zanna, 1979; Zanna & Aziza, 1976), suggesting that increased left frontal activity may be related to dissonance-related attitude change. Other research has found that left-frontal activation is increased during approach toward rewarding outcomes, whereas right-frontal activation is increased during withdrawal from aversive outcomes (Sobotka, Davidson, & Senulis, 1992). Thus, as approach-related action-oriented thinking increases, greater left frontal activation may occur. Moreover, individuals who are more action oriented may show increased left frontal activity following a dissonance-arousing decision.

In one experiment testing the hypothesis, participants were given low or high choice to engage in counterattitudinal behavior. Results indicated that immediately after individuals committed to writing a counterattitudinal essay (i.e., in the high-choice but not the low-choice condition), they showed increased left frontal activity (Harmon-Jones, Fearn, Gerdjikov, & Harmon-Jones, 2003). That is, a main effect of choice emerged, F (1, 38) = 4.33, $p < .05$, which indicated that high-choice participants evidenced greater relative left frontal cortical activity (midfrontal M = 0.141, SD = 0.156; lateral frontal M = 0.359, SD = 0.348) than did low-choice participants (midfrontal M = 0.076, SD = 0.143; lateral frontal M = 0.157, SD = 0.204).

In another experiment, participants made a difficult decision, and their EEG was recorded following the decision. Then, they rerated the decision alternatives. Finally, they completed Kuhl's (1993) trait measure of action control, which contains a subscale relevant to decision processes, the prospective and decision-related action orientation versus hesitation. We predicted that trait action orientation would relate to relative left frontal activity and spreading of alternatives. Results supported these predictions, with trait action orientation relating to relative left frontal activity (*partial r* = .31, $p < .05$, controlling for baseline activity) and spreading of alternatives ($r = .30$, $p < .05$; Harmon-Jones, Peterson, Hubbell, & Harmon-Jones, 2002).

Taken together, these two experiments suggest that the process of dissonance reduction involves the activation of the left frontal cortex. These results are consistent with research demonstrating that the left frontal cortex is involved in approach motivation processes, and with the action-based model of dissonance that predicts that the process of dissonance reduction involves an approach-related action orientation.

Emotion as Action-Tendency Experiment

To further test the action-based model of dissonance, we conducted an experiment to test the hypothesis that dissonance should be increased as the salience of the action implications of cognitions that are involved in a dissonant relationship are increased. Several perspectives consider emotions to involve action tendencies (Brehm, 1999; Frijda, 1986). To the extent that an emotion generates an action tendency, then as the intensity of one's current emotion is increased and is involved in a dissonant relationship with other information, dissonance should be increased.

Research has demonstrated that the emotion of sympathy (empathy) increases helping behavior because it evokes altruistic motivation, that is, motivation to relieve the distress of the person in need of help (see Batson, 1991, for a review). We have conducted one experiment that tested whether an inconsistency between the emotion of sympathy and knowledge about past failures to act in accord with the sympathy evoked motivation to reduce this inconsistency (Harmon-Jones, Peterson, & Vaughn, 2003).

In the experiment, we tested the hypothesis that after experiencing sympathy for a target person in need of help, individuals will be more motivated to help that person when they are reminded of times that they failed to help similar persons (see Batson et al., 1997, for evidence that feeling sympathy for one target person can transfer to the target person's group and cause attitude change toward the group). Participants were informed that they would be listening to a pilot broadcast for a local radio station and that the researchers would like students' reactions to the tape. Participants then listened to a tape-recorded message that was purportedly from a person in need of help (an adolescent with cancer). Before listening to the tape, participants were assigned to one of two conditions; one in which they tried to imagine how the person must feel (high-empathy set) or one in which they tried to remain objective as they listened to the tape (low-empathy set). Then they listened to the tape-recorded message, and afterward, completed questionnaires assessing self-reported emotional responses and evaluations of the tape-recorded message. Participants were then asked to list times when they failed to help other persons who were in need of help (to induce dissonance) or they completed a demographic survey (control condition). Finally, participants were given an opportunity to help by volunteering time to assist the person with addressing letters that would request money from possible donors or by donating money to the person's family. The design was a 2 (low vs. high empathy) × 2 (reminded of times that did not help or not reminded) between-subjects factorial. Consistent with predictions derived from the action-based model, results indicated that more helping occurred in the high-empathy/reminder of past failures condition than in other conditions.

FRONTAL BRAIN ASYMMETRY AND MOTIVATIONAL INTENSITY

In another line of research that has examined the motivational functions of the left and right frontal cortices, I have been influenced by Jack's theories of motivational and emotional intensity (Brehm, 1999; Brehm & Self, 1989). In this line of research, I have been comparing the emotional valence view of the frontal asymmetry with the motivational direction view of the frontal asymmetry (Harmon-Jones & Allen, 1997, 1998; Harmon-Jones & Sigelman, 2001). According to the emotional valence view, positive emotions are related to relatively greater left than right frontal cortical activity, and negative emotions are related to relatively greater right than left frontal cortical activity. According to the motivational direction view, approach motivation is related to relatively greater left than right frontal activity, and withdrawal motivation is related to relatively greater right than left frontal cortical activity.

State Anger and Relative Left Frontal Activity

Anger provides an optimal testing ground for these competing predictions because anger is a negative emotion that often generates approach motivation. To test the effect of anger on asymmetrical frontal brain activity, my colleagues and I manipulated anger and measured EEG and aggression. We predicted that anger would increase left frontal brain activity. Emotions such as anger can be conceived of as having motivational functions and as generating action tendencies (Brehm, 1999; Frijda, 1986). Of course, emotions may generate action tendencies that may not be manifest in overt behavior. However, anger often generates approach-related action tendencies that are generally aimed at resolving the anger-producing event. In the case of an insult, the action tendency may be aggression. If anger-induced relative left frontal activity is involved in approach motivational processes, then greater anger-induced left frontal activity may relate to increased aggression.

In the experiment, participants were randomly assigned to a condition in which they were either insulted or not insulted. Under the guise of a study concerning personality, psychophysiology, and perception, another participant gave them an insulting or neutral evaluation of an essay they had written. Immediately after the feedback manipulation, EEG was recorded. Then, in a "separate study" on taste perception, they selected one of six beverages for the "other participant." The beverages ranged from pleasant tasting to unpleasant tasting, and thus allowed us to obtain a behavioral measure of aggression. Aggression was calculated by assigning each beverage a value that corresponded to its unpleasantness. This measure of aggression is similar to a technique developed by other researchers (Lieberman, Solomon, Greenberg, & McGregor, 1999). Finally, self-reports of emotions experienced during the experiment were collected.

Results indicated that participants in the insult condition reported feeling more angry and were more aggressive than were participants in the no-insult condition. More importantly, participants in the insult condition evidenced greater relative left frontal activity than did participants in the no-insult condition. Finally, within the insult condition, participants who evidenced greater relative left frontal activity in response to the insult reported feeling more angry and they behaved more aggressively.

This research supports the prediction that anger is associated with relative left frontal brain activity. In conjunction with trait-based research (Harmon-Jones & Allen, 1998), the research demonstrates that asymmetrical frontal brain activity reflects motivational direction rather than emotional valence. In addition, results suggest that relative left frontal activity during an anger-evoking situation related to behavioral aggression.

Manipulating the Intensity of Approach Motivation in an Anger-Evoking Situation

According to the motivational direction model of asymmetrical frontal activity, approach motivation is related to left frontal activity and withdrawal motivation is related to right frontal activity. Thus, increased left frontal activation occurs in response to anger-inducing situations because the increase in relative left frontal activity increases approach motivational tendencies that would assist in behavior that may rectify the anger-inducing situation. From this perspective, it follows that if no approach behavior could be taken to deal with the anger-provoking situation, then this increase in relative left frontal activation should be less. In other words, if approach and withdrawal motivational tendencies do underlie asymmetrical frontal activity, then alterations in motivational intensity should affect the degree of activation in the frontal brain regions.

Jack's theories of emotional and motivational intensity predict that perceived task difficulty should affect motivational intensity (for reviews, see Brehm, 1999; Brehm & Self, 1989; Brehm, Wright, Solomon, Silka, & Greenberg, 1983; Wright & Kirby, 2001), with motivational intensity being highest for moderately challenging tasks and lower for easy or impossible tasks. For the emotion of anger, if a situation creates anger and the individual believes that she can, with some difficulty, successfully act to alter the situation, then motivational intensity should be relatively high. If, on the other hand, the individual believes that no action can be taken (i.e., that it is impossible to act to resolve the situation), then motivational intensity should be relatively low. A similar prediction follows from the idea of secondary coping (Lazarus, 1991). Negative emotions including anger, sadness, guilt, and fear occur when people find themselves in aversive situations. According to Lazarus (1991), the type of negative emotion evoked by a situation may be determined by coping potential—how people appraise their ability to deal with the aversive situation. If something can be done to resolve the situation, then anger, an active and negative emotion, should be aroused. In contrast, if nothing can be done to resolve the situation, then a passive and negative emotion, sadness, may be aroused.

Unfortunately, little research has addressed whether appraisals of higher coping potential lead to more anger. However, research by Levine (1995) found that when 5-year-old children were presented with scenarios in which a child experienced a negative outcome, they expected the protagonist to experience more anger and less sadness when they judged the possibility of goal reinstatement more likely, and less anger and more sadness when they judged goal reinstatement less likely. In addition, Brummett (1997; as cited in Brehm, 1999) found that the intensity of anger was greater when there were moderate amounts of deterrents to expressing anger and that the intensity of anger was reduced when the deterrents were greater.

Based on the integration of ideas from the motivational model of asymmetrical frontal activity with theories of motivational intensity and how coping potential relates to anger, we predicted that greater left frontal activation would occur in response to an anger-producing event when people believe that action can be taken to resolve the situation as compared to when people believe that no action can be taken to resolve the situation.

To test these predictions, university students who paid a sizable portion of their tuition and who were opposed to a tuition increase were invited to an experiment ostensibly concerned with reactions to pilot radio broadcasts. They then heard an editorial in which the speaker argued forcefully for a tuition increase. Immediately prior to hearing the editorial, participants were informed that the tuition increase may occur in the future and that petitions were being circulated to attempt to prevent the increase (action-possible condition), or they were informed that the tuition increase would definitely occur (action-impossible condition). Immediately after listening to the editorial, EEG was recorded, and then participants completed a self-report emotion questionnaire. Finally, participants in the action-possible condition were given the opportunity to sign a petition and take as many petitions as they wanted to have others sign.

Results revealed that participants in the action-possible condition evidenced greater relative left frontal activity than did participants in the action-impossible condition. Moreover, within the action-possible condition, this increase in relative left frontal activity directly related to self-reported anger and behaviors aimed at rectifying the anger-producing event (i.e., whether or not they signed the petition and number of petitions taken). Interestingly, self-reported anger did not differ between the action-possible and action-impossible conditions. Participants in both conditions reported feeling much angrier after hearing the editorial as compared to before hearing the editorial (Harmon-Jones, Sigelman, Bohlig, & Harmon-Jones, 2003). These results suggest that the appraisal of coping potential influenced relative left frontal activity but not angry feelings. Thus, the results for relative left frontal activity are consistent with predictions derived from Jack's (Brehm, 1999; Brehm & Self, 1989) theories of motivational and emotional intensity, which predict a "saw-tooth" relationship between motivational/emotional intensity and perceived task difficulty. Emotional intensity is expected to be highest when the task is perceived as moderately difficult and lower when the task is perceived as impossible.

Individual Differences That Predict Increased Relative Left Frontal Activity During Anger

The research suggests that trait and state anger are related to relative left frontal activity when anger is associated with approach motivational tendencies. Past research has revealed that individual differences in behavioral approach sensitivity (BAS) are related to relatively greater left frontal activity (Harmon-Jones & Allen, 1997). Thus, greater BAS should predispose individuals to respond with greater left frontal activity when angered. The BAS has been posited to be involved in predatory aggression (Gray, 1982). In addition, the BAS has been proposed to underlie types of psychopathology, with depression involving a hypoactive BAS (Fowles, 1988) and mania involving a hyperactive BAS (Depue & Iacono, 1989).

Based on these ideas, we conducted research to examine the relationship between proneness to hypomania/mania and anger-related left frontal activity (Harmon-Jones, Abramson et al., 2002). In the study, individuals with proneness toward hypomania/mania or depression symptoms were exposed to the anger-evoking radio broadcast used in the previously mentioned study (Harmon-Jones, Sigelman et al., 2003). Results indicated that individuals with proneness toward hypomania/mania evidenced greater left frontal activation when confronted with the anger-evoking situation, whereas individuals with proneness toward depression symptoms evidenced less left frontal activation when confronted with the same anger-evoking situation.

This research extends the past research on anger and frontal brain activity by revealing individual difference characteristics that predict who is more likely, as well as less likely, to respond with increased left frontal activity in anger-inducing situations. Individuals with proneness toward hypomania/mania symptoms evidence greater relative left frontal activity, whereas individuals with proneness toward depressive symptoms evidence lesser relative left frontal activity when confronted with an anger-evoking event. Thus, it seems plausible to predict that proneness toward hypomania/mania symptoms may predispose people toward responding with increased approach (and decreased withdrawal) motivational tendencies given challenging or frustrating situations, whereas proneness toward depressive symptoms may predispose people toward responding with decreased approach (and increased withdrawal) motivational tendencies given these same situations. These findings are consistent with the spirit of the Wortman and Brehm (1975) model that integrated reactance theory with learned helplessness theory. Wortman and Brehm predicted that reactance (which may be experienced as anger) should occur initially when an obstacle to a goal is encountered, but that, when a goal is frustrated repeatedly, learned helplessness should occur. Perhaps because of their differing expectancies of control over the situation, people prone to mania may persist longer in experiencing reactance when frustrated, whereas people prone to depression may more quickly experience learned helplessness. In other words, proneness toward manic symptoms may lead to reactance-like responses and proneness toward depressive symptoms may lead to helpless responses in the face of challenges.

CONCLUSION

In sum, Jack, beginning with his cognitive dissonance theory developments and extending to his recent theoretical statements on motivational intensity and the motivational function of emotions, has profoundly impacted a substantial portion of my research. Moreover, he has been a major influence on my approach to behavioral science. His persistent pursuit for truth, described in elegant theories that aim at explaining general mechanisms rather than specific problems, has stood as a shining example of how behavioral science should be done. I well remember observing his early research on emotional intensity (summarized in Brehm, 1999), and was quite impressed with his persistence. When the undergraduate student experimenters were having difficulties with some of the difficult-to-execute manipulations, what did Jack do? He began running his own participants so that he could understand why the manipulations were not working. And it is now clear that he worked things out, as several experiments have convincingly supported the theory of emotional intensity.

For Jack, science is about truth and elegant, parsimonious theories that are stated abstractly and apply to a wide range of phenomena. It is not about popularity among peers, number of publications, number and size of grants, or number of times cited. Although Jack has accomplished many of the feats deemed important by the field, his approach has always seemed motivated by the more important goal of determining truth. In fact, I never remember him saying a word about these other goals that have become so important in current behavioral "science." Perhaps that's why he appeared so noncompetitive (symbolically self-complete) when I first met him. As a field, we would benefit greatly by adopting his humble but bold approach.

ACKNOWLEDGMENTS

This research was partially supported by funds from a grant from the University of Wisconsin Graduate School, a grant from the Wisconsin/Hilldale Undergraduate/Faculty Research Fund, a grant from the National Science Foundation (BCS-9910702), and a grant from the National Institute of Mental Health (1 R03 MH60747-01). Thanks to Cindy Harmon-Jones for valuable comments provided on this chapter. Address correspondence concerning this manuscript to: Eddie Harmon-Jones, University of Wisconsin—Madison, Department of Psychology, 1202 West Johnson Street, Madison, WI 53706; or via the Internet: eharmonj@facstaff.wisc.edu.

REFERENCES

Batson, C. D. (1975). Rational processing or rationalization?: The effect of disconfirming information on a stated religious belief. *Journal of Personality and Social Psychology, 32,* 176–184.

Batson, C. D. (1991). *The altruism question: Toward a social–psychological answer.* Hillsdale, NJ: Lawrence Erlbaum Associates.

Batson, C. D., Polycarpou, M. P., Harmon-Jones, E., Imhoff, H. J., Mitchener, E. C., Bednar, L. L., Klein, T. R., & Highberger, L. (1997). Empathy and attitudes: Can feeling for a member of a stigmatized outgroup improve attitudes toward the group? *Journal of Personality and Social Psychology, 72*, 105–118.

Brehm, J. W. (1956). Postdecision changes in the desirability of alternatives. *Journal of Abnormal and Social Psychology, 52*, 384–389.

Brehm, J. W. (1999). The intensity of emotion. *Personality and Social Psychology Review, 3*, 2–22.

Brehm, J. W., & Cohen, A. R. (1962). *Explorations in cognitive dissonance*. New York: Wiley.

Brehm, J. W., & Self, E. (1989). The intensity of motivation. In M. R. Rosenzweig & L. W. Porter (Eds.), *Annual review of psychology* (Vol. 40, pp. 109–131). Palo Alto, CA: Annual Reviews, Inc.

Brehm, J. W., Wright, R. A., Solomon, S., Silka, L., & Greenberg, J. (1983). Perceived difficulty, energization, and the magnitude of goal valence. *Journal of Experimental Social Psychology, 19*, 21–48.

Brock, T. C., & Balloun, J. C. (1967). Behavioral receptivity to dissonant information. *Journal of Personality and Social Psychology, 6*, 413–428.

Brummett, B. H. (1997). The intensity of anger. *Dissertation Abstracts International: Section B: The Sciences & Engineering, 58*, 1590.

Burris, C. T., Harmon-Jones, E., & Tarpley, W. R. (1997). "By faith alone": Religious agitation and cognitive dissonance. *Basic and Applied Social Psychology, 19*, 17–31.

Cooper, J., & Fazio, R. H. (1984). A new look at dissonance theory. In L. Berkowitz (Ed.), *Advances in experimental social psychology* (Vol. 17, pp. 229–264). Orlando, FL: Academic Press.

Depue, R. A., & Iacono, W. G. (1989). Neurobehavioral aspects of affective disorder. *Annual Review of Psychology, 40*, 457–492.

Fowles, D. C. (1988). Psychophysiology and psychopathology: A motivational approach. *Psychophysiology, 25*, 373–391.

Frijda, N. H. (1986). *The emotions*. Cambridge: Cambridge University Press.

Gollwitzer, P. M. (1990). Action phases and mind-sets. In E. T. Higgins & R. M. Sorrentino (Eds.), *Handbook of motivation and cognition: Foundations of social behavior* (Vol. 2, pp. 53–92). New York, NY: Guilford.

Gray, J. A. (1982). *The neuropsychology of anxiety: An enquiry into the functions of the septo-hippocampal system*. New York: Oxford University Press.

Harmon-Jones, E. (1999). Toward an understanding of the motivation underlying dissonance: Is the production of aversive consequences necessary to produce dissonance? In E. Harmon-Jones & J. Mills (Eds.), *Cognitive dissonance: Progress on a pivotal theory in social psychology* (pp. 71–99). Washington, DC: American Psychological Association.

Harmon-Jones, E. (2000a). Cognitive dissonance and experienced negative affect: Evidence that dissonance increases experienced negative affect even in the absence of aversive consequences. *Personality and Social Psychology Bulletin, 26*, 1490–1501.

Harmon-Jones, E. (2000b). A cognitive dissonance theory perspective on the role of emotion in the maintenance and change of beliefs and attitudes. In N. H. Frijda, A. R. S. Manstead, & S. Bem (Eds.), *Emotions and beliefs* (pp. 185–211). Cambridge, England: Cambridge University Press.

Harmon-Jones, E., Abramson, L. Y., Sigelman, J., Bohlig, A., Hogan, M. E., & Harmon-Jones, C. (2002). Proneness to hypomania/mania or depression and asymmetrical frontal cortical responses to an anger-evoking event. *Journal of Personality and Social Psychology, 82*, 610–618.

Harmon-Jones, E., & Allen, J. J. B. (1997). Behavioral activation sensitivity and resting frontal EEG asymmetry: Covariation of putative indicators related to risk for mood disorders. *Journal of Abnormal Psychology, 106*, 159–163.

Harmon-Jones, E., & Allen, J. J. B. (1998). Anger and prefrontal brain activity: EEG asymmetry consistent with approach motivation despite negative affective valence. *Journal of Personality and Social Psychology, 74,* 1310–1316.

Harmon-Jones, E., Brehm, J. W., Greenberg, J., Simon, L., & Nelson, D. E. (1996). Evidence that the production of aversive consequences is not necessary to create cognitive dissonance. *Journal of Personality and Social Psychology, 70,* 5–16.

Harmon-Jones, E., Fearn, M., Gerdjikov, T., & Harmon-Jones, C. (2003). *Dissonance aroused by induced compliance increases relative left frontal activity.* Unpublished manuscript.

Harmon-Jones, E., & Harmon-Jones, C. (2002). Testing the action-based model of cognitive dissonance: The effect of action-orientation on post-decisional attitudes. *Personality and Social Psychology Bulletin, 28,* 711–723.

Harmon-Jones, E., Peterson, H., Hubbell, C., & Harmon-Jones, C. (2002). *Trait action-orientation relates to spreading of alternative and relative left frontal activity after a dissonance-arousing decision.* Unpublished manuscript.

Harmon-Jones, E., Peterson, H., & Vaughn, K. (2003). The dissonance-inducing effects of an inconsistency between experienced empathy and knowledge of past failures to help: Support for the action-based model of dissonance. *Basic and Applied Social Psychology, 25,* 69–78.

Harmon-Jones, E., & Sigelman, J. (2001). State anger and prefrontal brain activity: Evidence that insult-related relative left prefrontal activation is associated with experienced anger and aggression. *Journal of Personality and Social Psychology, 80,* 797–803.

Harmon-Jones, E., Sigelman, J. D., Bohlig, A., & Harmon-Jones, C. (2003). Anger, coping, and frontal cortical activity: The effect of coping potential on anger-induced left frontal activity. *Cognition and Emotion, 17,* 1–24.

Heckhausen, H. (1986). Why some time out might benefit achievement motivation research. In J. H. L van den Bercken, E. E. J. De Bruyn, & T. C. M. Bergen (Eds.), *Achievement and task motivation* (pp. 7–39). Lisse, the Netherlands: Swets & Zeitlinger.

Henriques, J. B., & Davidson, R. J. (1991). Left frontal hypoactivation in depression. *Journal of Abnormal Psychology, 100,* 535–545.

Jones, E. E., & Gerard, H. B. (1967). *Foundations of social psychology.* New York: Wiley.

Kosslyn, S. M., & Koenig, O. (1995). *Wet mind: The new cognitive neuroscience.* New York: Free Press.

Kuhl, J. (1984). Volitional aspects of achievement motivation and learned helplessness: Toward a comprehensive theory of action-control. In B. A. Maher (Ed.), *Progress in experimental personality research* (Vol. 13, pp. 99–171). New York: Academic Press.

Kuhl, J. (1993). Action versus state orientation: Psychometric properties of the Action Control Scale (ACS–90). In J. Kuhl & J. Beckmann (Eds.), *Volition and personality: Action versus state orientation* (pp. 47–59). Seattle, WA: Hogrefe & Huber.

Lazarus, R. S. (1991). *Emotion and adaptation.* New York: Oxford.

Levine, L. J. (1995). Young children's understanding of the causes of anger and sadness. *Child Development, 66,* 697–709.

Lieberman, J. D., Solomon, S., Greenberg, J., & McGregor, H. A. (1999). A hot new way to measure aggression: Hot sauce allocation. *Aggressive Behavior, 25,* 331–348.

Olson, J. M., & Zanna, M. P. (1979). A new look at selective exposure. *Journal of Experimental Social Psychology, 15,* 1–15.

Petrides, M., & Milner, B. (1982). Deficits on subject-ordered tasks after frontal- and temporal-lobe lesions in man. *Neuropsychologia, 20,* 249–262.

Robinson, R. G., & Downhill, J. E. (1995). Lateralization of psychopathology in response to focal brain injury. In R. J. Davidson & K. Hugdahl (Eds.), *Brain asymmetry* (pp. 693–711). Cambridge, MA: MIT Press.

Sobotka, S. S., Davidson, R. J., & Senulis, J. A. (1992). Anterior brain electrical asymmetries in response to reward and punishment. *Electroencephalography and Clinical Neurophysiology, 83,* 236–247.

Stone, J., Aronson, E., Crain, A. L., Winslow, M. P., & Fried, C. B. (1994). Inducing hypocrisy as a means for encouraging young adults to use condoms. *Personality and Social Psychology Bulletin, 20,* 116–128.

Tomarken, A. J., & Davidson, R. J. (1994). Frontal brain activation in repressors and nonrepressors. *Journal of Abnormal Psychology, 103,* 339–349.

Wortman, C. B., & Brehm, J. W. (1975). Responses to uncontrollable outcomes: An integration of reactance theory and the learned helplessness model. In L. Berkowitz (Ed.), *Advances in Experimental Social Psychology* (Vol. 8., pp. 278–336). New York: Academic Press.

Wright, R. A., & Kirby, L. D. (2001). Effort determination of cardiovascular response: An integrative analysis with applications in social psychology. In M. P. Zanna (Ed.), *Advances in experimental social psychology* (Vol. 33, pp. 255–307).

Wright, R. A., Tunstall, A. M., Williams, B. J., Goodwin, J. S., & Harmon-Jones, E. (1995). Social evaluation and cardiovascular response: An active coping approach. *Journal of Personality and Social Psychology, 69,* 530–543.

Zanna, M. P., & Aziza, C. (1976). On the interaction of repression-sensitization and attention in resolving cognitive dissonance. *Journal of Personality, 44,* 577–593.

5

Self-Awareness, Self-Motives, and Self-Motivation

Paul J. Silvia
University of North Carolina at Greensboro

Thomas Shelley Duval
University of Southern California

When people have problems understanding something—either because they feel incompetent or because the thing is new and complex—people explain the thing in terms of essences and categories, types and dispositions (Wicklund, 1999). When people understand something well, however, they explain its activity in terms of processes, contingencies, and interactions. For instance, when people explain the actions of strangers, they invoke broad essences known as "traits," such as "She said something nice because she's a friendly person." When people explain the actions of friends, in contrast, they invoke contingencies and interactions, such as "He's pretty friendly, although he can be aggressive when he's losing at sports" (Idson & Mischel, 2001).

Explanations in terms of dispositions versus contingencies extend beyond person perception into explanation more broadly. Kurt Lewin (1935) was among the first to note that scientific theories differ in their approach to explanation. Some theories search for variability in surface behavior, categorize behavior based on the observed variations, and then ascribe essences to the categories (Wicklund, 1990). Lewin traced this mode to Aristotle, who explained motion through different essential tendencies of objects. In the Galileian mode, in contrast, theories search for continuities underlying seemingly different events. Similarities in abstract principles thus take priority over similarities in concrete observations. A cart rumbling down a muddy path and a perfect sphere rolling down a smooth plane are different apparently but identical conceptually. The examples involve the same conceptual variables, such as friction and mass; they merely differ in the levels of the variables.

Motivation psychology is no stranger to essence explanations. Early theories of motivation posited instincts to explain variability in behavior. William McDougall (1908/1960), probably the most famous instinct theorist, inferred instincts from his observations of behavior. People sometimes explore their environments, so he assumed a "curiosity instinct." But sometimes people fear new things, so he further assumed a "flight instinct." Different behaviors reflect different motivations; similar behaviors reflect similar motivations. Things that seem different phenotypically are assumed to be different genotypically—no apparent differences are merely apparent. The notion that apparently antagonistic behaviors (like curiosity vs. anxiety, or approach vs. avoidance) might stem from the same set of processes was not considered.

The Aristotelian approach never quite left motivation psychology, and it recently found fertile ground in the study of self and motivation. The prevailing model of self-motivation posits a set of "self-motives"—self-enhancement, self-assessment, self-verification, and self-improvement—from which self-motivated activity derives (Sedikides & Strube, 1997). We hope to show that the self-motives approach to explaining self-motivation, like McDougall's instinct model, is inadequate—it infers the motive from behavior and then explains behavior with the motive. In the first part of our chapter, we review the premises of the self-motives approach and present some criticisms. We then present objective self-awareness (OSA) theory as a model of self-motivation. OSA theory assumes that seemingly diverse behaviors—such as accepting or denying responsibility for failure—stem from the same underlying dynamics. We argue that some phenotypic behavioral differences—like avoiding or seeking negative information, or approaching and avoiding one's failures—share genotypic dynamic identities. Models of self-motivation based on taxonomies are thus unnecessary.

SELF-MOTIVES AS A THEORY OF SELF-MOTIVATION

We take the SCENT model of self-motives (Self-Concept Enhancing Tactician; Sedikides & Strube, 1997) as our prototype for the self-motives approach. The SCENT model is specified in the most detail and represents the views of researchers working in the self-motives tradition. Research based on this tradition is widely known. In fact, a recent textbook on the social psychology of the self uses the SCENT model as the framework for its discussion of self-motivation (Hoyle, Kernis, Leary, & Baldwin, 1999).

So, whereas many researchers would disagree with some of the SCENT model's technical points, most would agree with its core premise: that self-motivation is founded on a small set of independent motives. The SCENT model proposes four motives, which we review briefly.

The Four Self-Motives

The self-enhancement motive leads people "to elevate the positivity of their self-conceptions and to protect their self-concepts from negative information" (Sedikides & Strube, 1997, p. 212). The motive is inferred from behaviors such as preferring downward social comparison, judging oneself as "better than average" on many dimensions, defining positive traits in terms of one's own abilities, and attributing failure to external causes and success to internal causes.

The self-assessment motive leads people "to obtain a consensually accurate evaluation of the self . . . People seek diagnostic information regardless of its positive or negative implications for the self and regardless of whether the information affirms or challenges existing self-conceptions" (Sedikides & Strube, 1997, p. 213). Self-assessment is inferred from seeking feedback about performance, creating tasks that enable feedback, preferring diagnostic tasks, and blaming self for failure.

The self-verification motive leads people "to maintain consistency between their self-conceptions and new self-relevant information" (Sedikides & Strube, 1997, p. 213). This is inferred from behaviors such as preferring self-consistent information and choosing interaction partners who verify one's self-image.

The self-improvement motive leads people to "improve their traits, abilities, skills, health status, or well-being" (Sedikides & Strube, 1997, p. 213). This motivates seeking genuine improvement and personal growth. The motive is inferred from behaviors such as actively approaching and coping with problems, seeking information that enables improvement, practicing existing skills, and choosing to work on remedial tasks that reduce deficiencies.

These four motives are distinct, so the motives can cooperate, conflict, or operate independently of each other. Conflict has received the most attention, particularly the clash between self-verification and self-enhancement (Swann, Pelham, & Krull, 1989) and between self-enhancement and self-assessment (Trope & Neter, 1994). The SCENT model assumes a hierarchical arrangement in which self-enhancement reigns over the others. The verification, assessment, and improvement motives are seen as local means of achieving the distal goal of making the self more positive (Sedikides & Strube, 1997, p. 225). Testing this assumption seems difficult. Assuming a hierarchy is not necessary for the self-motives approach, and other researchers in the self-motives tradition would disagree.

Criticisms of the SCENT Model

We think that the SCENT approach is inadequate for six reasons. First, it infers the motive from the behavior. If every different behavior were attributed to a different motive, psychology would degenerate into a chaotic eclecticism. There must be some continuities in motivation. Either we assume that things that seem different at the behavioral level always have different causes, or we assume that sometimes they have similar causes. If we assume the latter, then we need to specify the similar causes. The SCENT approach does not seek similarities among the motives (apart from subordinating them all to self-enhancement) and thus fails to consider the possibility of underlying dynamic continuities.

Second, the self-motives approach nears circularity. It infers self-enhancing tendencies from behavior and then explains behavior with the self-enhancing tendencies. It is not entirely circular, because the same observation is not used for both purposes. An earlier observation (past research) implies the self-motive, which then explains the present (and similar) observation. Either way, the four self-motives seem like descriptive labels for activity rather than explanatory concepts. Do people make external attributions for failure because they were motivated by self-enhancement, or is "self-enhancement" a description of this sort of activity?

Third, the self-motives approach cannot be contradicted by research. What happens when a study finds that people avoid performance feedback? This can be explained by self-enhancement motivation. But what if people seek feedback? This must have reflected self-assessment motivation. And what if nothing happened? Two motives must have conflicted. No matter what a study finds, one of the four motives can be invoked as the cause of the observed behavior. We suggest that the reader take a moment to consider how to design a study to show that self-enhancement motivation (or any of the four motives) was operating *without using seemingly self-enhancing behavior as the criterion*—it's an interesting methodological exercise.

Fourth, the SCENT approach cannot predict when one versus another motive will guide activity. Imagine an experiment in which people work on a task. The task's importance is manipulated (high vs. low), and everyone gets failure feedback. So how will importance affect interest in a remedial task, our dependent variable? Will people approach or avoid the task? It's hard for the SCENT model to make a prediction one way or the other—but it can explain either finding afterward. Instead of prediction, it can only compile a list of moderators observed after the fact (Freitas, Salovey, & Liberman, 2001; Trope & Pomerantz, 1998), but the prediction is not required by the self-motives approach. Finding moderators is an important part of research—but we think it matters whether the moderators stem from intuition or whether they're derived from a theory.

Fifth, the four self-motives are not circumscribed. For instance, people want to self-improve because there is a self-improvement motive. But when do they *not* want to self-improve? In our reading of the SCENT model, it seems people want to do so limitlessly, all the time, in all contexts—except inasmuch as they also want to self-enhance, self-assess, and self-verify. The only boundary for a given self-motive is the fact that three other self-motives exist. Like a four-party democracy, the four self-motives act as reciprocal checks-and-balances for the others.

Sixth, and finally, we wonder why there are only four self-motives. If we don't know the boundaries of the motives, then nothing keeps us from positing new ones. Indeed, if we're inferring motives from observed behaviors, then we can posit a new motive whenever we observe a (seemingly) new behavior. Why not a fifth "self-protective" motive to explain denial of responsibility for negative events? Why not a sixth "self-expansive" motive to explain including others in the self-concept? What conceptual reason prevents this? If observed behavior is the criterion for asserting a motive, rather than deeper conceptual continuities, then the diversity of motives is limited only by the diversity of observations.

Past Theories as Nonexamples

We can illuminate the problems with the SCENT approach by viewing what other theories would look like if they adopted the same explanatory structure. We'll use some of Jack Brehm's theories as nonexamples.

What would reactance theory (Brehm, 1966) look like if it followed the SCENT model? First, it would posit two independent motives: a "freedom motive" and a "conformity motive," creating an ASCII (Autonomy-Seeking *but* Conformity-Increasing Individual) model of reactance. The freedom motive is seen in the tendency to react against influence attempts; the conformity motive is seen in the tendency to comply. The ASCII model would have to posit these two motives because we have observed instances of failed and successful influence. Concrete variability requires conceptual variability, in the Aristotelian mode—different behaviors (like compliance and reactance) cannot reflect the same underlying processes. When formulated this way, ASCII reactance theory makes no predictions. Do attractive groups create reactance or compliance (Brehm & Mann, 1975)? Well, does the group arouse one or the other motive? We can't know unless we do the study. The real reactance theory, in contrast, makes subtle predictions because it specifies variables—such as the magnitude of the threat to freedom, the importance of the freedom, the implications for other freedoms, and whether people feel free to do something. Likewise, the ASCII reactance model cannot say when people will not react; it can only say that the antagonistic motives to react and to comply limit each other reciprocally. The real reactance theory, in contrast, can specify the boundaries of reactance using its variables.

What would cognitive dissonance theory (Brehm & Cohen, 1962; Wicklund & Brehm, 1976) look like if it followed the SCENT model's example? We observe times when people change their attitude in response to contrary information, and observe other times when people bolster the original attitude. So we would need to posit two independent motivational tendencies—attitudinal stability and attitudinal change—yielding the BOMBAST (Being Ostensibly Motivated to Bolster *and* to Shift Thoughts) model of cognitive dissonance. So when people must choose between two alternatives, how will their attitudes change? The BOMBAST model cannot make predictions because it derives the theoretical concepts from the observations, thus preventing predictions about new events. The real dissonance theory, however, describes processes and variables—such as commitment, resistance to change, and magnitude of the discrepancy—that enable the theory to extend beyond the observations that inspired it.

OBJECTIVE SELF-AWARENESS AS A THEORY OF SELF-MOTIVATION

In this section, we present objective self-awareness theory as an alternative model of self-motivation (Duval & Silvia, 2001; Silvia & Duval, 2001a). The revised theory builds on the original theory of self-awareness (Duval & Wicklund, 1972; Wicklund, 1975) by adding new assumptions about affect and causal attributions. In this section, we present an overview of the processes assumed by the theory; our recent book presents the theory in detail (Duval & Silvia, 2001, chaps. 2–7). The following section shows how objective self-awareness theory can reinterpret the four self-motives in dynamic terms, and, more importantly, can make new predictions about self-motivated activity.

Mechanisms of Self-Motivation

Self-Focused Attention and Self-Evaluation. Objective self-awareness (OSA) theory argues that self-motivation is founded on a small set of interacting elements. We assume that people have a concept of *self*, derived from encountering different social perspectives (Shibutani, 1961). The features of the self-concept can be compared to internalized *standards of correctness* that specify features the self ought to have. Standards can be unattainable, vague, abstract, perfectionistic, idiosyncratic, and inconsistent with other standards. Other theories have suggested different kinds of standards—such as ideals versus oughts (Higgins, 1987) or approach versus avoidance goals (Carver & Scheier, 1998)—but all standards share the functional quality of specifying a feature that the self should have.

People don't constantly monitor how self fares relative to its standards. Most self-theories go awry by assuming that simply failing to meet a standard will reduce self-esteem. Almost everything people do violates at least one standard, given the number, complexity, perfectionism, and abstraction of standards. People have so many features of self, and so many standards relevant to the features, that there must be a mechanism that connects a specific aspect of the self to a specific standard. OSA theory diverges from nearly every other self-theory by specifying when standards affect self-evaluation. People only compare self with standards to the extent that attention is *self-focused*. Unlike most animals, people can consider self as an object with features. This state of "objective self-awareness" promotes comparison of self with standards. If people aren't self-focused, then self-standard discrepancies won't impact activity. Self-awareness theory, in this sense, is primary over other theories of self-evaluation because so few theories consider when people self-evaluate in the first place.

Situational factors influence the momentary level of self-awareness (Duval & Silvia, 2001, chap. 2). Attention orients on self whenever the self stands out from the background formed by the social context or past experience. Being distinctive in some way—the one actor among a crowd of observers, the one woman in a group of men—will draw attention to self because of figure-ground principles of attention. Stimuli reminding the person of the self's object status—hearing recordings of one's voice or seeing one's image on TV—should also increase self-awareness, particularly if they involve experiencing the self in unusual ways. Finally, targeting the attention system directly, such as by priming self-relevant knowledge or consuming alcohol, will affect self-awareness. Much has been made of individual differences in self-focused attention, known as private self-consciousness (Buss, 1980). We suspect that "trait self-awareness" reflects enduring situational consistencies or enduring beliefs that self deviates from a reference group.

In short, self-evaluation requires self-focused attention. Many studies show that standards are inert when self-focus is low, even when people are preselected for extreme standards (e.g., Gibbons, 1978; Silvia, 2002) and when standards are explicitly induced and manipulated (e.g., Duval & Lalwani, 1999). People will only appraise how self relates to standards to the extent that attention is self-focused. Situational features influence the momentary levels of self-focused attention, and thus the degree of self-evaluation. But what happens once people begin self-evaluating?

Causal Attributions for the Experience of Discrepancies. When people are self-focused and thus comparing self with standards, they typically notice disparities between how the self is and how the self should be. OSA theory is rooted in consistency theories of motivated cognition (Heider, 1960; Wicklund & Brehm, 1976). We assume that people prefer congruity between different aspects of self, congruity between different standards, and congruity between self and standards. Self-standard discrepancies thus generate negative affect because the ideal state is maximal similarity between self and standards. The catch, however, is that people don't necessarily know *why* they feel bad. We assume that the experience of affect does not contain information about its cause. If it did, "misattribution" would be impossible—people would inherently know why they feel bad. If emotions don't immediately tell us why we feel the emotion, then we need another process to interpret the affective experience and connect it to a cause. This is the process of *causal attribution.* When events occur that are surprising, unexpected, inconsistent, complex, or imbalanced, people make attributions for why the event occurred (Weiner, 1985). When people suddenly experience negative affect, attributional processes will seek to connect this event to a likely cause. The attribution process is often automatic, and thus experienced as perception rather than as inference (Heider, 1958a).

Attributions are fundamental to self-motivation for two reasons. First, attributions direct action. If people don't know why they feel bad, then they also don't necessarily know what to do about it. If negative affect doesn't contain information about its cause, then it also doesn't contain information about specific situated actions that would make people feel better. Attributions for the problem give people a foothold into possible solutions for the problem. As Heider (1958b) argued, "attribution serves the attainment of a stable and consistent environment, gives a parsimonious and at the same time often an adequate description of what happens, and determines what we expect will occur and what we should do about it" (p. 25). By telling people what caused an event, attributions give people expectations about what might change the event. Attributions thus suggest *targets for action.* We assume that people will act on the perceived cause of the problem, all else being equal. If people think that they feel badly because their standards are too high, then they'll change the standards; if people think that self was the cause of failure, then they'll change self (Duval & Lalwani, 1999).

Second, attributions undergird self-motivation because they influence evaluations. Based on Heider's (1958a) analysis of tendencies toward congruity between unit and sentiment relations, we have suggested that attributions lead to attitude formation (Duval & Silvia, 2001, chap. 7). When people attribute the cause of failure to self—that is, connect the self to the negative event in a cause–effect unit relationship—then people will evaluate the self negatively because connected elements become similar in valence. This is one way of thinking about "state self-esteem." If people attribute their failure to another person, then they should dislike that person as well as anything similar to the person. By connecting positive or negative events to the self, to other people, to standards, or to anything else, attributions lead people to evaluate the perceived cause positively or negatively.

Interaction of Self-Evaluation and Attribution: Can the Person Meet a Standard?

Thus far, we've seen how self-focused attention leads people to recognize discrepancies between self and standards, and how people then make attributions for the negative affect aroused by the discrepancy. Self-standard comparison and causal attribution are the two core processes in objective self-awareness theory. But there's a catch—the comparison process can affect the attribution process. We assume that there are motives associated with attributional processes. People want to make coherent, simple, and consistent attributions (Heider, 1958a). Linking events to their "most plausible causes" accomplishes this general goal (Duval & Duval, 1983). But sometimes attributional simplicity conflicts with self-standard consistency. Imagine a case where a person fails and self is the most plausible cause of failure. Attributing the experience of failure to self will create discrepancies but it will also connect the event to the most likely cause. Attributing failure externally, in contrast, averts discrepancies but at the cost of making a less consistent attribution. The first attribution privileges the attribution system; the second, the comparison system. This conflict arises whenever the self is the most plausible cause for a negative event (more precisely, for any event that would create a self-standard discrepancy upon attribution to self).

So what happens when people are the most plausible cause for a negative event? We assume that this conflict is reconciled by people's perceived rate of progress toward reducing the discrepancy. People compromise. If people believe they can rapidly reduce the problem, then they'll attribute the problem to self. This promotes a consistent attribution *and* creates a discrepancy—but people expect the discrepancy to be quickly reduced. If people feel unable to reduce the problem, either at all or at too slow of a rate, then they'll attribute the problem externally. Blaming something else isn't the most consistent attribution, but it does avoid an intractable self-standard discrepancy. And people then attribute failure to the next most likely cause (Silvia & Duval, 2001b), which satisfies the attributional goal to some degree. Many studies support these predictions.

When perceived rate of progress is low, people blame the environment and other people for their failure (Duval & Silvia, 2002), disengage from the task (Carver & Scheier, 1998), and avoid remedial tasks (Duval, Duval, & Mulilis, 1992). When rate of progress is high, however, people blame themselves for failure, experience reduced self-esteem (Duval & Silvia, 2002), take responsibility for the problem (Lalwani & Duval, 2000), and actively try to reduce the discrepancy (Duval et al., 1992; Duval & Lalwani, 1999).

Summary. These are the concepts and dynamics posited by objective self-awareness theory. Self-focused attention can uncover self-standard discrepancies; attributions determine how people deal with the problem and how they feel about the perceived cause; and self-evaluation can sometimes affect attributions. Self-motivation thus rests in the interplay of two systems that reflect motives for consistent cognitive organization (Heider, 1960): a system that prefers congruity between self and standards, and a system that prefers simple attributional structure. Note that we described each concept without relying on past observations. We did not infer that self-focused attention leads to self-standard comparison because we have observed it in the past. Self-awareness theory makes assumptions about constructs and how they relate—this allows the theory to make predictions about new observations.

Reinterpreting the Self-Motives

In this section, we see how objective self-awareness theory reinterprets the four self-motives. We hope to show that apparently opposing behaviors stem from the same dynamics, not from opposing motives. Not only can the theory recast each motive in terms of dynamic processes, but it can specify boundaries and make new predictions.

Self-Enhancement. Self-enhancement motivation has been inferred from behaviors like attributing failure externally, defining traits in terms of the self's qualities, viewing oneself as better than average, and making downward social comparisons. But the boundaries of self-enhancement are poorly defined in the self-motives approach. Self-awareness theory, in contrast, makes firm predictions about when people will self-enhance. First, we recast self-enhancement in terms of comparing self with standards of correctness. Statements such as "people strive for self-concept positivity" are vague unless we know what indicates a positive self. As a more specific alternative, we argue that people want to be congruent with their internalized standards, which specify the qualities of "the good self."

Framing self-enhancement in terms of meeting personal standards makes new predictions. As a general rule, "self-enhancing" activity should be more likely when people are self-focused. If a person isn't comparing self with standards, then the person won't recognize or care about discrepancies—meeting standards won't be a concern. Failure feedback, for instance, has little impact on self-serving attributions and self-esteem when self-awareness is low (Duval & Silvia, 2002; Silvia & Duval, 2001b), a finding hard to reconcile with a blanket self-enhancement motive.

When people are self-focused and thus self-evaluating against their standards, then people's perceived ability to reduce the discrepancy influences "self-enhancing" activity. When self-focused people fail, they self-enhance when they feel unable to deal with the problem—they blame the environment and other people for their problem, have no change in self-esteem, avoid remedial tasks, and so forth. When self-focused people feel able to improve, however, they blame self for the problem, experience reduced self-esteem, and actively try to do something about the problem. And when people are not self-focused, very little happens. They admit that their performance was substandard, but they do not act defensively or experience changes in self-esteem (Duval & Silvia, 2002). Such findings are not easily explained within the self-motives approach, even after the fact, but they are predicted by OSA theory.

We suspect that other symptoms of self-enhancement—like self-serving trait definitions, better-than-average effects, and downward comparisons—follow the same dynamics. Research on trait definition usually involves self-relevant traits for which people have standards, and thus potentially have discrepancies (Dunning, 1999). If a person defines a standard (e.g., a good leader) in terms of the qualities that the self already has, then the person has effectively ensured that self will be consistent with the prototype. If the trait is irrelevant to a person's standards, or if the person feels discrepant but able to improve, then we suspect that people wouldn't define traits in terms of the self. Likewise, viewing the self as better-than-average probably reflects the fact that most standards are defined in terms of relative performance. Because many traits and abilities have no objective index, people judge the self through social comparison (Festinger, 1954). Perceiving self as better-than-average thus reduces a perceived discrepancy between self and a standard defined by relative performance. If so, then the effect should vary as an interactive function of self-focus and ability to improve the problem. Likewise, downward social comparison makes self seem closer to a standard due to the contrast with the unfortunate person's position. Consistent with our analysis, Wills (1981) found that people make downward comparisons only when they can't improve.

In short, people show "self-enhancing" activity according to the boundaries predicted by self-awareness theory. When self-awareness is low, people don't self-enhance. When self-awareness is high, people self-enhance when they feel unable to improve, and don't self-enhance when they feel able to improve. Rather than a blanket motive bounded only by other blanket motives, self-enhancement seems to have a circumscribed pattern of dynamics.

Self-Assessment. Although the idea of a general motive "to know oneself" has an intuitive appeal, research shows that "self-assessment motivation" applies rather narrowly. Sedikides and Strube (1997) found that signs of self-assessment appear only when people are highly uncertain about an important self-aspect. This hardly indicates a broad motive, self- or otherwise. We also doubt that studies forcing people to take or create tasks can show "self-assessment motivation," even when subsequent feedback is optional. Claiming a motive to understand the self seems premature unless we know how many people don't care and would rather not take the task at all.

Either way, the basic main effect is that people prefer diagnostic tasks and performance feedback when they are uncertain about an important ability. An underappreciated point is that "diagnosticity" of a task is confounded with the participant's attributions for task performance. If a task is diagnostic, then the feedback says something about one's ability—an internal attribution is implied. If a task is not diagnostic, then the feedback implies nothing about one's ability. Diagnosticity thus implies performance attributions. In fact, participants seem to understand this. People predict that their self-esteem will go up on tasks that are diagnostic of success and go down on tasks diagnostic of failure (Trope, 1986). Attributional processes, which we view as foundational to self-motivation, are thus lurking in the background of self-assessment.

OSA theory predicts that concerns about self's properties only come about when people are self-focused, as people are in the typical psychology experiment (Duval & Silvia, 2001, chap. 2). When self-focus is lowered, "self-assessment" motivation should be minimal. When self-focus increases, however, people recognize that self could fail to meet a standard. As before, the dynamics of self-awareness predict that if people feel capable of initially succeeding or eventually improving, then they should prefer diagnostic tasks because success on such a task will reveal self-standard congruity and thus boost self-esteem (Duval & Silvia, 2002, study 3). If people do not feel capable of initially succeeding or eventually improving, they should prefer the nondiagnostic task, avoid feedback, and generally wish to leave the field.

A study of private self-consciousness supports our analysis (Carver, Antoni, & Scheier, 1985). People were given success or failure feedback on a first test. They were then allowed to choose items for the second test.

Some items allowed feedback, and other items did not. People who succeeded on the first task probably expected to do well on the second similar task; people who failed probably expected to do poorly. When self-consciousness was high, people who succeeded chose more items with feedback, and people who failed chose more items without feedback. When self-consciousness was low, however, people seemed unmotivated by self-assessment. Other research has found that people seek feedback when they can improve and avoid feedback when they can't improve (Dunning, 1995). People also make upward social comparisons when they feel they can improve but not when they can't improve (Ybema & Buunk, 1993).

For self-assessment, then, the core variables asserted by self-awareness theory—self-focused attention, probability of improvement, and attributions—nicely cover extant findings and suggest new predictions. When people aren't particularly self-focused, potential successes and failures are insignificant because people aren't self-evaluating (Carver et al., 1985). When people become self-focused, they become concerned with possible failure, particularly for "diagnostic tasks," which imply that self is responsible for success and failure. As with other areas, probability of improvement should moderate defensive versus constructive activity. If people feel able to succeed, or if they feel able to improve should they fail, then they should seek feedback and approach the task. If people feel unable to improve, however, they should avoid diagnostic tasks and feedback.

As before, a seemingly blanket motive shows a coherent, circumscribed pattern of dynamics. And, interestingly enough, the dynamics of self-assessment resemble the dynamics of self-enhancement described earlier. Presumably contrary self-motives (like assessment and enhancement) and presumably contrary activities (like feedback seeking and avoidance) stem from the same set of processes. We thus begin to see why self-awareness theory is a general theory of self-motivation.

Self-Verification. Self-verification is inferred from activities such as choosing to interact with someone who confirms one's self-view and liking others who are similar, even when the self-view and the dimensions of similarity are negative (Griffitt, 1966; Swann et al., 1989). We interpret these effects in terms of the consistency motivation that leads people to prefer consistent, harmonious organizations of knowledge and experience. Objective self-awareness theory belongs to social psychology's group of "consistency theories." We assume that people prefer consistency between aspects of self, between their standards, and between self and standards. The theory focuses on self-standard consistency, but it argues for a broad cognitive consistency motive (Heider, 1958a, 1960). In a consistency model, enhancement becomes striving for consistency between self and standards, and verification becomes striving for consistency between different self-aspects and between incoming and existing self-knowledge. We thus view conflicts between enhancement and verification as chimerical. If both activities stem from cognitive consistency motivation, then any "motive conflict" is merely apparent.

OSA theory makes predictions concerning when people will "self-verify" versus "self-enhance." When people are self-focused and perceive a discrepancy, they are motivated to deal with the discrepancy. But if self-focused people do not perceive a discrepancy, then self-standard congruity isn't a concern. Other kinds of congruity can then become significant. So, if an experimenter shows the participant evaluations by two different people—one self-consistent and one self-inconsistent—then this creates inconsistency between existing and incoming self-information. People will try to resolve this incongruity by choosing exposure to the consistent information. So, increased self-focused attention should amplify "self-verification," interpreted here as consistency restoration, when people don't perceive a self-standard discrepancy. When self-focused people perceive a discrepancy, then the dynamics described earlier (appraising one's ability to improve, making attributions for performance) will occur.

It is surprising that self-awareness dynamics have never been intersected with self-verification. Some indirect support for our view comes from experiments on introspection and self-verification. People were asked to evaluate and select evaluations that matched or contradicted their self-concepts; no self-standard discrepancies were induced. When people could introspect about their choices—a process involving self-awareness—the preference for self-consistent evaluations was enhanced (Hixon & Swann, 1993).

Self-Improvement. Self-improvement motivation assimilates easily into the dynamics of OSA theory. The SCENT model's view of self-improvement fails to say when people don't care about self-improvement, and it fails to specify which self-aspects the person wants to improve. Human incompetence is vast. Most people freely admit they are bad at bowling, bad at mental math, bad at running, bad at avoiding unhealthy foods, and so on. If people know they're bad at so many things, why don't they want to self-improve all of these things? Why don't people drop everything to improve at topiary gardening? Perhaps "it isn't important"; but why isn't it important? The notion of a *general* motive to self-improve is too vague to be useful—people don't want limitless expertise at everything. A model of self-improvement must specify *when* people care about improvement, and *what* specific things they want to improve.

OSA theory argues that recognizing a discrepancy between self and a standard is a necessary condition for self-improvement. "Improvement" is impossible unless people (1) think improvement is needed (i.e., see a discrepancy), and (2) have some representation of what an improved self would look like (i.e., a standard). So, people don't self-improve their topiary gardening skills because they have no standards related to it. Discrepancies are impossible without standards, so motivation to reduce discrepancies is absent. Only when people have a standard for a self-aspect and feel they fall short of the standard does "self-improvement motivation" become an issue.

But OSA theory is even more specific than this. When people feel discrepant and think they can reduce the discrepancy, then they will attempt self-improvement. When people feel unable to improve their situation, they'll avoid the situation. A lot of research supports this prediction. Self-focused people who felt able to improve their deficient performance spent more time on remedial tasks and signed up for a second remedial session more quickly. When people felt unable to improve, they spent less time on the remedial tasks and procrastinated signing up for them when forced to do so (Dana, Lalwani, & Duval, 1997; Duval et al., 1992; Mulilis & Duval, 1995).

The effect of expected improvement on activity is moderated by *self-attribution* for the discrepancy. Earlier we argued that attributions undergird self-motivation because people try to change the perceived cause of their problem. When people see the self as responsible for failing and feel they can improve, they try to change the self to match the standard. When people feel their poor performance was caused by something else, they try to change that other thing. For instance, people who attributed failure to self worked significantly harder on a second practice trial. Self-attributions significantly mediated the effects of the manipulations on subsequent "self-improving" activity. But when people attributed failure to the standard, they changed the standard. They didn't try to change self, even though they felt able to do so (Dana et al., 1997; Duval & Lalwani, 1999). Research in other areas also finds that self-attributions mediate effects of feedback on interest in remedial tasks (Hong, Chiu, Dweck, Lin, & Wan, 1999).

Self-improvement effects, then, are easily predicted by self-awareness dynamics. Self-improvement only becomes an issue when people feel discrepant from a standard. This is why people don't try to improve all self-aspects simultaneously. Unlike the SCENT model, OSA theory can predict specifically when people care about improvement, what specific things they'll try to improve, as well as when people *avoid* improvement opportunities. And as before, the dynamics of self-improvement are identical to the dynamics of the other self-motives. The same processes—self-focused attention, perceived ability to improve, and attributions—predict the seemingly different effects. Once again, we see how OSA theory can be a general view of self-motivation.

Summary. Objective self-awareness theory offers a general system of self-motivation—it collapses qualitative distinctions between self-motives and supplants them with a dynamic analysis of underlying processes and their interactions. Do people perceive a discrepancy between self and their standards? If so, do they feel they can do anything about it? Is the experience of the discrepancy attributed to self or to something else? With just a few concepts and some assumptions about their relations, objective self-awareness theory shows how the dynamics of the four self-motives are basically identical. If apparently antagonistic behaviors—seeking and avoiding diagnostic tasks, or blaming self versus another person for one's failure—have the same dynamic underpinnings, then we can reject the claim that opposing behaviors stem from opposing motives.

Although objective self-awareness theory can reinterpret past research on self-motivation, we would like to emphasize the theory's new predictions. We can only allude to some of the predictions here (see Duval & Silvia, 2001), but most of them concern the role of attributions in self-motivation. We predicted that (self-focused) people who feel they can improve experienced reduced self-esteem because they attribute failure to self (Duval & Silvia, 2002); past work has argued that people simply brush off failure when they expect improvement (Dunning, 1995). We predict that attributions mediate between expecting to improve and trying to improve; other theories assume that improvement expectancies directly enhance motivation (Bandura, 1997; Carver & Scheier, 1998). Likewise, we predict when people will change standards rather than self, whereas other theories view standards as inflexible (Carver & Scheier, 1998; Higgins, 1987). And most significantly, we make predictions about when people will self-evaluate and when they will be unmotivated, whereas other theories imply that self-motivation is a continuous process (Sedikides & Strube, 1997). Many of our predictions have not yet been tested directly, and thus suggest directions for future research. We would particularly encourage direct tests of the self-awareness analysis of self-verification and self-assessment.

HOW MANY ANIMALS LIVE IN THE SELF-ZOO?

Tesser (2000) has described the social psychology of the self as a "self-zoo." Theories of the self abound—the price of admission to the self-zoo is merely the word *self* and a hyphen. In the interests of thinning the herd, we suggest that the social psychology of the self should emphasize the study of how the self relates to motivation and emotion. Social psychologists, like naive psychologists, want to know what people *do*—so how does the self relate to activity and experience? Ironically, the social psychology of the self started as the study of self and motivation, if we trace the field's roots to Aronson's (1969) self-esteem model of cognitive dissonance and Duval and Wicklund's (1972) original theory of objective self-awareness.

For this reason, there is much to respect about the self-motives approach, represented by the SCENT model (Sedikides & Strube, 1997). The study of self-motives has reoriented social psychologists toward issues of motivation, generated interesting research, and has brought issues of conflict back into self-motivation. Yet, we would like social psychology to view the self-motives model as a starting point rather than as a destination. Progress requires going beyond "different motives cause different behaviors." What are the core processes and mechanisms that lead people to accept or deny responsibility for negative events, to respond constructively or defensively to failure, to seek or avoid opportunities for improvement? What is the inner architecture of self-motivation?

Models look backward by inducting concepts from past observations; theories look forward by predicting new observations based on assumptions of how concepts should relate. By positing a few mechanisms capable of variation and interaction—like self-focused attention, standards, affect, and attributions—objective self-awareness theory enables complex predictions for superficially different but conceptually similar events. The theory accounts for existing findings and makes new predictions about self-motivated activity. In doing so, the theory unites seemingly different behaviors by showing their deeper dynamic continuities.

ACKNOWLEDGMENTS

We would like to thank Jack Brehm, Scott Eidelman, Guido Gendolla, and Jeff Greenberg for their comments on earlier versions of this chapter.

Correspondence should be addressed to Paul J. Silvia, Department of Psychology, P. O. Box 26170, University of North Carolina at Greensboro, Greensboro, NC, 27402–6170. Electronic mail can be sent to p_silvia@uncg.edu.

REFERENCES

Aronson, E. (1969). A theory of cognitive dissonance: A current perspective. *Advances in Experimental Social Psychology, 4,* 1–34.

Bandura, A. (1997). *Self-efficacy: The exercise of control.* New York: Freeman.

Brehm, J. W. (1966). *A theory of psychological reactance.* New York: Academic Press.

Brehm, J. W., & Cohen, A. R. (1962). *Explorations in cognitive dissonance.* New York: Wiley.

Brehm, J. W., & Mann, M. (1975). Effect of importance of freedom and attraction to group members on influence produced by group pressure. *Journal of Personality and Social Psychology, 31,* 816–824.

Buss, A. H. (1980). *Self-consciousness and social anxiety.* San Francisco: Freeman.

Carver, C. S., Antoni, M., & Scheier, M. F. (1985). Self-consciousness and self-assessment. *Journal of Personality and Social Psychology, 48,* 117–124.

Carver, C. S., & Scheier, M. F. (1998). *On the self-regulation of behavior.* New York: Cambridge University Press.

Dana, E. R., Lalwani, N., & Duval, T. S. (1997). Objective self-awareness and focus of attention following awareness of self–standard discrepancies: Changing self or changing standards of correctness. *Journal of Social and Clinical Psychology, 16,* 359–380.

Dunning, D. (1995). Trait importance and modifiability as factors influencing self-assessment and self-enhancement motives. *Personality and Social Psychology Bulletin, 21,* 1297–1306.

Dunning, D. (1999). A newer look: Motivated social cognition and the schematic representation of social concepts. *Psychological Inquiry, 10,* 1–11.

Duval, T. S., & Duval, V. H. (1983). *Consistency and cognition.* Hillsdale, NJ: Lawrence Erlbaum Associates.

Duval, T. S., Duval, V. H., & Mulilis, J. P. (1992). Effects of self-focus, discrepancy between self and standard, and outcome expectancy favorability on the tendency to match self to standard or to withdraw. *Journal of Personality and Social Psychology, 62,* 340–348.

Duval, T. S., & Lalwani, N. (1999). Objective self-awareness and causal attributions for self–standard discrepancies: Changing self or changing standards of correctness. *Personality and Social Psychology Bulletin, 25,* 1220–1229.

Duval, T. S., & Silvia, P. J. (2001). *Self-awareness and causal attribution: A dual systems theory.* Boston: Kluwer.

Duval, T. S., & Silvia, P. J. (2002). Self-awareness, probability of improvement, and the self-serving bias. *Journal of Personality and Social Psychology, 82,* 49–61.

Duval, T. S., & Wicklund, R. A. (1972). *A theory of objective self-awareness.* New York: Academic Press.

Festinger, L. (1954). A theory of social comparison processes. *Human Relations, 7,* 117–140.

Freitas, A. L., Salovey, P., & Liberman, N. (2001). Abstract and concrete self-evaluative goals. *Journal of Personality and Social Psychology, 80,* 410–424.

Gibbons, F. X. (1978). Sexual standards and reactions to pornography: Enhancing behavioral consistency through self-focused attention. *Journal of Personality and Social Psychology, 36,* 976–987.

Griffitt, W. (1966). Interpersonal attraction as a function of the self-concept and personality similarity–dissimilarity. *Journal of Personality and Social Psychology, 4,* 581–584.

Heider, F. (1958a). *The psychology of interpersonal relations.* New York: Wiley.

Heider, F. (1958b). Perceiving the other person. In R. Tagiuri & L. Petrullo (Eds.), *Person perception and interpersonal behavior* (pp. 22–26). Stanford: Stanford University Press.

Heider, F. (1960). The gestalt theory of motivation. *Nebraska Symposium on Motivation, 8,* 145–172.

Higgins, E. T. (1987). Self-discrepancy: A theory relating self and affect. *Psychological Review, 94,* 319–340.

Hixon, J. G., & Swann, W. B., Jr., (1993). When does introspection bear fruit? Self-reflection, self-insight, and interpersonal choices. *Journal of Personality and Social Psychology, 64,* 35–43.

Hong, Y., Chiu, C., Dweck, C. S., Lin, D. M. S., & Wan, W. (1999). Implicit theories, attributions, and coping: A meaning system approach. *Journal of Personality and Social Psychology, 77,* 588–599.

Hoyle, R. H., Kernis, M. H., Leary, M. R., & Baldwin, M. W. (1999). *Selfhood: Identity, esteem, regulation.* Boulder, CO: Westview.

Idson, L. C., & Mischel, W. (2001). The personality of familiar and important people: The lay perceiver as a social cognitive theorist. *Journal of Personality and Social Psychology, 80,* 585–596.

Lalwani, N., & Duval, T. S. (2000). The moderating effects of cognitive appraisal processes on self-attribution of responsibility. *Journal of Applied Social Psychology, 30,* 2233–2245.

Lewin, K. (1935). *A dynamic theory of personality.* New York: McGraw-Hill.

McDougall, W. (1908/1960). *An introduction to social psychology* (23rd ed.). London: Methuen.

Mulilis, J. P., & Duval, T. S. (1995). Negative threat appeals and earthquake preparedness: A person-relative-to-event (PrE) model of coping with threat. *Journal of Applied Social Psychology, 25,* 1319–1339.

Sedikides, C., & Strube, M. J. (1997). Self-evaluation: To thine own self be good, to thine own self be sure, to thine own self be true, and to thine own self be better. *Advances in Experimental Social Psychology, 29,* 206–269.

Shibutani, T. (1961). *Society and personality.* Englewood Cliffs, NJ: Prentice-Hall.

Silvia, P. J. (2002). Self-awareness and the regulation of emotional intensity. *Self and Identity, 1,* 3–10.

Silvia, P. J., & Duval, T. S. (2001a). Objective self-awareness theory: Recent progress and enduring problems. *Personality and Social Psychology Review, 5,* 230–241.

Silvia, P. J., & Duval, T. S. (2001b). Predicting the interpersonal targets of self-serving attributions. *Journal of Experimental Social Psychology, 37,* 333–340.

Swann, W. B., Jr., Pelham, B. W., & Krull, D. S. (1989). Agreeable fancy or disagreeable truth? Reconciling self-enhancement and self-verification. *Journal of Personality and Social Psychology, 57,* 782–791.

Tesser, A. (2000). On the confluence of self-esteem maintenance mechanisms. *Personality and Social Psychology Review, 4,* 290–299.

Trope, Y. (1986). Self-enhancement and self-assessment on achievement behavior. In R. M. Sorrentino & E. T. Higgins (Eds.), *Handbook of motivation and cognition* (Vol. 1, pp. 350–378). New York: Guilford.

Trope, Y., & Neter, E. (1994). Reconciling competing motives in self-evaluation: The role of self-control in feedback seeking. *Journal of Personality and Social Psychology, 66,* 646–657.

Trope, Y., & Pomerantz, E. M. (1998). Resolving conflicts among self-evaluative motives: Positive experiences as a resource for overcoming defensiveness. *Motivation and Emotion, 22,* 53–72.

Weiner, B. (1985). Spontaneous causal thinking. *Psychological Bulletin, 97,* 74–84.

Wicklund, R. A. (1975). Objective self-awareness. *Advances in Experimental Social Psychology, 8,* 233–275.

Wicklund, R. A. (1990). *Zero-variable theories and the psychology of the explainer.* New York: Springer.

Wicklund, R. A. (1999). Multiple perspectives in person perception and theorizing. *Theory and Psychology, 9,* 667–678.

Wicklund, R. A., & Brehm, J. W. (1976). *Perspectives on cognitive dissonance.* Hillsdale, NJ: Lawrence Erlbaum Associates.

Wills, T. A. (1981). Downward comparison principles in social psychology. *Psychological Bulletin, 90,* 245–271.

Ybema, J. F., & Buunk, B. P. (1993). Aiming at the top? Upward social comparison of abilities after failure. *European Journal of Social Psychology, 23,* 627–645.

6

Willful Determinism: Exploring the Possibilities of Freedom

Sheldon Solomon
Skidmore College

Tom Pyszczynski
University of Colorado-Colorado Springs

Jeff Greenberg
University of Arizona

Our long-term collaboration began in the late 1970s under Jack Brehm's mentorship at the University of Kansas, and the principles of experimental social psychology we learned from him have had a pervasive influence on all of our work. One key principle we learned from Jack is to focus on fundamental questions about human functioning. In this spirit, for this volume we decided to undertake a preliminary foray into what is for us a somewhat new direction. The fundamental questions we want to consider here concern the concepts of will and freedom.

Conceptions of the role of freedom and will in human affairs have swung back and forth like a giant pendulum across the millennia (for a historical overview, see Riley, 1982), between claims that human beings are passive subjects of the vagaries of fate in pre-Socratic Greek philosophy, to notions of free will in Aristotle and later Roman philosophers (e.g., Cicero and Seneca) and early Christian theologians (e.g., St. Augustine and St. Thomas Aquinas); from the mechanistic determinism of behaviorists like John Watson and B. F. Skinner to the more optimistic humanism of Carl Rogers, Rollo May, and more recently, Ed Deci and Richard Ryan.

Rather than enter the fray over whether voluntary control over human action exists, Jack Brehm's theorizing took a different tack, by focusing on the role played by the subjective sense of freedom and choice in human behavior. Brehm was perhaps the first psychologist to pursue an empirically based psychology of freedom, and to demonstrate the critically important role that a subjective sense of freedom plays in motivating human behavior. This can be seen in his early work on the cognitive dissonance-generating characteristics of free decisions (Brehm, 1956), through his later work that established a subjective sense of free choice and personal responsibility as necessary components for the arousal of dissonance (Brehm & Cohen, 1962; Wicklund & Brehm, 1976), to his development of the theory of psychological reactance that specified powerful motivational consequences of depriving people of the subjective sense that they are free agents (Brehm, 1966). Although Jack preferred questions of theoretical dynamics with clear implications for understanding the forces that motivate people to act, we believe his ideas about freedom have profound implications for the way we conceive of human nature, and we use them here as we approach questions concerning free will.

THE CASE FOR FREEDOM AND WILL AS ILLUSORY

> When we see and know the strength that moves us, we acknowledge necessity; but when we see not, or mark not the force that moves us, we then think there is none, and that it is not causes, but liberty that produceth the action. (Thomas Hobbes, as cited in Riley, 1982, p. 42)

> . . . men are deceived because they think themselves free, and the sole reason for their thinking so is that they are conscious of their own actions, and ignorant of the causes by which those actions are determined. (Bernard Spinoza, as cited in Riley, 1982, p. 49)

> The deeply rooted belief in psychic freedom and choice . . . is quite unscientific and must give ground before the claims of a determinism which governs mental life. (Sigmund Freud, 1917/1966, p. 95)

In addition to attention in philosophical debates, the role of free will in human affairs has long been a focus of psychological discourse. Freud's entire psychoanalytic enterprise was in part a response to the Enlightenment notion that rationality could be freely employed to effect substantial changes in the human estate. Instead, Freud insisted that human behavior is driven by biological instincts of which we are generally unaware, and that might not be controllable even if we were aware of them. On the other hand, Freud's psychoanalysis, and most other "talk" therapies influenced by it, are based on the premise that making the unconscious conscious offers some purchase on possibilities of control and change. In addition, in contemporary psychotherapy, the conscious desire to change is considered an important determinant of psychotherapeutic success (e.g., Prochaska, DiClemente, & Norcross, 1992).

Behaviorists such as John Watson and B. F. Skinner rejected just about every psychodynamic assertion about the nature of human behavior except that it is ultimately determined, albeit by environmental contingencies rather than biological imperatives. Indeed, the very notion of a scientific psychology can seem to demand that any notion of free will be banished from accounts of why people do the things they do. To paraphrase Skinner (1948), it is impossible to uncover the lawful relationships that govern behavior if you assume that the individual is able to negate these relationships as a matter of personal whim or fiat. At the same time, many of Skinner's own achievements and actions, such as his book of prescriptions for an ideal society, would be difficult to account for as mere products of shaping from environmental contingencies.

More recently, Dan Wegner and colleagues (e.g., Wegner, 2002; Wegner & Wheatley, 1999) have argued that although people certainly experience a *subjective* sense of will, this is an illusion in that this subjective experience has no actual direct effect on human activities:

> . . . will is not a psychological force that causes action. Rather, as a perception that results from interpretation, it is a conscious experience that may only map rather weakly, or perhaps not at all, onto the actual causal relationship between the person's cognition and action. (Wegner & Wheatley, 1999, p. 481)

From this perspective, the subjective experience of will is an interesting psychological phenomenon that is explained through principles very similar to Bem's (1967) self-perception theory: An inference that people make when one's behavior and the situational factors surrounding it imply that one's actions were likely caused by one's conscious mental activities.

A number of lines of research are consistent with the general proposition that will is a subjective illusion quite independent of any causal connection to action. First, although people are generally able to provide plausible accounts of their behavior when asked to do so, these explanations are often demonstrably false (Nisbett & Wilson, 1977). Second, a substantial proportion of very complex human activity that is often presumed to require conscious and willful effort (e.g., reasoning, social judgments, pursuit of behavioral goals), sometimes transpires without conscious awareness (e.g., Bargh, 1997; Jaynes, 1976). For example, Bargh, Gollwitzer, Lee-Chai, Barndollar, and Trotschel (2001, Study 1) primed high-performance goal striving by having participants locate words such as *win*, *strive*, and *attain* in a matrix of letters (control participants searched for neutral words of comparable familiarity and length such as *hat*, *ranch*, and *window*). High-performance primed participants subsequently performed better on a different set of word search puzzles although they were completely unaware that the priming manipulation played any role in their success. A second study demonstrated that cooperative behavior (on a simulated negotiation task) can be elicited by a similar priming procedure; again, participants were unaware that their behavior was in any way influenced by the priming task. Subsequent studies established that primed goal-directed behaviors persist despite delays, distractions, and the allure of more attractive alternative activities, leading Bargh et al. to dub these findings "The Automated Will."

A third line of research reveals the role of unconscious cerebral activity in voluntary action. Libet (1985) recorded brain readiness potential (RP) while asking participants to watch a clock and think about and then lift one of their fingers. Although the awareness of the intention to lift one's finger preceded actual finger movements, suggesting that the intention itself initiated the movement, the RP preceded the intention by almost ½ second, suggesting that the intention was itself the result of the activity of the brain rather than the direct cause of the finger movement. Brasil-Neto, Pascual-Leone, Valls-Sole', Cohen, and Hallett (1992) provided additional evidence for the irrelevance of conscious will by asking participants to choose to move either their right or left index finger following magnetic stimulation to the motor area of the right or left side of their brains. Participants perceived themselves as having chosen which finger to move, although there was a clear preference for moving the finger contralateral to the side of the brain that was stimulated.

Taken together, these findings indicate that the experience of will exists even when behavior is clearly influenced by external circumstances. Wegner and colleagues thus assert that the experience of conscious will is generated independent of the actual causal path between unconscious causes of action and action itself. According to their theory of apparent mental causation (Wegner, 2002; Wegner & Wheatley, 1999), the experience of conscious will occurs when *priority* (thought precedes action at proper interval), *consistency* (thought is compatible with action), and *exclusivity* (thought is the only apparent cause of action) factors imply such an interpretation. Thus, the experience of conscious will affecting one's actions is viewed as a causal misattribution that individuals make when their behavior and surrounding situational factors meet certain logical criteria. Wegner subsequently made this point even more forcefully at the end of his book, *The Illusion of Conscious Will* (2002, p. 342): "Our sense of being a conscious agent who does things comes at a cost of being wrong all the time."

TOWARD A SCIENTIFIC ANALYSIS OF FREE WILL

The foregoing considerations raise three basic questions: (1) Although much behavior is caused by environmental, biological, and unconscious processes that we apparently have little or no control over, does that mean that people have no conscious control over *any* of their behavior, and that the conscious experience of will is *always* illusory? (2) Is there any role for the concept of will (conscious or otherwise) and real freedom in a scientific psychology that assumes that all behavior is determined by a complex interplay of psychological forces?, and (3) If we accept the potential utility of the concept of will and perhaps even free will, how do the processes operate that give rise to such executive control over behavior?

It Ain't Necessarily So

To the first question, we feel confident that the answer is, quite simply, "no." The operation of a given causal process in some circumstances in no way implies that that same causal process must operate in all circumstances. Causal relationships virtually *always* depend on a series of contextual or moderating variables. Demonstrating that behavior is sometimes controlled by forces outside of awareness under particular circumstances in no way implies that behavior is always controlled by such forces. For example, although Bargh et al.'s (2001) provocative findings clearly show that unconscious forces influence behavior, they do *not* show that conscious forces exert no influence. Although we agree that much behavior occurs automatically with little or no need for conscious attention or willing, we suspect that many of Bargh and colleagues' findings reflect the impact of both unconscious and conscious sources of influence.

The Case for Freedom and Will

The second question is trickier. It is certainly possible that, as Hobbes, Spinoza, Freud, Skinner, Bargh, and Wegner suggested, concepts of freedom and will are merely placeholders that are destined to gradually recede from our analyses and eventually disappear as we learn more about the many forces that determine behavior. However, in our view, all humans have free will, and there is no inconsistency between asserting this and believing in science or determinism. At any moment in time, we humans have the possibility of engaging in a wide range of actions, from relatively trivial ones like what to wear when we awake in the morning, to very serious ones like whether to be or not to be. As existentialists such as Sartre and Camus have argued, each living human always has choices; even a prisoner chained to a dungeon wall can choose what to think about. Under virtually the same circumstances, two individuals will often engage in different actions. And the same person in virtually the same circumstances at two different times might engage in two different actions.

Let's take a trivial example. I just threw a pen in the air. I chose to do that and before having done it, I might have done many different things, but I chose that action. I willed it and had the freedom to do so—or not do so. Now, if our psychology were far more fully developed than it is, we might be able to fully explain the behavior (although not fully predict it because there is always an element of uncertainty or "luck"). To do so, we would refer to factors in the environment, such as the proximity of the pen, the nasty coeditors demanding we finish the chapter, and so on. Of course, this never fully explains human action because the characteristics of the individual person always play a role. If I had no right hand, or a better imagination, perhaps I would have done something different.

So the other part of the explanation would refer to my genetic make-up, my history of classical and operant conditioning, social learning experiences, and so on. Taking all those things into account, we might then decide that my behavior was fully determined by the combination of all of these factors. I would say I freely chose to throw the pen, the psychological scientist of the distant future might say that because of his genetic predispositions and his distal and proximal prior experiences, this behavior occurred. But at that particular moment in time, I was precisely the being who chose that behavior. When I say I chose to throw the pen, I am saying that the creature I was at that moment, which is indeed the sum total of all that made me what I was at that moment, chose to throw the pen. In other words, my will may have been determined by my genetics and past experiences, but that is what my will is; it's still mine and no one else's. Yes, I did what I did because of who I am, but that is my freedom—to be who I am and to act accordingly. And my actions will change over time and will rarely be predictable based solely on external factors. From this perspective, all animals have free will and make choices, but because humans have the widest range of possible responses to a given stimulus environment, they have the most freedom.

All that being said, if we are referring to conscious will, that is another matter. I willed the throwing of the pen, and the conditions that Wegner specified, priority, consistency, and exclusivity, are precisely the conditions under which I will usually be right in believing that I—the creature I was at that moment—willed that action. But it is quite another thing to argue that it was an act of purely conscious will, for, as Freud argued, consciousness is indeed the tip of an iceberg and there are always nonconscious processes involved in the generation of any thought or behavior—but in the case of the pen throwing, all those processes occurred in my brain and they generated the intention that sparked my behavior—so I willed it, but my consciousness surely did not do so "on its own."

The conscious perception of having willed the behavior is thus typically accurate, unless it is taken to mean that I choose the behavior entirely independently of any external influences or any processes occurring within my brain. Even the most naïve of naive psychologists seem to know that they often know they want or feel something ("I'm in love") and choose actions without being able to fully articulate why. So to say "I chose to throw the pen" or "I chose to quit smoking" is accurate unless in saying that one is claiming to know exactly all the factors that influenced that decision.

From this perspective, freedom and will do play important roles in human behavior, and the importance of these processes in determining human thought, emotion, and action will become increasingly clear as our understanding of the dynamics of human behavior improves. Note that we purposely refer to the role of freedom and will as *processes that determine human behavior*. We view freedom and will not as magical forces that operate capriciously, but rather as psychological phenomena to be subjected to rigorous scientific scrutiny in the hopes of uncovering the rules by which they operate. As William James (1890) very cogently argued, whereas keeping the construct of will theoretically viable will encourage empirical efforts to study it, rejecting it as illusory and/or antithetical to scientific analysis would tend to direct research away from key questions about the determinants of human behavior. Thus, we reject the dichotomy of free versus determined behavior, and suggest that one of the most daunting tasks facing psychology as we move into the 21st century is explaining the processes through which free will emerges and is exercised, and perhaps more importantly, the conditions that block the individual from behaving as a free and autonomous human being.

If We Grant the Utility of the Concept of the Will, What Function Does It Serve?

What does the will do? According to Peoples (2002, p. 1624):

> Willed control of behavioral selection involves dynamic emotional and cognitive analyses of past and expected events and the influence of these analyses on decisions about future actions. These influences may contribute to the initiation of actions, persistence of adaptive actions, and inhibition of impulses to engage in alternative but less beneficial behaviors.

Thus, the will is an executive control process that plays a role in the selection and enactment of behavior. We suggest that the will be viewed as an emergent process that results from the joint operation of a series of lower order regulatory processes, all of which ultimately function to keep the individual on track in his or her pursuit of various life goals. These life goals, which the will functions to achieve for us, are themselves, at least some of the time, creatively derived from an analysis and integration of life experiences and basic biological propensities. But human action and the goals toward which human action is directed are not always the result of willful activity. People vary in the extent to which their behavior is willful, and perhaps more elusively, free. In the following sections we explore some of the factors that contribute to and undermine this willfulness and freedom.

In addition to entailing executive control over behavior, the will is also a process that affirms the self as the phenomenological center from which behavior unfolds. It is through the exertion of the will that we experience ourselves as autonomous and free actors in what William James referred to as a "theatre of simultaneous possibilities." Martin Halliwell (1999, p. X) eloquently articulated James' position on these matters in his *Romantic Science and the Experience of Self: Transatlantic Crosscurrents from William James to Oliver Sacks*:

> . . . James splits self into two aspects: the adjusting 'nuclear' self which provides a sense of continuity, and the executing 'shifting' self which enables one to act upon the environment in the pursuit of future goals. In the dynamic interaction between these two, which is both conservative (the cumulative result of following habitual patterns) and projective (the revision of those patterns in the light of new experiences), James locates the primary mark of identity 'I'. This 'I' is both a linguistic structure which enables the individual to express him or her self in language, and a felt centre of activity which exists, despite the mutable fringes of experience, as 'the birthplace of conclusions and the starting point of acts'. In other words, the self is a site where remembering (retaining traces of past activities) and willing (forcing new perceptual stances) meet.

Exerting our wills provides us with the feeling of having a self. It also makes us feel free. The large literature on reactance processes documents the impact of the human motive to perceive ourselves as free (Brehm & Brehm, 1981). And a growing body of research documents the positive consequences of such feelings of autonomy for our mental health and well-being (for a review, see Deci & Ryan, 2002). Perhaps these positive psychological consequences of felt autonomy and willfulness feedback as reinforcers for acting in an autonomous manner, thus encouraging the individual to avoid mindless or externally influenced activities.

Otto Rank (see Leiberman, 1985; Menaker, 1982, for excellent overviews of Rank's work) based his entire approach to psychotherapy on trying to mobilize the individual's will to enable him or her to act in a freer, more self-determined manner. He defined the will as, "a positive guiding organization and integration of self which utilizes creatively, as well as inhibits and controls, the instinctual drives" (cf. Leiberman, 1985, pp. 357–358). Interestingly, for Rank, the will initially emerges as a result of the child's attempts to individuate himself or herself from the parents by behaving contrary to their wishes (counterwill). Early willful action, then, is a negation of the parents' demands or wishes for the child. Through this negation of the external control provided by the parent, the child begins to experience himself or herself as an independent locus of activity—a self or an "I"—that, within certain limits, is free to behave as he or she chooses. Interestingly, Benjamin Libet (1999), whose research on brain readiness potential (Libet, 1985) was used by Wegner and Wheatley (1999) as evidence that all willful activity is illusory, also viewed willful activity as entailing the negation of control.

Brehm's (1966) reactance theory takes the notion of resistance to control one step further by positing an active motivational process that counters the press of both external and internal forces likely to influence one's behavior. More recently, Kuhl (1985) proposed a theory of action control that specifies a series of mechanisms through which the individual ensures that an intended course of action is not disrupted or interfered with by other competing action tendencies. Even more recently, as discussed in the chapter in this volume by Oettingen, Bulgarella, Henderson, and Gollwitzer, Gollwitzer and colleagues have studied the role of implementation instructions in staying the course toward desired goals. These and other perspectives and research on will psychology converge in viewing willful control of behavior as functioning to resist or negate the influence of strong influences on one's behavior.

Consciousness and Willfulness. Although Wegner and colleagues equate the will with the conscious mental choice and initiation of behavior, there is nothing in the concept of the will, which we take to refer to the volitional control over behavior, that requires that *all* elements of willful processes operate under the full light of conscious awareness. Although the concept of will does seem to entail some degree of conscious analysis and activation of behavior sequences on the part of the individual, the contents of conscious processes likely interact with other processes that operate outside of consciousness to generate behavior. Even the most ardent supporters of a free will position would acknowledge that there are processes involved in the voluntary initiation of behavior that do not require conscious attention. Thus, we would suggest that it is not fruitful to inquire about the existence of conscious will (although it is useful to investigate the determinants of the perception of will). Rather, we should be focused on the nature and operations of will (energy and behavior directed toward chosen goals) and the precise roles of unconscious and conscious processes in such operations.

The phenomenological experience of voluntary action entails a sense of deciding to "make it so"—what William James referred to as a "heave of the will"—that is then followed by the seemingly "magical" emergence of the desired action. Clearly, the processes that intervene between the conscious intention to "make it so" and the unfolding of the action are part of the process of willful action, and just as clearly, many of these processes unfold outside of conscious awareness. Consistent with this view, Vallacher and Wegner's (1985) action identification theory posits that behavioral components are organized hierarchically, and that at any given point in time, individuals are aware of only one (or at most a few) of the various hierarchical components of their behavior. For example, although the behavior of driving to work can be construed at many levels of abstractions, all of which accurately describe the behavior (e.g., earning a living, going to a meeting, driving one's car, turning the steering wheel, adjusting muscle pressures in one's arms and legs) and all of which involve self-regulatory processes that compare current states with salient standards, people tend to identify their actions at a particular level of abstraction that is intermediate in the hierarchy (what Carver & Scheier, 1981, referred to as the program level). Thus, people are likely to be aware of their actions as driving to school or going to a meeting rather than turning the steering wheel, even though turning the steering wheel is part of the process of driving to the meeting. The more concrete components of an action sequence that are essential for turning an intention into an action are rarely the focus of one's attention.

Consciousness, Decision Making, and Goal-Directed Behavior. Similarly, although the decisional processes that lead to the formation of intentions often involve conscious deliberation and weighing of choice alternatives, the actual emergence of the choice or intention into consciousness is typically experienced as "just popping into one's mind." Clearly, this decision process also involves a good deal of processing that occurs outside of conscious awareness. Nonetheless, the process of conscious deliberation usually plays an important role in the emergence of a choice and/or intention. First, it seems highly likely that conscious contemplation often leads to thoughts, decisions, and/or recognitions that immediately feed back into nonconscious action-generating activities. Henri Poincare provides a well-known example of this process in his classic, *The Foundations of Science* (1913), in which he described the process of mathematical creativity based on his own experience leading to the discovery of Fuchsian functions while on a geological excursion (p. 387):

> The incidents of the journey made me forget my mathematical work. Having reached Coutances, we entered an omnibus to go some place or other. At the moment when I put my foot on the step, the idea came to me, without anything in my former thoughts seeming to have paved the way for it.

Poincare's famous experience is often alluded to (see e.g., Jaynes, 1976; Wegner, 2002) to support the contention that even the most sophisticated discoveries occur in a nonconscious and unwilled fashion; and indeed, it's hard to imagine how unexpected bursts of insight could be the result of conscious and willful effort. Poincare' himself seems to agree (p. 388):

> Most striking . . . is this appearance of sudden illumination, a manifest sign of long, unconscious prior work. The role of this unconscious work in mathematical invention appears to me incontestable . . .

However, Poincare also goes on to observe (p. 388):

> . . . this unconscious work . . . is only fruitful, if it is on the one hand preceded and on the other hand followed by a period of conscious work. These sudden inspirations . . . never happen except after some days of voluntary effort which has appeared absolutely fruitless and whence nothing good seems to have come, where the way taken seems totally astray. These efforts then have . . . set agoing the unconscious machine and without them it would not have moved and would have produced nothing. The need for the second period of conscious work, after the inspiration, is still easier to understand. It is necessary to put in shape the results of this inspiration, to deduce from them the immediate consequences, to arrange them, to word the demonstrations, but above all is verification necessary.

So for Poincare, human mental activity vacillates between willful conscious activity and automatic nonconscious activity. With regard to arriving at insight, Poincare appears to be talking about delayed effects of will rather than real time online processes that directly influence behavior in an immediate fashion. He argued that conscious will sets in motion nonconscious processes that over time then produce novel results. But he also notes the importance of conscious willful efforts for elaboration, application, and communication of the insight. Thus, for Poincare, willful activity involves an ongoing dialectic interplay between conscious and nonconscious processing.

When Is the Will Needed? A critical question for understanding the processes through which the will operates is when, if ever, would a capacity for exerting conscious online control over behavior be useful or functional for an individual? Clearly, there are many cases in which behavior is engaged with little requirement of conscious attention. Indeed, there are many situations in which conscious online control of behavior would be maladaptive. Having to actively consider every aspect of what one is doing would tax our capacities to a point where we would be unable to pursue complex long range goals. With repetition and practice, much human behavior becomes automatized (e.g., driving to a familiar destination). Although conscious processes play little role in automatized behavior, a conscious willful decision to instigate the action sequence often does occur, probably at a higher level of abstraction, say, in the case of the person deciding it's time to go home, to get something to eat, or to check her email. Furthermore, conscious online control can enter into the execution of such well-rehearsed action sequences under certain circumstances.

Most notably, conscious attention to lower level details is required for the successful completion of tasks when there is a disruption or anomaly in the execution of the automated activity. For example, although people are typically capable of driving home from work with little conscious attention devoted to the activity, icy road conditions, malfunctioning brakes, or a drunk driver swerving into our lane all require conscious attention and adjustments of our usually routine execution of the more concrete and specific behavior sequences involved in driving. Thus, one set of situations in which conscious willful attention to and control over behavior is needed are those in which novel or unexpected circumstances arise that require more thorough processing of situational cues so as to provide better guidance over one's behavior.

The general notion that novelty or disruption of routines engenders active conscious processing has been espoused by a wide range of theorists with respect to many aspects of human thought and behavior. Both William James (1890) and Julian Jaynes (1976) argued that conscious will is needed to direct action in novel and challenging circumstances. They pointed out that people are most acutely aware of themselves and their actions when they are in novel and uncertain situations and least conscious when they are engaged in habitual activity. Greenberg and Pyszczynski (1986) provided empirical evidence consistent with this proposition by showing that failure or other disruptions lead to an increase in self-focused attention, which presumably functions to encourage an evaluation of one's current state relative to one's goals or intentions. Focusing specifically on inferential processes, the biased hypothesis-testing model of causal inference (Pyszczynski & Greenberg, 1987) posits that active causal processing in which causal hypotheses are tested against available information is instigated when unexpected behavior occurs, whereas pre-existing causal theories are relied on to make attributions when expected events occur. In this latter case, there is often no awareness that a causal explanation has even been sought. Research has supported this analysis by showing that unexpected events instigate more "why questions" (Wong & Weiner, 1981), more explanations being spontaneously offered (von Hippel, Sekaquaptewa, & Vargas, 1997), and more interest in attribution-relevant information (Pyszczynski & Greenberg, 1981). Thus, there seems to be a convergence of theories and research showing that novel and unexpected events capture one's conscious attention, presumably in the service of facilitating more intensive processing that is used to guide later thoughts and action.

The idea that conscious control of behavior is needed when automatized control is disrupted leads to an interesting converse notion. Automatized control of behavior in routine circumstances functions to free up the resources that enable us to exert willful control over other aspects of our lives. Without automatization, we may simply lack the capacity for willful activity. Conserving resources by delegating much of the control over our behavior to automatic unconsciously controlled processes may free up our time and energy for those decisions that really matter. For example, although we likely often "decide" to change lanes when we encounter a slow-moving vehicle ahead of us, with little conscious deliberation, the troublesome dispute with a spouse, employer, or journal editor that is occupying our attention as we quickly zoom past the farm vehicle is important enough that conscious attention is delegated to it, and that conscious attention undoubtedly plays an important role in the way we resolve the conflict.

Brehm's (1956) conception of freedom in decision-making situations implies another situation where conscious willful deliberation is likely to be adaptive: When there is no clearly dominant motive that unambiguously compels a particular response. Brehm's (1956) original free choice decision-making research (and follow-up research, see Wicklund & Brehm, 1976) shows that freedom is greatest, and therefore the highest levels of dissonance are aroused, in situations where one's choice alternatives are equal in attractiveness. Similarly, in his later work on reactance, Brehm (Brehm & Brehm, 1981; Wicklund, 1974) argued that people facing difficult but important decisions can threaten their own freedom by beginning to show a preference for one alternative over the other—that is, when the attractiveness of the two alternatives begin to diverge from each other. Research has provided strong support for these contentions (for a review, see Wicklund, 1974) by showing that in the predecisional state, when freedom to move in any direction is highly valued, the emergence of a preference for one choice alternative arouses reactance that leads to a compensatory increase in the attractiveness of the other alternative or a leveling off of any preference that is emerging.

Taken together, these two lines of thinking imply that conscious volitional choice is most needed when one is maximally free, when one is able to move in any possible direction, and there are no forces compelling or restricting such movement. This could occur either in situations where the opposing options are all highly valenced (either highly desirable or undesirable) or where the options have little motivational pull. Under these conditions, freedom makes the exercise of will necessary.

WILL AND DESIRE

> For the mind in most cases, as is evident in experience, has a power to suspend the execution and satisfaction of any of its desires; and so all, one after another; is at liberty to consider the objects of them, examine them on all sides, and weigh them with others . . . This seems to me the source of all liberty; in this seems to consist that which (as I think improperly) is called free-will. For, during this suspension of any desire, before the will be determined to action . . . we have opportunity to examine, view, and judge of the good or evil of what we are going to do; and when, upon due examination, we have judged, we have done our duty, all that we can, or ought to do, in pursuit of our happiness; and it is not a fault, but a perfection of our nature, to desire, will, and act according to the last result of a fair examination . . . This, as seems to me, is the great privilege of finite intellectual beings . . . That they can suspend their desires, and stop them from determining their wills to any action, till they have duly and fairly examined the good and evil of it. (Locke, as cited in Riley, 1982, pp. 80–81)

Perhaps a more general claim could be made here: Strong motivational forces tend to undermine freedom. When one is under the influence of strong motivational states, one's behavior has little voluntary character. A starving woman can hardly be thought of as "choosing" to eat, just as a frightened man can hardly be thought of as "choosing" to flee from that of which he is afraid. Following Rank (1936/1978), Becker (1973), and others, we have previously argued that fear generally limits freedom, in that fear tends to dominate the psychological field and push other goals and intentions aside. Fear can also lead to a distorted expression of other motives, as many terror management studies have shown. For example, reminders of one's mortality have been shown to increase biased responding to those whose beliefs and values impinge on one's own (e.g., Greenberg et al., 1990), to increase risky behavior that might in fact threaten one's life (Taubman-Ben-Ari, Florian, & Mikulincer, 1999), and to lead to the avoidance of pleasurable stimulation among those high in neuroticism (Goldenberg, Pyszczynski, Warnicke, & Landau, 2002).

Becker (1973) suggested that the human proclivity to orient one's life around living up to cultural values and standards was essentially a result of the emergence of the fear of death, which he viewed as a side effect of the emergence of intellectual abilities that were favored by natural selection because they reduced our reliance on fixed response patterns and therefore rendered us, at least potentially, more free. The irony of this increased potential for freedom, however, is that it led to a heightened potential for anxiety, which led humankind to give up their freedom by clinging to cultural dictates as a way of managing their fears. As Otto Rank put it, "out of freedom . . . man creates a prison" (1936/1976, p. 13).

One could argue that a similar dynamic exists with respect to understanding other affect-driven motivational states, such as reactance. Reactance presumably functions to preserve perceived freedoms. However, as noted earlier, Wicklund and Brehm (1976) have shown that the emergence of preferences in a predecisional state leads to a reduction in attraction to the more preferred alternative and an increase in attraction to the less preferred alternative. Thus, although reactance functions to preserve freedoms, in some instances it ironically pushes the individual away from alternatives that he or she finds attractive, and in that sense, limits his or her freedom by making it more difficult to act on his or her preferences. It also often allows external threats to influence attitudes and behavior.

It could also be argued that cognitive dissonance has a similar freedom-reducing effect. As Brehm (1956) has shown, the aversive tension state of cognitive dissonance is aroused when one must choose between alternatives of roughly equal attractiveness (i.e., when one's choice is maximally free), and the more equal the alternatives are in attractiveness, the more dissonance is aroused. This dissonance leads to a distortion of the appeal of the two alternatives, with the chosen alternative increasing in attractiveness and the rejected alternative decreasing in attractiveness. This spreading of the attractiveness of choice alternatives is far from a rational process and the available research strongly suggests that it occurs without any conscious awareness or willful consideration. Indeed, Pyszczynski, Greenberg, Solomon, Sideris, and Stubing (1993) have shown that if participants are made aware of their feelings of dissonance, the attitude change that typically functions to reduce the aversive tension is eliminated. Thus, cognitive dissonance, too, can be thought of as an irrational motivational force that pushes a person away from a rational or willful assessment of his or her true preferences. The point is that the irrational freedom-limiting tendencies instigated by reactance and dissonance are both responses to the problem of freedom, and both push the individual away from a rational, conscious, willful assessment of the psychological situation.

In this sense, there may be parallels with the impulse to escape from freedom that Erich Fromm (1941) discussed in his classic book. Fromm argued that despite its allure and despite the psychological benefits that accrue from it, freedom can be frightening. When we are maximally free, in the sense of not having clear forces pushing us in one direction or the other, we lack a clear basis for action. We simply don't know what to do or which way to turn. As Fromm, Becker, and others have suggested, action can break down in the absence of clear motives or external direction. Furthermore, with freedom comes responsibility for one's actions, and as Brehm and others have shown, with responsibility comes cognitive dissonance, which is an aversive tension state that people are highly motivated to escape and avoid. Fromm argued that the aversive feelings that freedom produces push us to turn to authoritarian policies and leaders as a way of "escaping from freedom."

FREEDOM AS SELF-CREATION OF SELF

Although conscious volitional control over behavior is most needed in situations where one is not being compelled to move in any particular direction, the foregoing analysis shows that the very existence of such freedom sets in motion a set of complex motivational forces that sometimes push us away from rational decision making. In what sense, then, can a person be free? A wide range of theorists, from Rank to Piaget to Deci and Ryan have argued that people actively create themselves by creatively integrating new experiences with existing psychological schemas and structures. This is the essence of human growth and development.

We and others have previously argued that this process of development is a motivated one that is energized by the state of positive affect or exhilaration that is an intrinsic part of the process of integrating new information with existing structures (Frederickson, 2001; Greenberg, Pyszczynski, & Solomon, 1995; Pyszczynski, Greenberg, & Solomon, 1997). Integration requires and generates energy that is experienced as positive affect or exhilaration, which then serves as an incentive for future integrative activities. Through this integrative process, we actively transform ourselves and take new experiences and information into our selves. If this integrative process is an unconstrained, self-generated, creative response to experience, we can be thought of as playing an active role in the self-creation of our selves. Of course, much of this integrative processing occurs automatically and takes place outside of conscious awareness. Still, to the extent that it is we who are doing the processing, and to the extent that this processing is unconstrained by strong motivational forces that compel a particular form of distortion of experience, the result of this process can be said to be an authentic form of self-creation:

> . . . though our character is formed by circumstances, our desires can do much to shape those circumstances; and that what is really inspiriting and ennobling in the doctrine of free-will, is the conviction that we have real power over the formation of our own character; that our will, by influencing some of our circumstances, can modify our future habits or capabilities of willing. (Mill, as cited in Bonaparte, 1975, p. 56)

Unfortunately, the integrative processing of new information and experience is rarely, if ever, completely unconstrained. Basic needs and fears impinge on how we integrate new experience with existing psychological structures, and lead to systematic distortions in the service of controlling anxiety (for a more thorough discussion, see Pyszczynski, Greenberg, & Goldenberg, 2002). The end result is at best only a partially authentic self that is not fully self-determined but rather is the result of a compromise with our needs and fears.

Following Deci and Ryan (2002), we suggest that people can be thought of as being autonomously self-determined to the extent that their regulatory systems and the standards and values they contain are relatively self-determined, that is, the result of unconstrained integrative processing. To the extent that these standards and values are constrained by external forces or strong internal motive states like fear and anger, however, the contents of the self-regulatory system are not self-determined and thus the person is unable to act in a free and authentic way. From this perspective then, individuals are neither free nor slaves, but some combination of the two that varies from situation to situation and from person to person, and may also change across the life span.

CONCLUSION

Conscious perception and thought almost always play a role in determining our choices and actions. Even a cursory consideration of research in social psychology supports the role of content of consciousness in many attitudes and behaviors, such as the effects of cognitive load, accuracy instructions, self-awareness manipulations, and awareness of primes, models, and self-threats on phenomena such as persuasion, aggression, moral decisions, thought suppression, and social perceptions and judgments. Although people are not always aware of how contents in consciousness influence them, they often are. When a man punches a guy who hits on his girlfriend, he willed that action and the awareness of what the guy was doing influenced that decision. The fact that the few drinks he had had may have also contributed through nonconscious effects on his neurotransmitter receptor sites, and that he might have no awareness of that influence, does not mean the behavior was not willed.

In this chapter, we attempt to make a persuasive case for three general points. First, Wegner's (2002, p. 342) claim that "Our sense of being a conscious agent who does things comes at a cost of being technically wrong all of the time" is provocative but dubious. Our sense of being an agent who does things is usually accurate, and understanding how this agency operates is of immense importance for understanding human behavior. Second, although the current focus in experimental social psychology on the role of unconscious processes in a host of human activities is surely important (albeit an ironic return to a notion championed long ago by Freud but fervently rejected by most academic research psychologists until recently), it would be most unfortunate if these lines of research moved the field back toward mechanistic or reductionist models of human behavior and encouraged dismissal of the role of conscious as well as unconscious aspects of will in human affairs. Third, there is already great richness in the theoretical and empirical work on the psychology of will and freedom, and likely even greater riches yet to be uncovered if we continue to study, rather than dismiss as illusory, concepts of freedom and will. We are hopeful that our preliminary analysis of the conditions under which will operates and freedom is maximal offers one fruitful direction for such further study.

REFERENCES

Bargh, J. A. (1997). The automaticity of everyday life. In R. S. Wyer, Jr. (Ed.), *Advances in social cognition* (Vol.10, pp. 1–61). Mahwah, NJ: Lawrence Erlbaum Associates.

Bargh, J. A., Gollwitzer, P. M., Lee-Chai, A., Barndollar, K., & Trotschel, R. (2001). The automated will: Nonconscious activation and pursuit of behavioral goals. *Journal of Personality and Social Psychology, 81*, 1014–1027.

Becker, E. (1973). *The denial of death.* New York: Free Press.

Bem, D. J. (1967). Self-perception: An alternative interpretation of cognitive dissonance phenomena. *Psychological Review, 74*, 183–200.

Bonaparte, F. (1975). *Will and destiny: Morality and tragedy in George Eliot's novels.* New York: New York University Press.

Brasil-Neto, J. P., Pascual-Leone, A., Valls-Sole', J., Cohen, L. G., & Hallett, M. (1992). Focal transcranial magnetic stimulation and response bias in a forced-choice task. *Journal of Neurology, Neurosurgery, and Psychiatry, 55*, 964–966.

Brehm, J. W. (1956). Post-decision changes in the desirability of alternatives. *Journal of Abnormal and Social Psychology, 52*, 384–389.

Brehm, J. W. (1966). *A theory of psychological reactance.* New York: Academic Press.

Brehm, S. S., & Brehm, J. W. (1981). *Psychological reactance: A theory of freedom and control.* New York: Academic Press.

Brehm, J. W., & Cohen, A. R. (1962). *Explorations in cognitive dissonance.* New York: Wiley.

Carver, C. S., & Scheier, M. F. (1981). *Attention and self-regulation: A control theory approach to human behavior.* New York: Springer-Verlag.

Deci, E. L., & Ryan, R. M. (Eds.). (2002). *Handbook of self-determination research.* Rochester, NY: University of Rochester Press.

Frederickson, B. L. (2001). The role of positive emotions in positive psychology: The broaden-and-build theory of positive emotions. *American Psychologist, 56*, 218–226.

Freud, S. (1917/1966). *Introductory lectures on psychoanalysis.* New York: Norton.

Fromm, E. (1941). *Escape from freedom.* New York: Farrar & Rinehart.

Goldenberg, J., Pyszcynski, T., Warnicke, G., & Landau, M. (2002). *Death, neuroticism, and aversion to physical sensations, both the painful and pleasurable.* Unpublished manuscript, Boise State University, Boise, Idaho.

Greenberg, J., & Pyszczynski, T. (1986). Persistent high self-focus after failure and low self-focus after success: The depressive self-focusing style. *Journal of Personality and Social Psychology, 50,* 1039–1044.

Greenberg, J., Pyszczynski, T., & Solomon, S. (1995). Toward a dual motive depth psychology of self and social behavior. In M. Kernis (Ed.), *Self, efficacy, and agency* (pp. 73–99). New York: Plenum.

Greenberg, J., Pyszczynski, T., Solomon S., Rosenblatt, A., Veeder, M., Kirkland, S., & Lyon, D. (1990). Evidence for terror management theory II: The effects of mortality salience on reactions to those who threaten or bolster the cultural worldview. *Journal of Personality and Social Psychology, 58,* 308–318.

Halliwell, M. (1999). *Romantic science and the experience of self: Transatlantic crosscurrents from William James to Oliver Sacks.* Brookville, VT: Ashgate.

James, W. (1890). *Principles of psychology.* New York: Holt.

Jaynes, J. (1976). *The origin of consciousness in the breakdown of the bicameral mind.* Boston, MA: Houghton Mifflin.

Kuhl, J. (1985). From cognition to behavior: Perspectives for future research on action control. In J. Kuhl & J. Beckmann (Eds.), *Action control from cognition to behavior* (pp. 267–276). New York: Springer-Verlag.

Leiberman, E. J. (1985). *Acts of will: The life and work of Otto Rank.* New York: Free Press.

Libet, B. (1985). Unconscious cerebral initiative and role of conscious will in voluntary action. *Behavioral and Brain Sciences, 8,* 529–566.

Libet, B. (1999). Do we have free will? *Journal of Consciousness Studies, 6,* 47–57.

Menaker, E. (1982). *Otto Rank: A rediscovered legacy.* New York: Columbia University Press.

Nisbett, R. E., & Wilson, T. D. (1977). Telling more than we can know: Verbal reports on mental processes. *Psychological Review, 84,* 231–259.

Peoples, L. L. (2002). Will, anterior cingulate cortex, and addiction. *Science, 296,* 1623–1624.

Poincare, H. (1913). Mathematical creation. In *The foundations of science* (G. B. Halsted, Trans.). New York: Science Press.

Prochaska, J. O., DiClemente, C. C., & Norcross, J. C. (1992). In search of how people change: Applications to addictive behaviors. *American Psychologist, 47,* 1102–1114.

Pyszczynski, T. A., & Greenberg, J. (1981). The role of disconfirmed expectancies in the instigation of attributional processing. *Journal of Personality and Social Psychology, 40,* 39–46.

Pyszczynski, T., & Greenberg, J. (1987). Toward an integration of cognitive and motivational perspectives on social inference: A biased hypothesis-testing model. In L. Berkowitz (Ed.), *Advances in experimental social psychology* (Vol. 20, pp. 297–340) Hillsdale, NJ: Lawrence Erlbaum Associates.

Pyszczynski, T., Greenberg, J., & Goldenberg, J. (2002). Freedom vs. fear: On the defense, growth, and expansion of the self: Freedom in the balance. In M. Leary & J. Tangney (Eds.), *Handbook of self and identity* (pp. 314–343). New York: Guilford Publications.

Pyszczynski, T., Greenberg, J., & Solomon, S. (1997). Why do we need what we need? A terror management perspective on the roots of human social motivation. *Psychological Inquiry, 8,* 1–20.

Pyszczynski, T., Greenberg, J., Solomon, S., Sideris, J., & Stubing, M. J. (1993). Emotional expression and the reduction of motivated cognitive bias: Evidence from dissonance and distancing from victim's paradigms. *Journal of Personality and Social Psychology, 64,* 177–186.

Rank, O. (1936/1978). *Truth and reality.* NewYork: Knopf.

Riley, P. (1982). *Will and political legitimacy: A critical exposition of social contract theory in Hobbes, Locke, Rousseau, Kant, and Hegel.* Cambridge, MA: Harvard University Press.

Skinner, B. F. (1948). *Walden two.* New York: Macmillan.

Taubman-Ben-Ari, O., Florian, V., & Mikulincer, M. (1999). The impact of mortality salience on reckless driving: A test of terror management mechanisms. *Journal of Personality and Social Psychology, 76,* 35–45.

Vallacher, R. R., & Wegner, D. M. (1985). *A theory of action identification.* Hillsdale, NJ: Lawrence Erlbaum Associates.

Von Hippel, W., Sekaquaptewa, D., & Vargas, P. (1997). The linguistic intergroup bias as an implicit indicator of prejudice. *Journal of Experimental Social Psychology, 33,* 490–509.

Wegner, D. M. (2002). *The illusion of conscious will.* Cambridge, MA: MIT Press.

Wegner, D. M., & Wheatley, T. (1999). Apparent mental causation: Sources of experience of will. *American Psychologist, 54,* 480–492.

Wicklund, R. A. (1974). *Freedom and reactance.* Hove, UK: Lawrence Erlbaum Associates.

Wicklund, R. A., & Brehm, J. W. (1976). *Perspectives on cognitive dissonance.* Hove, UK: Lawrence Erlbaum Associates.

Wong, P. T., & Weiner, B. (1981). When people ask "why" questions, and the heuristics of attributional search. *Journal of Personality and Social Psychology, 40,* 650–663.

7

The Role of Distance in Valuing Another Person[1]

Robert A. Wicklund
University of Trieste

What is the psychological role of temporal or spatial distance between humans? Is the person who is available, reachable, that is, in proximity, inevitably the one who is preferred? Are attraction and satisfaction optimal among people who are mutually accessible?

These questions are addressed here in the context of three very diverse psychological perspectives, each of the perspectives bearing on the relation between the distance separating two or more people and the degree of their mutual attraction, as well as the relation between distance and their mutual satisfaction.

SOCIAL NEEDS AND RAPID NEED SATISFACTION

The implicit model of communication and interpersonal contact that is transmitted via the social psychological literature is this: Adult humans carry a variety of easily describable needs, chronic and acute, that demand satisfaction. The needs move the person toward instrumental, goal-oriented actions, toward consummatory behavior. This far-reaching implicit model would seem to apply no matter whether the needs in question border on having an instinctual character (e.g., Bowlby, 1973) or a more derived, secondary character. Needs such as those for physical contact, to

[1]This chapter was inspired by Marcella Rao.

feel superior to others (i.e., self-esteem and related concepts), to express emotions, to firm up or confirm one's own perceptions and opinions, or to sense that one belongs, all carry the person toward demanding a solution. The motivation to take up contact with another person can thus be seen as accompanied by a certain impatience, and this implies that a "goal" (another person) that is readily accessible will be preferred, will be more attractive than a person who is distant. The person nearby temporally and spatially will in turn deliver the quicker, more controllable satisfactions.

By this line of thought, contentment in communication and in social relations, as well as preferences and attractions, will be found among people who have ready access to one another. However, this line of thought, which seems to guide nearly all analyses of communication and social relations, overlooks three important considerations, to be delineated later. These three perspectives, these theoretical points of view, lead us in quite an opposite direction, in that each of them implies directly that spatial or temporal distance is a fundamental antecedent of attraction and of contentment in interpersonal relations. The first of these regards distance as a motivating force, one that enhances the subjectively perceived quality of the other person.

Perspective I: Nonavailability as a Motivating Force

Research dating back to the period of H. F. Wright (1937) points us toward thinking about a possible positive relation between nonavailability and the attractiveness of food. Wright varied the physical distance between the subject and the food items (desserts), over a distance varying between 2 and 32 inches. He found a curvilinear effect, such that moderate distances maximized subjects' preferences for desserts. He described the effects in terms of his pressure theory, which was not far removed from Lewin's (1926) ideas about the effect of interruptions or nonavailability on the continuation of tension states.

A subsequent theoretical direction made these distance analyses more explicit, within the context of a theory about freedom (Brehm, 1966). Reactance theory has generated numerous studies and observations with respect to the attractiveness-enhancing effects of interruptions, distances—or more generally—the effects of curtailing a person's expected freedom to move toward one or another desired state of affairs.

To be sure, the theory has been brought to the issue of distance between people. A study by Wicklund and Ogden (in Wicklund, 1974) showed the following: If a person expects to be able to choose among several possible partners, for a brief encounter, the partner who is reported as showing up late, or as unable to show up, tends to become more attractive to the person doing the choosing. Such tendencies were present only among participants who expected freedom to choose a partner. If subjects expected to receive a partner by assignment, the lateness/absence did not result in increments in the other's attractiveness.

The further implications of reactance theory for distance between people are evident. An individual who expects freedom or control over an encounter with another will become increasingly motivated to approach the other when distances interfere with immediate contact. A long waiting time, the other's preoccupation with other people, a complicated detour to reach the other should all make the other more subjectively attractive, desired, and serve to increase persistence in trying to take up contact with the other.

A theory published slightly earlier (cognitive dissonance theory, Festinger, 1957), and later elaborated on by Brehm and Cohen (1962) bears equally on nonavailability of the other person (or object) on motivation to pursue that person. In contrast to reactance theory, the evolved dissonance theory (Brehm and Cohen) stipulates that a certain commitment is necessary before the effects of dissonance become clear. For example, once a person has decided to join a group, barriers to successful participation in the group will set in motion a process of dissonance reduction, which often takes the form of justifying one's commitment to the other person. The result, then, is increased subjective attractiveness of the other person who is difficult to reach, who requires efforts, who is costly, who is relatively unavailable. For instance, Kiesler and Corbin (1965) showed that, among subjects who had a commitment to continue in the group, rejection by the other members resulted in subjects' elevating their attraction to the group.

Subsequently, Brehm developed a more general and elaborated theory of motivation (Brehm, Wright, Solomon, Silka, & Greenberg, 1983; Brehm & Self, 1989; Wright, 1996; Wright & Brehm, 1989). As applied to the topic of this chapter, Brehm's energization notion implies that spatial–temporal distance between people will produce increased motivation or desire to reach the other person, and in turn, this motivation or desire will be reflected in increments in the subjective attractiveness of the other (Brehm et al., 1983).

However, such effects are said to take place only when it is functional for the organism to be energized. If the other person is immediately available, then from a functional point of view, the organism should not mobilize energy in order to reach the other. Translated into measures that reflect the motivated state, this means that the immediately available other will not be the most attractive other. As distance increases, and thus as the effort or strain required to reach the other person grows, the person will be increasingly energized and feel more attracted to the other. As the distance becomes insurmountable, this functional view indicates that it is no longer functional for the organism to be energized in regard to the distant

other, and so motivation will drop, thus implying a drop in the other's attractiveness, relative to the case in which the other is perceived as moderately difficult to reach.

These theories have in common that the person must first have an interest in the goal object, that is, in the other person. There must be an initial desire to pursue, or approach the other. Given this initial prerequisite, each of the models indicates that an increment in distance, in difficulty of reaching the other, will heighten motivation to approach that other. Each model brings its own variables to bear on the case of interpersonal relations, but the most important commonality among them is that *some degree* of distance serves to motivate the person who is interested in another. With a certain degree of distance, the other person thereby gains in attractiveness. The person who is interested will be more prone to persist, to show continued interest in the other, to find value in the other.

Further, the three theories share a common kind of field of application, in that none of them refers explicitly to the motivated person's switching to another goal (person), nor to a substitute. Central in every analysis is a single other person (goal), whose subjective appeal waxes and wanes as a function of distance.

Perspective II: Delay of Gratification

Delay of gratification, as well as tolerance of frustration (Lawson, 1965), is a school of theory and research that revolves around temporal distance between a person who desires and the objects or persons that are desired. The research field has been defined largely by Mischel (1974, 1996), whose research entails, for the most part, children's ability to wait before consuming.

In his experimental contexts, Mischel defined distance in terms of the waiting period, and characteristically set up situations in which the youthful participant is seated before two food objects. One of them is clearly superior (e.g., a candy bar vs. two peanuts), and the subjects are told that they must wait until the experimenter returns if they want to have the more desirable food item. Then a waiting period ensues, and if the subjects cannot tolerate the seemingly long wait, they are given the inferior item.

Mischel's measure is not parallel to that of the motivational schools previously described, in that attractiveness or goodness of taste are in fact not measured. Instead, the outcome of interest is the subject's ability or willingness to wait, to endure a distance in order to procure the superior food items. It is the theory underlying this measure that is central to this chapter.

By Mischel's recounting of the literature, children must come to learn that value is generally associated with distance. Desserts come only after the boring potatoes and meat, a high salary comes only after years of preparation, important or attractive people are scarce, and we must wait in order to gain access to them. Going a bit beyond Mischel, it is fair to say that the learned associations between distance and the perceived value can come about via two routes; (a) through direct experience with naturally occurring events, in the sense that the more attractive objects and people tend to be rare, and (b) through cultural experiences, by which the dominant educational influences point toward the advantages of waiting, of enduring hardships, in order to arrive later at a superior status for oneself and to experience high quality generally.

This kind of thinking implies that a person, when confronted with an immediately available other person and a person who is more distant, will ascribe more value to the distant person. This ascription can take place independent of the person's actual desire for the other person, because the basis for the ascription is in learning experiences. The individual, as a product of cultural influences, has learned that waiting, struggling, and physical distance are intimately tied up with the value of one's pursuits.

When will the individual in fact choose the more difficult of two alternative, potential partners? One of Mischel's central variables, given his child developmental perspective, is age. As his research shows, with increasing age people are more able to wait the required time interval in order to receive the higher quality product. A further variable is salience: Waiting is much more difficult when people are confronted directly—visually—with the food item.

To summarize: Mischel provides a clear answer, from his perspective, to our central question regarding the relation between distance and value. As a result of actual experience with the relation between delay and receipt of goal objects of various quality, children come to learn the idea that value is associated with distance. Further, as a result of education, thus emersion in one's cultural influences, there is a generalized expectation of distance being associated with value.

Applying Mischel's principle to interpersonal relations, we should therefore expect a monotonic relationship between a person's perception of another as difficult to reach and the subjective value, or attractiveness, ascribed to that person. In contrast, the determinants of a person's actually pursuing someone who is more difficult to reach are more complex. Based on Mischel's research, the salience of the person who is immediately available should push the person to renounce a delay. In other words, Mischel would suggest that the immediate (auditory, visual) salience of another would override the tendency to wait for someone who may ultimately possess more valued qualities.

Perspective III: Distance, Communication, and Accepting "Part" of the Other Person

In applying the preceding two perspectives to distance and interpersonal relations, there is the implicit assumption that "the goal is the goal." That is, it is assumed implicitly that the actual form of contact between persons does not become transformed as a result of distance. For instance, thinking in terms of examples appropriate to cognitive dissonance theory, or to delay of gratification, the distance simply means a physical distance to be traversed, or a waiting period, before contact is established. The form of the contact, and the nature or components of the other person, are not thought to be transformed by factors of distance, costs, or struggling to reach the other.

But to the contrary, it is possible to suppose that distance and proximity bear on whether the ultimate contact with the other is complete or less complete. Thus, the issue becomes one of the relation between distance and the quality or extensiveness of contact between two or more people.

This analysis (Wicklund & Vandekerckhove, 2000) begins with the assumption that communication or relations with others vary substantially with regard to the dimensionality of contact. In pointing to "original interaction forms," we have noted that many forms of traditional contact, as between infants and their mothers, or between family members or neighbors, are complete in the sense of using all of the sensory modalities. Thus, the focus of Bowlby (1973) on the formative contact between mother and infant is on the simultaneity of the visual, auditory, tactile and olfactory dimensions. It is similar to Locke's (1998) depiction of traditional social relations. People know others, and in turn come to know themselves, by the mutual presence of cues that employ all of the sensory modalities.

Drawing on the interruption and substitution notions of Lewin (1926) and colleagues (e.g., Lissner, 1933; Mahler, 1933), we have attempted to delve into the issues that arrive when "original" forms of interaction are difficult or impossible, and when quicker, alternative forms of interaction are presented in place of the social forms entailing multidimensionality of sensory stimulation. For instance, let's assume that two people—collaborating colleagues, friends, parent + child, or two lovers—have experienced increased distance. A job or a required schooling has moved them apart, to two separate cities. Assume further that the distance is surmountable (several miles), such that traversing the distance is possible, but with effort and considerable planning. Based on the preceding Perspectives I and II, we might think that this increment in distance would make the relations between these two people more appealing. They should come to show more interest in one another; mutual attraction should go upward. However, the analysis of the effects of distance changes substantially when we introduce the idea of *substitute contact* (Wicklund & Vandekerckhove): As the research of Lissner (1933) and Mahler (1933) so well demonstrates, people willingly undertake substitute activities when the original activity is blocked, and to various degrees, they evidence satisfaction with those substitute activities. That is, according to the findings of their experiments, a substitute activity is frequently satisfying or tension reducing, sufficiently satisfying that people do not necessarily return to the original activity when they are given an opportunity to do so. Whether or not they return, that is, whether or not a tension state remains after completing the substitute activity, depends on several pertinent factors, including the similarity of the substitute to the original activity.

In the case of our example of distance between two colleagues or between two lovers, the Lewinean concept of substitute can be used to refer to alternative forms of communication/contact, forms that carry a reduced dimensionality. Concretely, this means that when there is physical separation, each of the two parties to the separation is free to use the telephone, write letters, send e-mails, or pass along a message via a third person. And given that such alternatives offer a kind of immediate contact, it should come as no surprise that people readily use them.

Whether or not long-term satisfactions arise from using communication of reduced dimensionality is a grand and interesting question, one that has received negative answers from such critics of fast communication as Locke (1998) and Postman (1982), and one that has received positive answers from authors who see advantages in the immediate availability of the other (McKenna & Bargh, 2000; Rheingold, 1993).

The experience of distance, or of encountering barriers between two people is necessarily more frequent within the context of the "original" interaction form. Because numerous circumstances require traversing long distances or undergoing delays in order to arrive at these original sorts of interactions, we are confronted with the reality that the human impatience, deriving from the various needs for contact, lead to taking quicker routes. Thus, the unreachable "full dimensional" other is transformed into a "partial" other, given that the quicker routes, rendering the other more or less immediately accessible, entail a reduced dimensionality. The impatient person, confronted with a spatial or temporal distance, picks up the telephone and talks with the other, leaves a message on the answering machine, sends an express letter, sends a fax or e-mail, or the like. If the distances are so quickly eliminated by taking substitute forms of contact, then we eliminate the possibility that distance can work to enhance the other's appeal, to generate increased motivation to interact with the other. This is simply because the person has "been reached"; the "contact" has come about. And if this reduced form of contact is satisfying, there is no reason in psychological theory to suppose that the other will therefore become more attractive or appealing. Distance, as a factor underlying motivation to pursue the other and as a factor that stands for value of a hard-to-reach other, has been eliminated.

Two Separate Forms of Satisfaction

Locke (1998), who criticized a society in which contact is mediated mechanically or electronically, or eliminated altogether, makes repeated reference to a human that demands full-dimensional contact for its long-term satisfactions. The full expression of emotions, the elaborated sense of who one is as a person, desires for direct physical contact and sexuality, everyday rituals among humans—all of these, including even physical health, would seem to depend on direct, physical, face-to-face contact with others.

Obviously there are hosts of needs that do not require such intense, elaborated contact, needs pertaining more to gaining information, to obtaining facts, to procuring material objects. But if we follow Locke's arguments, it becomes plausible that certain, rather chronic human needs are best addressed by the full-dimensional presence of others.

However, there is a qualitatively different kind of satisfaction associated with human interaction. This is the satisfaction gained by reaching, also predicting and controlling, the other. Given a desire to have some form of contact with the other, the first moment of reaching the other is obviously satisfying and tension reducing. What transpires after that moment, for the duration of the contact, is a separate question and has to do with needs of a different quality—needs akin to those depicted by Locke and Bowlby. If the interaction that ensues, following the initial moment of contact, is devoid of sensory cues, there may well be no satisfactions other than the tension-reducing, initial moment of "reaching" the other.

SUMMARY

Distance between humans is a factor that can produce increments in motivation to be with the other person. This motivation, as described in the first perspective discussed here, is then the antecedent of enhanced attraction to the other, of increments in persistence to be with the other. In a parallel fashion, Mischel's approach to delay of gratification implies that distance is associated with value; the person who is hard to get will be valued relative to someone within reach.

However, when we consider the third perspective, we see that seemingly impossible distances can be eliminated rapidly by mediated contact with the desired person. The implication is that the relation between distance and value in social relations will often be nonexistent once contact is established with the "partial" other person. Finally, this latter analysis raises the question of satisfaction in communication and social relations, satisfaction based on full-dimensional contact with others as compared to satisfactions that are possible within a relationship of limited dimensionality.

REFERENCES

Bowlby, J. (1973). *Attachment and loss: Vol. 2. Separation: Anxiety and anger.* London: Hogarth Press.

Brehm, J. W. (1966). *A theory of psychological reactance.* New York: Academic Press.

Brehm, J. W., & Cohen, A. R. (1962). *Explorations in cognitive dissonance.* New York: Wiley.

Brehm, J. W., & Self, E. (1989). The intensity of motivation. *Annual Review of Psychology, 40,* 109–131.

Brehm, J. W., Wright, R. A., Solomon, S., Silka, I., & Greenberg, J. (1983). Perceived difficulty, energization, and the magnitude of goal valence. *Journal of Experimental Social Psychology, 19,* 21–48.

Festinger, L. (1957). *A theory of cognitive dissonance.* Stanford, CA: Stanford University Press.

Kiesler, C. A., & Corbin, L. (1965). Commitment, attraction, and conformity. *Journal of Personality and Social Psychology, 2,* 890–895.

Lawson, R. (1965). *Frustration: The development of a scientific concept.* New York: Macmillan.

Lewin, K. (1926). Untersuchungen zur Handlungs- und Affekt-Psychologie. II: Vorsatz, Wille und Beduerfnis [Investigations in behavior- and affect-psychology. II: Intention, will and need]. *Psychologische Forschung, 7,* 330–385.

Lissner, K. (1933). Die Entspannung von Beduerfnissen durch Ersatzhandlungen [The reduction of needs through substitute behaviors]. *Psychologische Forschung, 18,* 218–250.

Locke, J. L. (1998). *Why we don't talk to each other anymore: The de-voicing of society.* New York: Touchstone.

Mahler, W. (1933). Ersatzhandlungen verschiedenen Realitaetsgrades [Substitute behaviors of differing degrees of reality]. *Psychologische Forschung, 18,* 27–89.

McKenna, K. Y. A., & Bargh, J. A. (2000). Plan 9 from cyberspace: The implications of the internet for personality and social psychology. *Personality and Social Psychology Review, 4,* 57–75.

Mischel, W. (1974). Processes in delay of gratification. In L. Berkowitz (Ed.), *Advances in experimental social psychology* (Vol. 7, pp. 249–292). New York: Academic Press.

Mischel, W. (1996). From good intentions to willpower. In P. M. Gollwitzer & J. A. Bargh (Eds.), *The psychology of action: Linking cognition and motivation to behavior* (pp. 197–218). New York: Guilford.

Postman, N. (1982). *The disappearance of childhood.* New York: Vintage.

Rheingold, H. (1993). *The virtual community: Homesteading on the electronic frontier.* New York: Harper.

Wicklund, R. A. (1974). *Freedom and reactance.* Potomac, MD: Lawrence Erlbaum Associates.

Wicklund, R. A., & Vandekerckhove, M. M. P. (2000). Delay of gratification in interaction rituals. In T. Postmes, R. Spears, M. Lea, & S. Reicher (Eds.), *SIDE issues centre stage: Recent developments in studies of de-individuation in groups* (pp. 191–202). Amsterdam: Koninklijke Nederlandse Akademie van Wetenschappen Verhandelingen, Afd. Letterkunde, Nieuwe Reeks, deel 183.

8

The Diamond in the Stone: Exploring the Place of Free Behavior in Studies of Human Rights and Culture

Stephen Worchel
University of Hawai`i at Hilo

There is an Armenian folk tale about a young traveler whose eye is captured by an interestingly shaped stone on the side of the road. He walks past the stone, but can't quite shake its image from his mind. He retraces his steps, picks up the stone, and stuffs it in his pocket, not having any thought about what he will do with it. Throughout his journey, he finds inventive uses for the stone, including as a projectile to slay a fierce dog that attacks him. At the end of the story, the traveler happens to break the stone, finding a valuable diamond inside it. The story's lesson, I think, is that we should embrace those things (ideas or stones) that grab our interest, even if we are not sure of their immediate value.

Although reactance theory had an immediate appeal (for me) from the time of its introduction (Brehm, 1966), one concept was especially intriguing. In fact, that concept was one of the least developed in the theory, and it has largely escaped the eye of researchers. Brehm postulated that individuals have a set of free behaviors, acts in which they could engage either at the moment or at some time in the future, and that he or she has the necessary physical or psychological ability to perform. The elimination or threat of elimination of a free behavior triggers the motivational state of psychological reactance, and ignites efforts to protect or regain the freedom.

The vast majority of the research on reactance has focused on reactions to threats to or elimination of freedom (Brehm, 1972; Hammock & Brehm, 1966). In the best empirical tradition, freedom (and the importance of these freedoms) is generally controlled by or granted in the experimental setting. Individuals are led to believe that they have the freedom to choose between various alternatives or objects (Brehm, Stires, Sensenig, & Shaban, 1966), only to have one of the alternatives cruelly snatched away. Or they are told that they have access to a communication, only to have it censored (Worchel, Arnold, & Baker, 1975). The importance of the freedom and the type of threat are manipulated by the experimenter, and the victim's reaction is examined. The large body of research embracing this paradigm offers important insight into how people respond to barriers to their free behavior.

But hidden in the theoretical closet of the theory is the intriguing concept of *freedom*. How do people arrive at the perception that specific acts constitute their free behaviors? In many of the experiments, individuals are explicitly assigned freedom by the omnipotent experimenter. But how do these perceptions develop outside the laboratory? A related issue concerns why freedom is important. Why is an individual less than elated to be told that he will have to settle for the Porsche, when he would have chosen this option anyway? One can only stare in amazement at the individual who scurries around the barnyard of life like a chicken rounding up her wayward chicks, trying to protect freedom, when the goals of these free behaviors can be guaranteed by others. Why does the promise of America as the land of freedom, have more appeal than the presentation of America as the land of milk, honey, and guaranteed riches?

Brehm and others (Brehm, 1966; Brehm & Brehm, 1981) take a glancing blow at addressing these and related questions. My interpretation of their position is that freedom allows people to adapt to the changing demands of their world. Freedom equates with adaptation in a way that objects (even a red Porsche) do not. Freedom (of choice or action) allows people to meet their changing needs. Because of this, a freedom "is important to the degree that it might lead to the satisfaction of needs that are central to the person's life" (West & Wicklund, 1980, p. 251). Unfortunately, the importance of freedom has often been equated with the attractiveness of the alternatives involved in a choice or decision. The more attractive the ultimate objects, the more important the freedom. Brehm and Brehm (1981) opened the curtain of possibilities a bit further by relating freedom to control. Control is encased in the rock of freedom, and the elimination of a free behavior not only takes away the opportunity to have the cookie (Worchel, Lee, & Adewole, 1975) or the blender, but it also reduces the individual's control over outcomes. Wortman and Brehm (1975) emphasized the importance of control in examining the conditions that lead to reactance (trying harder) and those that result in learned helplessness (reducing effort). Reactance is generated when control is challenged, but learned helplessness occurs when the individual accepts that he or she no longer has control (usually after repeated elimination of a freedom). The ultimate utility of control is not completely addressed in reactance theory, but several other investigators have suggested that control equates with predictability and security (Pervin, 1963; Rodin & Langer, 1977).

According to reactance theory, individuals learn through experience what their freedoms are (or are not), or they are specifically given freedom by a powerful other. Exactly how this process occurs remains somewhat unclear. And one can wonder whether experience in one situation leads to the perception of freedom in another or how a figure attains the right to dole out freedom to others.

Like many of my colleagues, I accepted these positions as sufficient and focused my own research on how people reacted to threats to freedom and/or regained lost freedom. But like a rock in the pocket of the Armenian wayfarer, the issues surrounding the concept of freedom continued to find their way into my consciousness and my research in areas that seemed far removed from reactance theory. Why is freedom important? Is freedom unique to the single individual or to a specific situation? What influences the perception of freedom? I devote the remainder of this chapter to these questions.

The general plot of the chapter is to explore and expand the concept of free behavior. This goal requires going well beyond the original and concise use of the concept of free behavior employed by Brehm in proposing reactance theory. Brehm viewed free behavior as being situation specific and limited to the domain of the individual. I venture into uncharted waters by exploring the value of possessing free behaviors, suggesting that free behaviors are important because they relate to the individual's sense of identity. Further, I suggest that many of the individual's free behaviors are granted by the groups to which he or she belongs, and, therefore, they become lynchpins in the relationship between individuals and groups. In taking this perspective, the possibility that groups, like individuals, have free behaviors is proposed. This approach leads to considering free behaviors in the context of rights and duties that characterize the interface between individuals and groups. Given that the individual–group relationship has been defined as a foundation for culture, I conclude the chapter by exploring the role of culture in determining the free behaviors that are most important to individuals and groups. My ultimate aim is to demonstrate that concepts introduced by reactance theory have broader implications than those traditionally embraced by research on reactance.

FREEDOM AND PERSONAL IDENTITY

It is difficult to argue with the adaptive function of free behaviors. Just as the wise hunter packs extra ammunition when entering a foreboding forest, the intelligent wayfarer would be reluctant to start down the path of life without ensuring a full load of free behaviors. Although not specifically proposed by reactance theory, it is not a far stretch to suggest that there may be a lure to securing free behaviors that can be used to gain control over outcomes. One never knows when the freedom to resist eating spinach or the freedom to choose a specific candy bar (Hammock & Brehm, 1966) might be necessary to preserve life or the comforts of life. Therefore, I suggest that individuals are attracted to situations or groups that offer them increased behavioral freedom. But the role of behavioral freedom may not be confined to enhancing the individual's ability to adapt to and thrive in a variety of situations.

Along with the struggle for survival, one of the most basic human endeavors is the search for identity (Erickson, 1959; Wylie, 1961). Individuals search in the most unusual places to develop the self-concept. They peer into the "looking glass" of social interaction (Cooley, 1902) to identify the self. And Festinger (1954) argued that individuals measure themselves against a yardstick of social comparison to develop their self-concept in domains that have no physical reality. Explorations in cognitive dissonance theory suggest that individuals might actually choose impoverished options to retain a self-concept once it is developed (Aronson & Carlsmith, 1962; Festinger, 1957).

Tajfel and his colleagues (Tajfel, 1970; Tajfel & Turner, 1979, 1986) argued that one's self-concept is based on two pillars. One, the social identity, arises from the social groups to which one belongs. In an effort to enhance this social identity, individuals strive to join attractive groups and/or to enhance the position of their group relative to groups to which they do not belong. The other pillar is personal identity, which is built on characteristics unique to the individual. The concept of personal identity was given a secondary role because of Tajfel's abiding interest in the relationship between groups. However, personal identity was generally viewed as including physical characteristics (height, weight, etc.), personality variables (friendly, hard working, etc.), and unique personal experience. My colleagues and I have also argued that a third foundation of identity includes the roles one occupies within groups and organizations (Worchel, Iuzzini, Coutant, & Ivaldi, 2000). People are defined (and define themselves) by the titles and positions they occupy within the groups to which they belong. In fact, the may retain those titles (Captain, Senator, President) after they leave the group, because these titles have become a critical part of their identity.

I now offer a fourth foundation on which an individual's identity and esteem are based. That foundation includes the number and nature of free behaviors that one believes he or she has. For example, I suggest that an individual's view of self changes when he or she perceives that they have the freedom to choose between a number of alternatives (jobs, mates, vacation destination, automobiles) rather than when no such freedom exists. Similarly, a child's perception of himself or herself changes, not only with age, but because age often is accompanied by new behavioral freedoms.

The role of freedom in developing an identity was raised by Apfelbaum (1979) in her discussion of power and dominance in intergroup relations. In keeping with Wortman and Brehm (1975), Apfelbaum separated the concept of power from material outcome. She argued that the possession of power allows the dominant group to determine the rights and privileges of the subordinate group. The dominant group, in other words, determines the free behaviors that will be possessed by the subordinate group. Played out over time, the subordinate group develops a dependency on the dominant group. The subordinate group loses its autonomy and is defined by its relation to the dominant group. The subordinate group ultimately adopts the norms, standards, and values established by the dominant group. Indeed, these norms and values are accepted as legitimate. Even when its physical needs are adequately met, *the group without power loses its unique identity as do members of that group.* The loss of power is equated with a loss of identity.

Apfelbaum's insightful analysis of power begs introduction to Brehm's treatment of freedom (free behaviors). If power/control is equated with one's freedom, Apfelbaum's position suggests that the *freedom to control one's outcomes is a foundation of individual identity.* And the threat to or elimination of freedom causes injury to the individual's sense of personal identity. In fact, Apfelbaum argued that power is the currency used by individuals to purchase personal rights and control the rights of subordinates. Taking this perspective, free behaviors not only facilitate adaptation to and control over one's environment, they define the essence of the individual. And the psychological reactance that is ignited by threat to or elimination of freedom is a motivational state designed not only to restore freedom, but also to reestablish identity.

This position is congruent with Sharon Brehm's (1983) suggestion that individuals are especially sensitive to threats to freedom that reduce their social distinctiveness. Brehm's focus was on the fact that some specific free behaviors such as the freedom to chose one's clothing or to choose a profession are directly connected with one's distinctiveness. The threat to one of these free behaviors is perceived as a direct threat to one's unique self-image. However, a threat to a more benign behavior, such as choosing what to eat for lunch, may also threaten one's image through the implication it has for one's power. Andreoli, Worchel, & Folger (1974) found that a threat to one free behavior could be perceived as implying threats to other free behaviors, thereby initiating a high degree of reactance. A threat to a seemingly unimportant behavior may be viewed as a general threat to one's control over environmental outcomes. Therefore, the possession and protection of free behaviors can have important links to self-image and individual identity (see also Brockner & Elkind, 1985).

The plausibility of this freedom–identity link is evident in data that my students (William Webb, Dawna Coutant, Michelle Grossman, Frankie Wong, Judy Oulette) and I have collected on the self-concept of people in 12 different cultures over a number of years. Respondents were given a variety of instruments (Who am I?, self-ideal discrepancy, Cantril's Self Anchoring Scale) that ask them to describe themselves and their group (nation). Preliminary analyses of the data revealed several interesting patterns and differences between cultures. Our scoring approach was initially designed to code responses on the basis of adjectives that respondents used to describe themselves. Although specific traits comprised many of the responses, a surprising number of responses (especially in individualistic cultures; see pp. 120–122) involved free behaviors that individuals felt were characteristic. For example, when asked to respond to an open-ended version of the Who Am I questionnaire, responses included the "free behaviors" listed in Table 8.1.

The point of this discussion is to suggest that free behaviors are important because they play a critical role in defining self-identity and in establishing the uniqueness of the individual. The motivational state of reactance results when personal identity and uniqueness are threatened by the elimination of free behaviors. More generally, I would argue that relating reactance theory to individual identity can both expand the scope of the theory and explicate processes related to establishing identity.

TABLE 8.1
Examples of Free Behaviors Used to Describe "Who Am I?"

"I am a 21-year old who can finally buy beer on my own, but I really find I'm not as motivated to drink like I did when I was younger."

"I am the owner of a 1987 Honda Civic. I have freedom! I drove to Houston yesterday just to show that I could."

"I love to jog because it is one thing I can do on my own without interference of others."

"I live on a ranch which gives me the chance to ride horses when I want. My friends would love to have this opportunity."

"I am free, independent, and 18!!! My parents can't tell me what to do."

"I am a Christian. My special relationship with Jesus frees me from the daily worries that others have. No one can interfere with this feeling."

"I am the only person who can tell me what to do!"

"I go to class when I feel like it, not like these students who feel they have to go."

"I am a bird who can fly when she wants to."

"I dream because no one can stop me from dreaming. My dreams are like no one else."

"I am unique because I choose to act different than others do."

Pushing the Limits: Free Behaviors for Groups

It may be only a figment of my imagination, but when I remember my days in graduate school, I have a vague picture of the graduate students lining up in the early morning to chant the mantra, "Psychology is the study of *individuals*!" Utterances about groups, teams, or collectives would bring the graduate school equivalent of solitary confinement. But the 1960s was the period of the Civil Rights Movement, the Vietnam War, and the Cold War. Ideological lines in the sand separated individual from individual. But these same lines of demarcation also divided groups from each other. Whether it was Black/White, North Vietnam/South Vietnam, or communist countries/democratic countries, identifiable groups or nations stood in opposition to other groups or nations. Groups declared war on other groups, and groups entered into treaties that bound both existing and future members to defined courses of action. Concepts such as group ideology, national identity, and group beliefs made their appearance (Bar-Tal, 1990; P. Worchel, 1967). As a kid, Muzafer and Carolyn Sherif were frequent visitors in my home, and they often spoke of their camp studies that involved creating distinct groups from the collection of campers that arrived on the first day of the sessions. Groups were viewed as distinct entities that behaved.

Research on social identity theory (Turner, 1987) has demonstrated that individuals will act to advantage their own group (such as giving it a disproportional share of points or money), even when the individuals do not directly share these rewards. Admittedly, SIT argues that enhancing the status of the group ultimately augments the individual's social identity. But there are a plethora of examples where individuals willingly sacrifice their lives for their group, suggesting that egoistic motivations are not the only forces that drive the desire to protect one's group.

Building on research by McGrath and Kelly (1986), LaCoursiere (1980), and others (Moreland & Levine, 1988), my students and I conducted several longitudinal studies on groups and their members (Worchel, Coutant-Sassic, & Grossman; 1992; Worchel, Coutant-Sassic, & Wong, 1993). We found that groups develop through stages, and that the stages occur even though members enter and leave groups. The results also showed that groups have distinct identities that are evident in the adoption of group names (Red Devils, Hell's Angels), symbols, and language. These identities are separate from the identities of the individual group members, and they outlive any individual members. Included in these group identities is the perception that groups have free behaviors, actions in which the group can engage in either at the moment or at some point in the future. These free behaviors might include entering into treaties with other groups, controlling territory or resources, governing group members, and being recognized as a legitimate body by other groups.

A threat to the group's freedom leads to a host of responses, several very similar to those identified in individuals by research on reactance theory. My own research with ongoing groups showed that groups focus attention on the threat, and the threatened "freedom" takes on increased importance. For example, groups reacted with anger and protest when an experimenter instructed them on how to arrange their chairs, after first leading them to believe that seating arrangements could be decided by the group. An analogy might be the reaction of one nation to the incursion (even accidental) by another nation on territory that was heretofore deemed uninhabitable. Threats to a group's freedom (either by other groups or physical situations) often lead to perceptible changes in group structure. Group cohesiveness increases in the face of threats (Sherif, Harvey, White, Hood, & Sherif, 1961) Leadership becomes more centralized (Worchel & Shackelford, 1992). We need only examine reactions in the United States following the terrorist attacks of September 11 to see that individuals sacrifice individual freedoms (e.g., criticizing leadership) to restore group freedoms following a threat to these freedoms. It is difficult to resist offering the observation that a "threat to a group's freedom leads to a motivational state (within that group) aimed at restoring that freedom."

Another interesting direction for this discussion concerns threats to an individual's freedom that also imply threats to the freedoms of one's group. Research on ethnic identity (Worchel, 1999) found that whereas individuals reacted negatively to threats to their person, they were especially hostile toward threats that appeared to also have implications for their ethnic group. For example, an Israeli settler in the West Bank may be distressed at being told that he or she cannot occupy a specific piece of land. However, if the individual views this prohibition as implying that Israelis have no right to settle this land, the reaction is much more exaggerated. Tajfel (Tajfel & Turner, 1979) echoed this point from a different perspective by suggesting that threats to one's group were viewed as threats to the self. I am suggesting that threats to one's personal freedom may be viewed as implying a threat to one's group. In other words, there is a clear perception that groups do have freedom and individuals will respond to protect this freedom.

The point of this discussion is to suggest that reactance theory need not be limited to the psychology of individuals. Groups, too, may be characterized as having free behaviors. These behaviors not only enhance the group's control over its environment and enhance its ability to adapt (survive), but also help define its identity (and power). The threat to or elimination of these free behaviors leads to a motivational state designed to restore the freedom. Indeed, lurking in the shadows of the volumes of research on reactance theory may be a rich treasure trove of ideas that relate to group dynamics and intergroup relations.

The Intersection of Individual Psychology and Group Dynamics: Rights and Duties

Although I may have committed an unpardonable sin by introducing reactance theory to the domain of group dynamics, I suggest that this unholy partnership can open up intriguing new research vistas. One interesting direction, suggested by Rex Wright in his review of this chapter, is that group membership can define the individual's freedoms. For example, certain social clubs offer membership to "couples only"; a single individual does not have the freedom to join these clubs. The Kamehameha schools in Hawai`i are only open to kids of Hawaiian ancestry. Hence, being in a group, either by choice or birth, may define the free behaviors available to an individual. Individuals gain (or lose) freedom by membership in groups. Further, when an individual moves from one group to another, the menu of free behaviors may change. A man may have the freedom to light up a good cigar and savor a cold beer when with his softball team, but such behaviors are outside the realm of possibility when he meets with his bible study group.

Another area of interest opened by the assumption that groups have free behaviors concerns the conflicts that may occur between individual and group free behaviors. As an independent individual living in a tropical paradise in the middle of the Pacific Ocean, I have the freedom of choosing whether to vacation in Bali or Palau. However, my family feels that it, too, has the freedom to determine the destination of our vacation site. I'm not only horrified to learn that the family is considering Tallahassee and Tampa as vacation destinations, but the situation deteriorates further when I realize that my individual freedom clashes with my group's freedom. Indeed, the price of group membership can be measured by the freedom(s) that the individual sacrifices to join the group. This dilemma is at the root of the enduring psychological conflict between independence and interdependence (Brewer, 1991; Worchel & Coutant, 2001), and it helps explain why group membership is so rarely stable (Levine, Moreland, & Choi, 2001). Indeed, one of the major factors that determines group membership may be the free behaviors that individuals are willing to relinquish to join a group, and the freedoms that groups are willing to forgo to attract certain members. Such ignoble human behaviors as infidelity and defection may be the result of the latent reactance that results from this bargaining ritual.

Although this line of reasoning can be taken into many domains, including traditional research on group dynamics, one of the more intriguing paths to follow takes us into the area of human rights. Sadly, the examination of human rights has largely escaped the microscope of social psychology. Social psychologists have had only a fleeting relationship with the concept of human rights, largely under the guise of justice (Austin, 1979; Thibaut & Walker, 1975). More recently, Doise (Doise, Spini, & Clemence, 1999; Doise, Staerkle, Clemence, & Savory, 1998) and Moghaddam (Moghaddam, 2000; Moghaddam & Vuksanovic, 1990) have directly examined the concept of human rights. However, despite social psychology's reluctance to embrace human rights as a research focus, the concept of human rights has been one, if not the major, social issue on the global agenda for the last half century.

Spurred by the atrocities of the Nazis during World War II, the members of the United Nations set aside economic, social, and political differences long enough to craft the *Universal Declaration of Human Rights* (1948). This bold document spelled out the rights of each human in the form of 30 articles. The rights included such actions as the rights to own property, to seek political asylum, to freely express opinions, to work, marry and begin a family, and to be educated. Although the concept of "right" was not explicitly defined, its implicit definition is akin to Brehm's concept of "free behavior"; the freedom to engage in specified behaviors. A human right within any specific group may be viewed as a "free behavior" that is shared by all or most members of that group. This definition separates rights from idiosyncratic free behaviors that are unique to a specific individual and his or her personal experience. The UN Declaration attempts to delineate universal rights as those freedoms that belong to all individuals because of their membership in the human race. Although Brehm suggested that individuals learn which behaviors are "free behaviors" and these freedoms may be situation specific, the UN Declaration placed few such restrictions on the universal human rights.

The one interesting caveat reserved for Article 29 was that "Everyone has duties to the community in which alone the free and full development of his personality is possible." Although the "duties" were not specifically identified, it is important to note the reference of duties "to the community". I (Worchel, in press-a) have suggested that the concept of duties involves the obligations of the individual to the group. Whereas rights grant the individual independence, duties define the boundaries of interdependence. It is this combination of rights and duties that comprise the individual's personal and social identities (à la SIT). I further suggest that individuals ultimately "purchase" their rights by agreeing to accept the obligations/duties imposed by the group. Rights, even those identified by the UN as universal, are guaranteed only to the extent that individuals fulfill their duties to their group.

From the perspective of expanding the domain of reactance theory, the process by which individuals accumulate rights (or free behaviors) through accepting duties to their social groups stands as an interesting focus on its own. Not only would research on this issue flesh out one of the more underdeveloped areas of reactance theory (the process of accruing free behaviors), but it would also forge the link between individual freedom and group membership. In addition, this research could identify another motivation for joining and remaining in groups. If free behaviors are related to group membership and purchased by accepting obligations to the group, the rupture of the individual–group relationship introduces uncertainty into the domain of free behaviors. Although a new set of free behaviors may become open to the individual who leaves a group, others are eliminated. For example, divorce may eliminate the individual's freedom to attend certain social functions or interact with certain individuals. Research on individuals in abusive relationships does show that one reason that individuals remain in these relationships, despite recognizing them as dysfunctional, is the recognition that "opportunities" outside the relationship will disappear with the demise of the relationship (Duck, 1984; Imber-Black, Roberts, & Whiting, 1988). The organizational literature also reports that individuals state that one of the benefits considered in choosing a job is the options (meeting people, joining clubs, vacation) outside the workplace associated with the job (Roberts, 1998). Indeed, it is no accident that the United States presents itself as the land of "freedom and opportunity," rather than as the place of riches and security. Groups attract members by offering rights and freedoms in exchange for the performance of duties, and this issue could be fertile grounds for research relating reactance theory to group dynamics.

Group Rights and Duties. Given the fact that both psychology and the Western world are preoccupied with the individual, it is only natural to focus on individual rights and duties. However, the flip side of the coin, the rights and duties of the group, is equally interesting and important. As my research has suggested, groups are viewed (both by members and nonmembers) as having a cafeteria of rights that guarantee their ability to survive and thrive (Worchel, 1996; Worchel et al., 1992). Among these rights is the right to control members by granting and limiting their free behaviors, often through rules and laws (Worchel & Coutant, 2001). This is a challenging process. At first glance, it might appear that groups have the upper hand over the individual member. The group generally has more resources and more power than the individual. Hence, any conflict between group rights and individual rights should be decided in favor of the group. However, the group is constantly faced with the task of attracting new members (Levine et al, 2001). It must, therefore, present an attractive situation to perspective members. One way to accomplish this is to offer these individuals free behaviors that they could not find in other groups.

A second challenge to groups is the need to adapt and develop (Worchel, 1995; Worchel et al, 1992). To a large degree, this can be achieved by giving members the freedom to exercise their unique talents and to reach their individual potential. These goals are achieved by presenting these members the environment (freedom) to develop their skills. Because individuals have different skills, interests, and potentials, each individual requires different freedom in order to develop and thrive. Hence, groups are faced with the conundrum of how to preserve their own freedom and satisfy members' demands for equal and fair treatment, while granting individual members unique freedoms that are suited to their needs and aspirations.

The stew of individual–group relations is completed by adding the final ingredient; group duties. Groups may gain power over individuals by possessing physical or social weapons to ensure compliance by the individual. However, coercive power (French & Raven, 1959) is both expensive to maintain and requires constant surveillance of individuals. Aside from creating an arsenal of coercive weapons, groups can capture the loyalty and compliance of individuals by meeting their needs. In addition to granting individuals rights and freedoms, groups administer to the needs of individuals by taking obligations or duties to those individuals. In some cases, these duties prescribe actions by the group (e.g., provide security and/or services to individuals). In other cases, these duties prohibit the group from specific activities: "Nothing in the Declaration may be interpreted as implying for any State, group, or person any right to engage in activity or perform any act aimed at the destruction of any of the rights and freedoms set herein (Article 30, UN Universal Declaration of Human Rights)." Regardless of whether action is prescribed or prohibited, group duties limit or eliminate group freedom.

The relationship between the group and individual is inherently unstable and fraught with conflict because of the bargaining over the rights and duties of each. Worchel and Coutant (2001) compared this bargaining process to dancers engaged in an intricate tango. It is further suggested that this conflict over establishing and maintaining free behaviors contributes to the instability of group membership. Individuals choose to leave groups when freedoms are threatened or eliminated by the group, and groups reject or expel members who do not respect the free behaviors of the group.

Implications for Reactance Theory. The system of individual and group rights and duties not only defines the relationship between individuals and groups, but it also opens up new opportunities for reactance theory. This perspective suggests that the roots of many, if not most, individual free behaviors reach deep into the fertile ground of groups. Groups, whether the UN or the University of Kansas, grant to individuals prescribed "free behaviors." Threats to these freedoms may create reactance that motivates the individual to change the group or leave the group. Likewise, groups are granted free behaviors by other groups and/or by their individual members. Threats to these freedoms ignite actions to change their relationship with other groups and/or their members. For example, the actions of a single deviate may not necessarily injure the group, but they may imply a threat to the group's "right" to control individual members. The surprisingly harsh and often public punishment of deviates may, therefore, be interpreted as efforts by the group to regain its free behavior (Asch, 1956). The application of reactance theory to individual–group relationships may help predict and explain behaviors that result in these situations.

Another interesting issue addressed by the examination of freedom (rights) and limits to freedom (duties) involves social order and predictability. From the perspective of the individual, the possession of "free behaviors" implies individual control. The freedom to choose when I will arrive at work gives me control over my daily life. However, from the perspective of the group, individual freedom invites chaos and unpredictability. Individuals and groups detest unpredictability (Baum, Singer, & Baum, 1981). Therefore, social order requires limits to individual freedom. Likewise, individuals would face a difficult life if they could not predict the actions of their group or representatives of their groups. If I hear a strange noise outside my house, I want to be confident that the police will exercise their duty to investigate when I place my frantic call to them. Predictability in social relations requires a clear understanding of the freedoms and duties of individuals and groups, and a system to ensure that behavioral freedom is not expanded without mutual consent.

The role of free behavior in determining predictability and social order is an interesting domain of study. Worchel and Coutant (1997) ventured into this arena in an examination of patriotism and nationalism. Their discussion showed that during periods of threat (war, natural disaster) to either individual or group, predictability becomes extremely important. During these times, individual freedom is often suspended in favor of group rights and duties. The resulting increase in social order allows the group to act quickly and effectively. Complaints about the loss of personal freedom are viewed as traitorous, and met with swift punishment. However, during periods of stability and low threat, the emphasis may swing to individual rights and freedoms. Order and predictability are less important, and individuals "doing their own thing" (exercising personal freedom) is viewed as acceptable, if not healthy.

For the most part, research on reactance theory has not dealt with the negotiations between individuals and groups over freedom (or duties) or how social conditions affect this negotiation. However, the work on implied threat and implied restoration of freedom has interesting implications for this question. For example, Andreoli et al. (1974) found that individuals experienced reactance when they observed the freedom of another person being threatened. In this study, a decision alternative that participants viewed as being unfairly removed in one discussion group was accorded increased importance in another group. In other words, when participants observed a group expanding its freedom at the expense of a member's freedom, they reacted in their own group to protect that freedom. In another study (Worchel & Brehm, 1971), reactance responses by an individual were reduced when they observed a member of a discussion group regaining his decisional freedom that had been unfairly usurped by a group. These data suggest that individuals are sensitive to freedoms of groups and individual members, and actions by others within the group affect the individual's response and the experience of reactance. This analysis could be expanded to directly explore the development of individual and group rights and duties and responses to events that dishonor these.

The Role of Culture in Determining Rights and Duties . . . and Reactance

It is no accident that psychology has flourished in industrialized Western countries such as the United States, Great Britain, and Germany, whereas the field of sociology has been more keenly embraced in communist countries such as the Soviet Union and the Peoples Republic of China. In a comparative analysis of the constitutions of the United States and the Soviet Union, I (Worchel, in press-a, in press-b) found that the former document was preoccupied with the rights of the individual, whereas the latter document enumerated the rights of the State rather than those of the individual. The United States Bill of Rights explicitly grants individuals the rights of free speech, privacy, and bearing arms. In fact, in the Declaration of Independence, Thomas Jefferson proclaimed that it is the "Right of the People to alter or abolish" the government when it exceeds its authority and infringes on individual rights. On the other hand, the 1977 Constitution of the Soviet Union clearly elevates the group over the individual: "The Soviet state and its bodies function on the basis of socialist law, ensure the maintenance of law and order, and safeguard the interests of society and the rights and freedoms of citizens (Article 3)." In Article 8, the Soviet Constitution gives to groups (not individuals) the right to discuss and decide state and public affairs. And in Article 17, the individual is further ignored in the proclamation that "The state makes regulations for such work to ensure that it serves the interest of society."

In an examination of responses from over 100,000 employees around the world, Hofstede (1980) found similar differences between cultures in their emphasis on the individual and group. Hofstede classified cultures along a continuum ranging from highly individualistic to low emphasis on individualism (collectivism). The highly individualistic cultures such as the United States and Germany emphasize personal autonomy and independence. Individuals in these cultures are typically viewed as responsible for their actions, and causal attributions emphasize individual choice and personal causality. Although groups are important to personal identity, individuals easily and frequently change groups to satisfy personal needs and desires (Worchel, in press-b). Quite the opposite picture is found in cultures low in individualism, often labeled collective cultures. In these cultures, the group reigns paramount. Individuals "serve" the group, and personal achievement is valued to the extent that it advances the needs of the group. Behavior is highly situational, and personal consistency is not stressed. Unlike individualistic cultures where social comparison is common between group members, social comparisons in collective cultures are frequently between members of different groups (Worchel, 2001). Individuals in collective cultures are expected to preserve group harmony, even when this conflicts with personal desires.

In my analysis of group and individual rights and duties, I found that individualistic cultures stress individual rights and group duties (Worchel, in press-a). On the other hand, collective cultures emphasize group rights and individual duties in their laws and social customs. This analysis has several interesting implications for reactance theory's conceptualization of "free behaviors." First, it suggests that freedom in individualistic cultures will often be based on personal desires, whereas the group should be viewed as the grantor of personal freedom in collective cultures. This difference will be especially evident when the free behaviors in question are social in nature and have the potential to affect the group. For example, distinct cultural differences occur in such domains as the choice of mate, occupation, or place to live, but it can also be found in more individual-based areas such as the determining how to dress or occupy leisure time. According to Hofstede (1980), groups in collective cultures are especially sensitive to any action that can threaten the harmony of the group, and they are reluctant to give individuals control over these behaviors (i.e., have them defined as "free behavior"). Further, individuals in individualistic cultures should take personal action to capture freedom, and the range of free behaviors should differ widely between individuals, even members of the same group. In collective cultures, individuals should be less predatory in gaining free behaviors, and the freedom of individual members of the same group should be relatively homogeneous, especially when those members occupy the same roles.

In addition to differences in the base of free behaviors, culture should affect the experience of reactance. In individualistic cultures, individuals should be particularly prone to threats to their freedom, and reactance should be quickly aroused whether threats arise from the action of other individuals or groups. On the other hand, individuals in collective cultures should be less likely to experience reactance when their personal freedom is threatened. However, reactance should be quickly ignited when their group's freedom is threatened. Although they may not experience strong reactance when their freedom is threatened by the actions of their own group, reactance should be quickly aroused by threats from other groups or outgroup members to their freedom. Finally, these individuals should be more susceptible than people in individualistic cultures to experiencing reactance when observing other in-group members having their freedom threatened. And, the restoration of freedom (implied social restoration) by the actions of other in-group members should be more effective in reducing reactance in collective cultures than in individualistic cultures.

I must confess that these predictions are highly speculative, and I am not aware of cross-cultural research on reactance theory. However, questionnaire data that I have collected from students in several cultures offer some support for my reasoning. As part of a larger survey, students in psychology classes at several universities responded to several questions relating to the relationship between individuals and groups (Worchel, in press-a). As Table 8.2 indicates, students from individualistic cultures in comparison with those from collective societies generally perceived individual rights as more important than group rights. Indi-

TABLE 8.2
The Impact of Culture on the Perception of Human and Group Rights

Agree = 1 Disagree = 7	*Individualistic Cultures*	*Collective Cultures*
The rights of the individual should be respected at all costs	2.21	4.63
The rights of a group are more important than the rights of individual members	5.06	2.62
Some individuals deserve more rights and opportunities than others	6.02	1.79
Some groups deserve more rights and opportunities than others	2.06	1.92
The most important conflicts are the ones that occur between individuals	2.77	4.02
The most important conflicts are the ones that occur between groups	3.92	1.66
Individuals need to be protected from the tyranny of groups	1.30	5.97

vidual rights were viewed as applying to all individuals, rather than being selectively doled out based on the group or position one occupied. Further, the students from individualistic cultures indicated that individuals needed protection from the group. Clearly, culture affected how students conceptualized individual freedom and the dangers posed to these freedoms by social institutions.

I tread on the thin ice of speculation for two reasons. The first reason is to make the point that reactance theory, possibly more than many psychological theories, could benefit from a coordinated program of cross-cultural research. This research could directly address the universality of reactance theory, and identify the limits of the theory. Reactance theory is particularly suited to cultural issues because of its dealing with personal freedom, an issue that appears to define and separate different cultures. The second motive behind my reckless wandering is to refocus attention on the conceptualization of freedom, an emphasis that has remained relatively obscure in reactance theory's preoccupation with the restoration of freedom. No psychological theory has dared address the issue of personal freedom to the extent found in reactance theory. The juxtaposition of individual and group freedom lies at the root of human cultures. Culture defines whether freedom is the domain of groups or individuals, and determines the source of personal freedom (group or individual). Cultural differences in the experience of reactance and the response to threatened freedom may offer critical dimensions for identifying and classifying cultures. With increasing emphasis being placed on the understanding of human cultures, reactance theory may offer a critical perspective.

THE DIAMOND IN THE STONE: CONCLUSION

It is difficult to overemphasize the importance of examining human rights in a theoretical and empirical context. In nearly every domain of human life, the issue of human rights stands at the forefront. "The right to life" versus "the right to control one's body" divides those who seek to prohibit abortion from those who feel it should be available. The advances in cloning and genetics have sparked controversy over who and how human life should be initiated. Charges and countercharges about human rights abuses continue to litter the international political landscape and add uncertainty and tenseness to the relationship between superpowers China and the United States. The terror unleashed on the World Trade Center pulled back the veil of the Taliban regime in Afghanistan and raised troubling questions about the rights of women and freedom or religion in distant lands. The world hungers for a voice that will add some clarity to the debates on issues surrounding the identification and protection of human rights.

Although students of philosophy, law, political science, and sociology have long grappled with these issues (Dworkin, 1978, 1996; Etzioni, 1993; Glendon, 1991), social psychology has largely avoided associating with these issues. Research on justice, fairness, and morality (Austin, 1979; Greenberg & Cohen, 1982; Kohlberg, 1978) have provided interesting insight, but they have also demonstrated the difficulty of developing concrete hypotheses that can be tested with empirical investigations. Reactance theory stands out as an effort to directly confront issues surrounding individual freedom and responses to threats of this freedom. Research on reactance has demonstrated that empirical research can shed light on these issues.

From the perspective of the debate over human rights, the diamond in the stone is Brehm's basic premise that individuals have free behaviors. In this chapter, I attempt to identify several critical questions surrounding the concept of free behavior that can bring reactance theory to center stage in the debate over human rights. These questions concern how individuals come to perceive specific actions as being their free behavior, how individual freedom relates to group freedom, and how culture affects the identification of individual and group free behavior. Reactance theory and the research on hypotheses derived from it have carefully avoided confronting the larger, and admittedly, more murky, subjects of individual and group rights and duties. This course of action has accorded the research a degree of scientific rigor and respect. However, continuing along this path may ultimately damn the theory to the stable of social psychological efforts that have been declared academically interesting by socially irrelevant.

Reactance theory provides an extremely useful framework for examining issues related to human rights. The theory sets the stage for questioning the foundation of freedom and the host of reactions to threats to the freedom. Equally illuminating has been the consideration of free behavior within a cultural context. For the past several years, I have worked with the Seeds of Peace International Camp, a camp that brings together kids from cultures engaged in violent and protracted conflict. The campers include Palestinians, Israelis, Egyptians, Jordanians, Greek and Turkish Cypriots, Serbs, Croats, Bosnians, Indians, and Pakistanis. During coexistence groups, it has been a fascinating experience to observe differences in the reactions of the highly individualistic Israelis and the more collective Arabs to threats to individual and group freedom.

The preparation of this chapter and the review of reactance theory has led me to the conclusion that the issues raised by reactance theory are as current today as they were in the 1960s. The field of social psychology has expanded to embrace issues such as the influence of culture on human social behavior and the expanded base for individual and group identity. Reactance theory offers important insights into these new directions, and these new directions offer the challenge to revisit and increase the reach of reactance theory. I have tried to address some of the possible avenues that can be explored. Future research will determine whether this effort is mere speculation from the confines of an isolated island or real opportunity.

ACKNOWLEDGMENTS

This manuscript was prepared with support of a National Science Foundation grant BCS-0078867 and a NIOSH grant. I would like to thank Dawna Coutant and Laura Stevens for their help.

REFERENCES

Andreoli, V., Worchel, S., & Folger, R. (1974). Implied threat to freedom. *Journal of Personality and Social Psychology, 30,* 765–771.

Apfelbaum, E. (1979). Relations of domination and movements for liberation: An analysis of power between groups. In W. Austin & S. Worchel (Eds.), *The social psychology of intergroup relations* (pp. 121–143). Monterey, CA: Brooks/Cole.

Aronson, E., & Carlsmith, J. (1962). Performance expectancy as a determinant of actual performance. *Journal of Abnormal Social Psychology, 65,* 178–183.

Asch, S. (1956). Studies of independence and conformity. I. A minority of one against a unanimous majority. *Psychological Monographs, 70.*

Austin, W. (1979). Justice, freedom, and self-interest in intergroup conflict. In W. Austin & S. Worchel (Eds.), *The social psychology of intergroup relations* (pp. 141–143). Monterey, CA: Brooks/Cole.

Austin, W., & Worchel, S. (Eds.). (1979). *The social psychology of intergroup relations.* Monterey, CA: Brooks/Cole.

Bar-Tal, D. (1990). *Group beliefs.* New York: Springer-Verlag.

Baum, A., Singer, J., & Baum, C. (1981). Stress and the environment. *Journal of Social Issues, 37,* 4–35.

Brehm, J. (1966). *A psychological theory of reactance.* New York: Academic Press.

Brehm, J. (1972). *Responses to loss of freedom: A theory of psychological reactance.* Morristown, NJ: General Learning Press.

Brehm, J., & Brehm, S. (1981). *Psychological reactance: A theory of freedom and control.* New York: Academic Press.

Brehm, J., Stires, L., Sensenig, J., & Shaban, J. (1966). The attractiveness of eliminated choice alternatives. *Journal of Experimental Social Psychology, 2,* 301–313.

Brehm, S. (1983). Psychological reactance and social differentiation. *Bulletin de Psychologie, 37,* 471–474.

Brewer, M. (1991). The social self: On being the same and different at the same time. *Personality and Social Psychology Bulletin, 17,* 475–482.

Brockner, J., & Elkind, M. (1985). Self-esteem and reactance: Further evidence of attitudinal and motivational consequences. *Journal of Experimental Social Psychology, 21,* 346–361.

Cooley, C. (1902). *Human order and social order.* New York: Scribner.
Doise, W., Spini, D., & Clemence, A. (1999). Human rights as social representations in a cross-national context. *European Journal of Social Psychology, 29,* 1–29.
Doise, W., Staerkle, C., Clemence, A., & Savory, F. (1998). Human rights and Genevan youth: A developmental study of social representations. *The Swiss Journal of Psychology, 57,* 86–100.
Duck, S. (1984). Perspectives on the repair of personal relationships: Repair of what, when? In S. Duck (Ed.), *Personal relationships: Vol. 5. Repairing personal relationships.* Orlando: Academic Press.
Dworkin, R. (1978). *Taking rights seriously.* Cambridge, MA: Harvard University Press.
Dworkin, R. (1998). *Freedom's law: The moral reading of the American constitution.* Cambridge, MA: Harvard University Press.
Erickson, E. (1959). Identity and the life cycle: Selected papers. *Psychological Issues, 1,* 50–100.
Etzioni, A. (1993). *The spirit of community: Rights, responsibilities, and the communitarian agenda.* Lanham, MD: Rowman & Littlefield.
Festinger, L. (1954). A theory of social comparison processes. *Human Relations, 7,* 117–140.
Festinger, L. (1957). *A theory of cognitive dissonance.* Palo Alto, CA: Stanford University Press.
French, J., & Raven, B. (1959). The bases of social power. In D. Cartwright (Ed.), *Studies in social power.* (pp. 150–167). Ann Arbor: University of Michigan Press.
Glendon, M. (1991). *Rights talk: The impoverishment of political discourse.* New York: Free Press.
Greenberg, J., & Cohen, R. (Eds.). (1982). *Equity and justice in social behavior.* New York: Academic Press.
Hammock, T., & Brehm, J. (1966). The attractiveness of choice alternatives when freedom to choose is eliminated by a social agent. *Journal of Personality, 34,* 546–554.
Hofstede, G. (1980). *Culture's consequences: International differences in work-related values.* Beverly Hills, CA: Sage.
Imber-Black, E., Roberts, J., & Whiting, R. (Eds.). (1988). *Rituals in families and family therapy.* New York: Norton.
Kohlberg, L. (1978). Revisions in the theory and practice of moral development. *New Directions in Child Development, 2,* 83–88.
LaCoursiere, R. (1980). *The life cycle of groups.* New York: Human Sciences Press.
Levine, J., Moreland, R., & Choi, H. (2001). Group socialization and newcomer innovation. In M. Hogg & S. Tinsdale (Eds.), *Blackwell handbook of social psychology: Group process* (pp. 86–106). Oxford, England: Blackwell.
McGrath, J., & Kelly, J. (1986). *Time and human interaction: Toward a social psychology of time.* New York: Guilford.
Moghaddam, F. (2000). Toward a cultural theory of human rights. *Theory and Psychology, 10,* 291–312.
Moghaddam, F., & Vuksanovic, V. (1990). Attitudes and behavior toward human rights across different contexts: The role of right-wing authoritarianism, political ideology, and religiosity. *International Journal of Psychology, 25,* 455–474.
Moreland, R., & Levine, J. (1988). Socialization in small groups: Temporal changes in individual group relations. In L. Berkowitz (Ed.), *Advances in experimental social psychology* (Vol. 15, pp. 137–192). New York: Academic Press.
Pervin, L. (1963). Performance and satisfaction as a function of individual–environment fit. *Psychological Bulletin, 69,* 56–68.
Roberts, G. (1998). Perspectives on enduring and emerging issues in performance appraisal and job selection. *Public Personnel Management, 27,* 301–320.
Rodin, J., & Langer, E. (1977). Long-term effects of control relevant intervention with institutionalized aged. *Journal of Personality and Social Psychology, 35,* 891–902.
Sherif, M., Harvey, O., White, B., Hood, W., & Sherif, C. (1961). *Intergroup conflict and cooperation: The Robber's Cave experiment.* Norman: University of Oklahoma Press.

Tajfel, H. (1970). Experiments in intergroup discrimination. *Scientific American, 223,* 96–102.

Tajfel, H., & Turner, J. (1979). An integrative theory of intergroup conflict. In W. Austin & S. Worchel (Eds.), *The social psychology of intergroup relations* (pp. 33–47). Monterey, CA: Brooks/Cole.

Tajfel, H., & Turner, J. (1986). The social identity theory of intergroup behavior. In S. Worchel & W. Austin (Eds.), *The psychology of intergroup relations* (pp. 7–24). Chicago: Nelson Hall.

Thibaut, J., & Walker, L. (1975). *Procedural justice: A psychological analysis.* Hillsdale, NJ: Lawrence Erlbaum Associates.

Turner, J. (1987). *Rediscovering the social group: A self-categorization theory.* Oxford, England: Blackwell.

West, S., & Wicklund, R. (1980). *A primer of social psychological theories.* Monterey, CA: Brooks/Cole.

Worchel, P. (1967). Social ideology and reaction to international events. *Journal of Conflict Resolution, 11,* 414–430.

Worchel, S. (1995). The seasons of a group's life . . . and their impact on intergroup relations. In F. Morales, D. Paez, & J. Deschamps (Eds.), *Perspectives on social identity and social categorization* (pp. 53–75). Barcelona: Anthropos.

Worchel, S. (1996). Emphasizing the social nature of groups in a developmental framework. In J. Nye & A. Brower (Eds.), *What's social about social cognition?* (pp. 261–284). Thousand Oaks, CA: Sage.

Worchel, S. (1999). *Written in blood: Ethnic identity and the struggle for human harmony.* New York: Worth.

Worchel, S. (2001). *Mirror, mirror on the wall: A reexamination of the role of social comparison in the formation of social identity.* European Association of Experimental Social Psychology (small group meeting), Sardinia, Italy (September 7).

Worchel, S. (in press-a). The rightful place of human rights: Relating rights and duties to individuals and groups within a cultural context. In N. Finkle & F. Moghaddam (Eds.), *Human rights and duties: Psychology's contributions, the law's commentary.* Washington, DC: American Psychological Association.

Worchel, S. (in press-b). No man is an island: A system perspective on human rights. In C. Serino (Ed.), *Diritti umanie pregiudizio.* Milano, Italy: Edizioni Unicopli.

Worchel, S., Arnold, S., & Baker, M. (1975). The effect of censorship on attitude change: The influence of censor and communication characteristics. *Journal of Applied Social Psychology, 5,* 227–239.

Worchel, S., & Brehm, J. (1971). Direct and implied social restoration of freedom. *Journal of Personality and Social Psychology, 18,* 294–304.

Worchel, S., & Coutant, D. (1997). The tangled web of loyalty: Nationalism, patriotism, and ethnocentrism. In D. Bar-Tal & E. Staub (Eds.), *Patriotism in the life of individuals and nations* (pp. 190–211). Chicago: Nelson Hall.

Worchel, S., & Coutant, D. (2001). It takes two to tango: Relating group identity to individual identity with the framework of group development. In M. Hogg & S. Tinsdale (Eds.), *Blackwell handbook of social psychology: Group process* (pp. 461–481). Oxford, England: Blackwell.

Worchel, S., Coutant-Sassic, D., & Grossman, M. (1992). A developmental approach to group dynamics: A model and illustrative research. In S. Worchel, W. Wood, & J. Simpson (Eds.), *Group process and productivity* (pp. 181–202). Newbury Park, CA: Sage.

Worchel, S., Coutant-Sassic, D., & Wong, F. (1993). Toward a more balanced view of conflict: There is a positive side. In S. Worchel & J. Simpson (Eds.), *Conflict between people and groups: Causes, processes, and resolutions* (pp. 76–92). Chicago: Nelson Hall.

Worchel, S., Iuzzini, J., Coutant, D., & Ivaldi, M. (2000). A multidimensional model of identity: Relating individual and group identities to intergroup behavior. In D. Capozza & R. Brown (Eds.), *Social identity process* (pp. 15–32). London: Sage.

Worchel, S., Lee, J., & Adewole, A. (1975). Effect of supply and demand on the ratings of object value. *Journal of Personality and Social Psychology, 32*, 906–914.

Worchel, S., & Shackelford, S. (1992). Preparing groups for stress: The impact of environmental stress and group structure on performance. *Personality and Social Psychology Bulletin, 17*, 640–647.

Wortman, C., & Brehm, J. (1975). Response to uncontrollable outcomes: An integration of reactance theory and the learned helplessness model. In L. Berkowitz (Ed.), *Advances in experimental social psychology* (Vol. 8, pp. 278–336). New York: Academic Press.

Wylie, R. (1961). *The self-concept: Theory and research on selected topics* (Vol. 2). Lincoln: University of Nebraska Press.

9

Responses to Scarcity: A Commodity Theory Perspective on Reactance and Rumination

Timothy C. Brock
Philip J. Mazzocco
Ohio State University

Impending scarcity can instigate extreme evaluation as well as reactance. Consider two examples.

• Clinton-era efforts to declassify sensitive government documents have been reconsidered since the World Trade Center destruction of September 11, 2001. Some already declassified documents that date back to the early cold-war period contain information relevant to the construction of biological weapons (e.g., anthrax). Reclassification has been proposed to prevent such information from getting in the hands of potential terrorists. However, reclassification may augment interest in the to-be-withheld information (reactance theory) and it may also increase estimates of the magnitude of the danger of biological weaponry (commodity theory, Brock, 1968).

• In commenting on his book-length indictment of child pornography (Jenkins, 2001), the author acknowledges that he has not seen any of the pictures that are the focus of his book because those "pictures would be criminal to view" (Jenkins, 2002, p. B17). In reactance against the viewing ban, Jenkins proposed "some kind of journalistic exemption" (p. B17), concluding that, "What's out there [on the Internet] is more damaging than we might imagine, in terms of the activities depicted and the children's ages" (Jenkins, 2002, p. B17). Again, in this second example, reactance and extreme evaluation are intertwined responses to unavailability.

PURPOSE, CORE QUESTIONS, OVERVIEW

We provide an updating of the commodity theory (Brock, 1968) literature in order to demarcate the domains of reactance theory (Brehm, 1966) and commodity theory. To what extent do the theories offer distinct derivations and to what extent is reactance theory subsumed under commodity theory? What mechanisms, motivational and/or cognitive, best explain how unavailability effects are mediated?

The core premise of commodity theory (Brock, 1968) is that to the extent that a "commodity" is scarce, it will be valued more extremely by an individual. "Commodity" might be a consumer product (Lynn, 1989), a health condition (Ditto & Jemmott, 1989), some attitude-relevant information (Brock & Becker, 1965), a trait (Brock & Brannon, 1992)—indeed anything for which there exists the possibility of possession by the individual. A meta-analysis of the literature found sufficient evidence to conclude that scarce commodities are indeed valued more extremely than their common counterparts (Lynn, 1991). However, despite the fact that the "scarcity effect" is well established, the mechanisms responsible for this phenomenon are still not agreed upon. A number of accounts have been based on motivational theories. For example, Fromkin (1969, 1970a, 1970b) proposed that negative feelings of indistinctiveness would lead to the preference for uncommon attributes. People would be motivated to become more distinctive by owning "unique" commodities. Reactance theory (Brehm, 1966) may also offer an account for many scarcity-related effects. When scarcity threatens, or removes, freedoms (in this case, the freedom to own or obtain a commodity), individuals may be motivated to reestablish those freedoms and, in so doing, increase their valuations of the threatened commodity.

Motivational accounts of scarcity effects have difficulty accounting for certain results. For example, research has demonstrated that scarcity leads to decreased valuation, "worsened ratings," of commodities such as diseases (Ditto & Jemmott, 1989). Thus, it seems that scarcity may act not to increase positive valuation, but to make valuation more extreme regardless of valence. To explain the evaluative polarization phenomenon, a number of cognitive accounts for scarcity effects have been offered. One debate contrasts opposing cognitive accounts. Some authors have proffered a simple heuristic-cue account whereby information about scarcity acts as a mindless, "knee-jerk," cue to the value of a commodity (Cialdini, 1985, 2001; Ditto & Jemmott, 1989; Lynn, 1992a; Verhallen & Robben, 1995). At the other end of the thinking continuum (from less thinking to more thinking) is an increased-elaboration account whereby scarcity is thought to instigate rumination, namely, processing information in a more thoughtful and elaborate fashion (Bozzolo & Brock, 1992; Brannon & Brock, 2001a, 2001b; Brock & Brannon, 1992).

A review of studies and theoretical work related to the reactance and commodity accounts of scarcity effects is provided. We also consider the aforementioned debate between heuristic and elaboration accounts of scarcity effects. Finally, some future directions in the study of scarcity effects are discussed.

BASICS OF COMMODITY THEORY—ORIGINAL FORMULATION

Commodity theory (Brock, 1968) was originally cast to stem from humans' automatic sensitivity to prevalence (or frequency, Hasher & Zacks, 1984) and to scarcity (Alchian & Allen, 1967). A commodity was defined as anything that has usefulness to the possessor and that can be conveyed (object) or communicated (message, information) from person to person. Usefulness was broadly defined as potential relevance to the needs and interests of a person. The two main premises were: (1) any commodity will be valued to the extent that it is unavailable; and (2) that threat increases both commodity-seeking behavior and the tendency to withhold commodities from others. For the purposes of the 1968 chapter, the discussion of commodity theory was limited to information, experiences, and messages in which the interested individual was the communicator, the recipient, or both. Eight propositions delineated the mechanisms of "commodification." These were broken into four basic categories: scarcity, effort, delay, and restriction (see Table 9.1). Each proposition described a condition under which entities would become viewed as valued commodities. Although Lynn (1991) reviewed evidence that supported the basic premises of commodity theory, still missing was a set of mechanisms to explain how unavailability effects are mediated. One obvious mechanism is, of course, reactance.

JACK BREHM CONTRIBUTIONS

Reactance Theory

Reactance theory stated that when a freedom is eliminated or threatened, people will evaluate the freedom more positively and take steps to protect or secure it. Although the overlap between reactance theory and commodity theory seems obvious, research has suggested that the theories are not redundant. Consider two early reactance studies by Brehm, Stires, Sensenig, and Shaban (1966). In Study 1, participants rated four musical selections on the dimension of attractiveness. Ostensibly, the

TABLE 9.1
Original Commodity Theory Propositions

Scarcity
A. Perceived number of recipients, relative to the total number of potential corecipients, declines
B. Perceived number of communicators is few

Effort
C. The greater the degree of coercion upon the communicator needed to elicit the message
D. The greater perceived effort involved by the communicator to conceal the information or to transmit it
E. The greater the magnitude of the recipient's effort to obtain the information or to understand it

Restriction
F. The greater the amount of opposing reasons accompanying disclosure
G. The greater the restrictions set by the communicator on further transmissions

Delay
H. The greater the delay by the communicator

next day they would be allowed to choose a gift copy of any album they liked. When participants returned on the next day, half were told that whatever option had been rated as the third most attractive the previous day had become unavailable as a gift option. The other half were not given this information. Finally, all participants rated the attractiveness of the four musical selections a second time. Results showed that the unavailable option (third selection) increased in attractiveness relative to the initial rating. Both reactance theory and commodity theory would take this result as confirmatory evidence. In Study 2, however, a new condition was added in which participants did not expect to be able to choose their gift selection (no prior freedom). In this case, the unavailability of the third selection was not associated with increased attractiveness ratings. In fact, participants in the no prior freedom condition evaluated the eliminated selection as less attractive after it was made unavailable. This particular result was predicted by reactance theory, but could not be explained by commodity theory. Perhaps because of such discrepancies, reactance theory and commodity theory were viewed for some time as alternative accounts.

Consider a line of studies on censorship and restriction (see Worchel, 1992 for a similar treatment). Noteworthy among a number of articles appearing in the 1970s was that they fell into two camps; those that invoked commodity theory but not reactance theory (Fromkin & Brock, 1973; Pincus & Waters, 1976; Zellinger, Fromkin, Speller, & Kohn, 1975), and those that invoked reactance theory but not commodity theory (Worchel & Arnold, 1973; Worchel, Arnold, & Barker, 1975).

Fromkin and Brock (1973) tested straightforward implications of commodity theory for the restriction of erotic materials. Proposition G (see Table 9.1) states, to the extent that restrictions are placed on a commodity, that commodity will be perceived as more valuable. Proposition F (Table 9.1) states that increased delays in commodity availability will also increase valuation. Thus, if teenagers perceive great delay involved in their access to erotic materials, commodity theory would predict their increased appetite for such materials. Zellinger et al. (1975) had male undergraduates evaluate pornographic materials that were either accompanied by age restrictions (restricted to those 21 years of age or older), or were not. They found that such materials were evaluated as more desirable when age restrictions were present. Pincus and Waters (1976) replicated this basic pattern, although only for materials that were not explicitly defined as erotic. In these three articles, reactance theory was not acknowledged as a possible explanation of the effects of restriction on the evaluation of erotic materials.

At the same time, Worchel and colleagues were engaged in research on the effects of censorship. Worchel and Arnold (1973) informed participants that a speech they were about to hear had been censored. Results showed that censorship increased desire to hear the speech and subsequent attitude change. The results were interpreted in terms of reactance theory; commodity theory was not referenced. The Worchel and Arnold (1973) study was replicated and extended by Worchel, Arnold, and Baker (1975) without citing commodity theory.

Although it seemed that reactance theory and commodity theory were traveling along parallel paths, Worchel, Lee, and Adewole (1975) recognized the overlap between reactance theory and commodity theory: Worchel et al. (1975) was the "classic" attempt to delineate the common and separate domains of the two theories. Careful analysis of the design and results of this study affords the best tutorial about the relationship between the two theories. In Study 1, participants were led to believe they would be tasting some cookies as part of a consumer behavior study. Participants were seated at a table with a glass jar initially containing either 2 or 10 cookies (a scarce or abundant amount respectively). Before the session started, a confederate experimenter entered the room ostensibly to check on the cookie supply. In the change conditions, the experimenter exchanged 2 cookies for 10 (scarce change) or 10 cookies for 2 (abundant change). In a third condition, the experimenter merely checked on the supply and left (no change). When change occurred, it altered the participants' scarcity status in the experimental design. Hence, a participant who was originally in the scarce condition, but had cookies added, was analyzed as a member of the abundant condition.

When change did occur, the experimenter gave one of two reasons for the switch. In a demand condition, the experimenter explained that the change occurred because his other participants had eaten so many cookies (in the scarcity condition), or that the change occurred because participants were not eating as many cookies as expected (in the abundance condition). In an accidental condition, the experimenter explained that the jars had accidentally been switched. In addition to this 2 × 3 design, a third factor was present. Half of the participants in each condition were told that only a small number of participants would participate in the study, ostensibly because consumer research experiments are expensive. The other half were informed that a large number of participants were yet to be run through the study. This manipulation was included as another manipulation of scarcity. According to Brock's (1968) original conceptualization, scarcity should be increased to the extent that the perceived number of recipients of some commodity, relative to the total number of potential corecipients, declines.

After all manipulations were complete, participants were allowed to taste the cookies. After the tasting, participants rated the cookies in terms of their desire for more (lower numbers correspond to increased desire). The results of the study are reprinted in Table 9.2. Overall, the cookies were desired significantly more in the scarcity-no change condition ($M_{\text{scarcity-no change}} = 4.23$) than in the abundance-no change condition ($M_{\text{abundance-no change}} = 5.55$). Thus, the basic proposition of commodity theory was supported. However, within the scarcity condition, scarcity was associated with increased desire in the two change conditions in which participants had initially expected an abundant amount ($M_{\text{scarcity-change}} = 3.09$; $M_{\text{scarcity-no}}$

TABLE 9.2
Mean Liking of Cookies

	Reason for Change in Supply[a]		
Participation Level	*Demand*	*Accident*	*No Change*
Scarcity			
High Participation	2.25	3.27	4.08
Low Participation	3.00	3.75	4.40
Abundance			
High Participation	7.17	6.30	5.64
Low Participation	6.82	6.64	5.46

Note. From "Effects of Supply and Demand on Ratings of Object Value," by S. Worchel, J. Lee, and A. Adewole, 1975, *Journal of Personality and Social Psychology, 32*, pp. 906–914. Copyright 1975 by the American Psychological Association. Reprinted with permission.

[a]The lower the number, the more favorable the evaluation.

$_{change}$ = 4.23). Within the scarcity conditions, scarcity due to demand ($M_{scarcity\text{-}demand}$ = 2.63) produced increased desire relative to scarcity due to accident ($M_{scarcity\text{-}accident}$ = 3.51). In the abundant condition, there was a nonsignificant trend for abundance due to demand ($M_{abundance\text{-}demand}$ = 7.00) to be associated with decreased desire relative to the accidental condition ($M_{abundance\text{-}accident}$ = 6.48). The participation manipulation had no effect on desire to eat the cookies ($M_{high\ participation}$ = 4.79; $M_{low\ participation}$ = 5.00). The authors suggested that the participation manipulation was likely to have been ineffective because it had no bearing on the participants' actual access to cookies.

Although Worchel et al. (1975) utilized a commodity theory framework to interpret their results, reactance theory was proposed as the likely mediator of the differences between the scarcity-change conditions and the scarcity-no change condition. In effect, those in the change conditions had a potential freedom (to eat cookies to their heart's content) removed. Reactance theory could not explain all obtained effects however. For example, scarce cookies were desired more than abundant cookies even in the no change condition, when no existing freedoms had been removed. Furthermore, reactance theory could not easily account for the increased desire in the scarcity due-to-demand versus scarcity due-to-accident conditions. The same freedom had been removed in both cases. Commodity theory, however, could easily explain this difference by assuming that cookies that were in greater demand were more scarce than those that, relatively speaking, were not. Finally, reactance theory would not make predictions about abundance, whereas, in commodity theory, abundance is the other end of the prevalence continuum upon which commodity theory is based. These considerations led Worchel et al. (1975) to suggest that reactance may have mediated some commodity theory effects but that it could not account for others.

In their scrutiny of the relationship between reactance theory and commodity theory, Brehm and Brehm (1981) relied heavily on the Worchel et al. (1975) experiment and concluded that "although there is some overlap between commodity theory and reactance theory, this overlap is not complete. Both can address scarcity, but they do so with different prerequisites in mind and formulate a somewhat different set of predictions" (pp. 342–343). Furthermore they advised that "both may be of value in understanding consumer reactions to situations of scarcity" (p. 343). The dual theory acceptance by Brehm and Brehm (1981) has been reiterated by subsequent authors (Snyder, 1992; Worchel, 1992).

Verhallen (1982) subsequently reported a detailed analysis of the factors that would lead to a reactance account of scarcity effects. As in the Worchel et al. (1975) experiment, Verhallen focused on the reasons for scarcity. Participants in the experiment were given a choice between three books that had ostensibly been sent by a publisher. These books varied in their level of availability (6, 16, or 30 copies). Furthermore, participants were given one of four reasons for the difference in availability. In one condition, they were told that it was an accident. In another condition, they were told that fewer copies remained of the more popular books. In a third condition, participants were told that the differences in numbers of copies were due to differences in the sizes of the edition (fewer books for editions that were in limited supply). Finally, some participants were told that the differences were due to both differences in edition size and in popularity. After receiving this information, participants ranked the books according to the order of their preference. Participants were initially split into two groups: those that had prerated books as an attractive product type, and those who prerated the books as unattractive. Results showed that the basic scarcity/unavailability proposition of commodity theory held, but only for the group of participants who had prerated books as an attractive commodity. Furthermore, the unavailability effect, in contrast to the Worchel et al. study, was found only when the scarcity was due to market forces (all conditions but the accident condition). Interestingly, in the nonattractive source condition, unavailability was associated with decreased preference. This pattern of results is revisited later in this chapter.

Although some authors continued to force the choice between reactance theory and commodity theory (Madey et al., 1996), it is now generally accepted that, within the framework of scarcity studies, reactance theory and commodity theory are not competing explanations. In fact, Verhallen and Robben (1995) have even offered a list of the conditions under which reactance theory would be a likely mediator for scarcity effects. They predict that reactance will be aroused only when (1) unavailability exists due to some type of regulation, or when (2) restricted availability of a commodity that was once available has been imposed by a group of which the target is not a member.

In conclusion, reactance theory serves as an important mechanism within the general rubric of commodity theory and under certain conditions. Worchel et al. (1975) showed that perception of preexisting freedoms was necessary to invoke reactance effects. As just reviewed, Verhallen and Robben (1995) provided even more detailed freedom-related conditions for reactance effects. Finally, Verhallen (1982) showed that reactance would only occur when the commodity in question was rated a priori as at least somewhat attractive. Commodity theory certainly made predictions given a priori attractiveness and these predictions were very similar to those of reactance theory. However, commodity theory also applies to a wide range of phenomena in which preexisting freedoms need not be present, and in which the commodity is not only not liked, but is disliked (e.g., rare diseases). Thus, reactance theory should be thought of not as an alternative account of scarcity effects, but as one of several potential mediational accounts under the wider rubric of commodity theory. This statement should not be seen as reducing the importance of reactance, or the voluminous research literature that has examined the reactance phenomenon. The majority of the remainder of the chapter examines other potential mediators of scarcity effects.

Energization Theory

Wright (1992) showed how energization theory (Brehm, Wright, Solomon, Silka, & Greenberg, 1983) may be related to commodity theory. Energization theory is based on two concepts: potential motivation and actual effort. Potential motivation to engage in some goal-relevant instrumental behavior is due to such factors as level of need, perceptions of incentive value, and the perceived degree to which engaging in the instrumental behavior is likely to lead to motive satisfaction. The degree of actual effort expended will be greater to the extent that energization is higher. The level of energization is determined jointly by potential motivation and task difficulty, however not in a monotonic fashion. In general, task difficulty is assumed to be associated with increased energization. However, this effect is constrained by the level of potential motivation. At lower levels of potential motivation, even moderately difficult tasks will be associated with reduced energization. At very high levels of potential motivation, it is predicted that task difficulty will be associated with increased motivation up to the point at which difficulty passes into the realm of impossibility.

Wright (1982) discussed how energization theory could act as a framework for a number of the proposed mediators of scarcity effects. In addition to a reactance theory account, Wright also discussed scarcity as a heuristic cue to value and to the tendency to desire scarce objects to increase self-uniqueness (discussed later). The effects of each mediator were examined in light of energization theory. Reactance theory effects could be explained as increased energization resulting from the difficulty in obtaining an unavailable commodity. The scarcity heuristic cue effect could be explained as increasing incentive value and, thus, potential motivation. Finally, and most obviously, aversive feelings of undistinctiveness would be expected to increase the motivational need to be unique and, thus, to own unique commodities. As Wright (1992) pointed out, there have been no direct tests of the efficacy of energization theory for explaining scarcity effects. However, it seems likely that energization theory could act as a general mechanism standing in between commodity theory and many of the more specific mediators of unavailability effects that are related to motivation.

In sum, contribution to the understanding of commodity theory stems from both reactance theory and energization theory. Furthermore, the potential for energization theory to shed light on commodity theory seems promising.

SELECTIVE LITERATURE REVIEW

A Summary

It is most efficient to point to Lynn's (1991) meta-analysis that examined 41 separate tests of commodity theory predictions. Although the analysis did include some failures (e.g., Shippee, Mowen, & Gregory, 1981), the positive relationship between unavailability and commodity valuation was found to be highly reliable ($z = 8.39$; $p < .0001$). The meta-analysis appeared shortly before a special issue of *Basic and Applied Social Psychology* (*BASP*, 1992, vol. 13) that was wholly dedicated to commodity theory. The issue featured a number of perspectives that attempted to shed light on commodity theory or that were conceptually related to commodity theory. Perhaps most notable was an article in which the original commodity theory was liberalized (Brock & Brannon, 1992) via (1) extension of "commodities" to include traits and skills, (2) extension of commodities to include negative elements, and (3) proposal of a scarcity-elaboration-polarization (SEP) model. The SEP model proposes that unavailability information produces differences in the amount or extent of cognitive elaboration about a commodity. If the commodity is initially thought of as highly valuable, it will be thought of as more valuable due to elaboration, and the reverse if the commodity was thought of as not valuable (e.g., a disease). Before examining the SEP model more closely, a number of other accounts may be mentioned.

Motivational Accounts

In the *BASP* issue, Lynn (1992b) reviewed many mediators posited for commodity theory. These factors can be broken into those that are motivational in nature and those that are cognitive in nature. The most prominent of the motivational accounts was reactance theory, which has already been considered. However, Lynn also mentioned several other possible motivational mediators. For example, it is possible that scarce resources may confer power in interpersonal relationships (Emerson, 1962). It is also possible that people would be motivated to obtain scarce resources because they think that scarce resources may indicate status (Veblen, 1965) or that possessing scarce resources may allow downward comparisons (Wills, 1981).

Personal equity-comparison theory (Seta & Seta, 1992) assumes that scarcity implies cost incurrence, and further states that when individuals perceive cost, they will want equitable payback. In order to do this, people will compare the expected outcome with the actual outcome and attempt to calibrate the positive qualities of the actual outcomes so that they match the expected outcomes (assimilation to the expected outcome). If this cannot be done (if the object actually cannot be positively accentuated) contrast will occur. Thus, personal equity-comparison theory can predict instances in which scarce commodities will be both more and less positively valued—depending on the actual attributes of the commodity itself.

Among other motivational accounts is the idea that people desire ownership of scarce commodities in order to reduce a need for uniqueness (Brock, 1968, p. 272; Lynn & Snyder, 2002). The challenge of developing this theory and of conducting early empirical tests was taken up initially by Fromkin (Fromkin, 1968; Fromkin, 1970a, 1970b; Fromkin & Snyder, 1980). As delineated in Fromkin (1968), the theory states that people can vary in their need to feel unique. When this need is high, it is predicted that people will be motivated to secure scarce commodities in an attempt to become more "unique." In a supportive empirical test, Fromkin gave individuals varying levels of uniqueness feedback (high, medium, or low). Participants were then given an opportunity to enter into "psychedelic" chambers that were either described as available or unavailable to others, and that ostensibly produced novel or familiar feelings. When participants had been given low uniqueness feedback, they preferred the unavailable chambers that produced novel feelings.

Lynn's (1991) meta-analysis examined 11 prior tests of the relationship between need for uniqueness and the preference for scarce commodities. Although a significant relationship was obtained ($p < .001$), the predicted effect was reliable in only 4 of the 11 tests. This disparity is not necessarily troubling because need for uniqueness is only one of many factors that can affect preferences for scarce products. There is no clear way to predict when need for uniqueness might be overwhelmed by other motives. In experiments that are not properly controlled, or in which need for uniqueness is not the target variable of interest, it is not surprising that the need for uniqueness relationship would not always be obtained. In fact, Verhallen and Robben (1995) made the prediction that need for uniqueness would only be a likely explanation for the desire for scarce products under conditions of limited availability, due to market or nonmarket circumstances, accompanied by increased demand/limited supply. In other words, when a commodity is potentially available to everyone, but difficult to obtain, need for uniqueness would be a likely explanation for scarcity effects. A review of the literature on need-uniqueness theory included factors expected to moderate the size of the effect (cf. Snyder, 1992).[1]

Although many of the early accounts of scarcity effects have been motivational, recently, cognitive mechanisms have received the lion's share of theoretical and empirical attention.

Cognitive Accounts

Scarcity as an Expensiveness Cue. Motivational theories assume behaviors and preferences are produced in order to satisfy some need or drive. In contrast, the cognitive accounts assume that scarcity influences valuation by altering the way information is processed, or the way in which commodities are perceived. The alterations, in turn, result in relatively "cool" (rational) decision processes. One cognitive account involving a scarcity-heuristic was offered by Lynn (1989, 1992a). Lynn held that scarcity, at least in the case of material goods, might act as a cue to expensiveness or to the level of demand for an object. Therefore, people would be predicted to desire scarce products simply because they would be perceived as better products, all else equal, than common ones. In one study, Lynn (1989, Study 1) showed that scarcity enhanced the desire for art prints, but only when subjects had previously been primed to think about the expensiveness of art prints in general. Study 2 in the same article showed that scarcity effects with respect to bottles of wine could be eliminated by informing participants of the actual price of the wine. In this case, information about scarcity could not be used to influence perceptions of expensiveness because the actual price was already known.

Scarcity as a Simple Value Heuristic. In slight contrast to the expensiveness heuristic, it has been proposed that scarcity might act as a simple cue to value. The roots of this perspective can be found in Cialdini's (1985, 2001) work on the automatic operation of six compliance mechanisms. The six basic compliance principles (consistency, liking, reciprocity, social proof, authority, and scarcity) were conceptualized as exogenous cues. When one of these cues impinged on an actor, the actor was thought to respond to it in a mindless and patterned way. Cialdini analogized humans to tape recorders. The cue causes a behavioral tape to commence ("click"), which then runs to completion ("whir"; Cialdini, 2001, p. 3). In the case of scarcity, scarce commodities were thought to automatically elicit increased liking.

[1]It is interesting to note that need for uniqueness theory was a large part of the inspiration for Brewer's theory of optimal distinctiveness (Brewer, 1991).

A pair of studies by Ditto and Jemmott (1989) extended this simple cue idea to include instances in which scarcity is associated with decreased liking. In the first study, participants evaluated a medical condition called *thioamine acetylase presence* (TAA). Some participants were led to believe that the presence of TAA had positive health outcomes, whereas others were led to believe it had negative health outcomes. Furthermore, in each valence condition, some participants thought the condition was quite common, whereas others thought it was quite rare. The dependent measure was a scale tapping the perceived "healthfulness" of the condition. Interestingly, the effect of scarcity was to polarize judgments of healthfulness. When participants thought TAA was positive, scarcity was associated with increased ratings of healthfulness relative to abundance. When participants thought TAA was negative, scarcity was associated with decreased ratings of healthfulness relative to abundance. Study 2 replicated Study 1 with slightly different procedures and measures. These results were interpreted in terms of a simple scarcity-extremity heuristic whereby scarcity causes an extremitization of preexisting valuations.

Scarcity Increases Elaboration. In contrast, Bozzolo and Brock (1992; see also Brock & Brannon, 1992; Folger, 1992) theorized that scarcity information would actually increase the amount of rumination about the focal commodities. In the Ditto and Jemmott experiment (1989) it is possible that scarcity information actually caused participants to ruminate more about the medical condition. If so, then it makes sense that rumination about a negatively valenced condition should make the condition seem worse, and rumination about a positively valenced condition should make the condition seem even better. In each case, rumination should produce thoughts of predominantly similar valence to the overall impression of the medical condition. Increased rumination may also stand as an explanation for the mixed results obtained by Verhallen (1982). Recall that Verhallen gave housewives a choice between three books that varied in their level of availability. The classical scarcity-increases-desirability effect was found only for participants who had prerated books as an attractive commodity in general. For those who had prerated books as unattractive, however, unavailability was associated with decreased preference.

Unfortunately, the Ditto and Jemmott experiment and the Verhallen experiment contained no measures or manipulations that would allow the cue-heuristic account to be disentangled from the increased rumination account. For this reason, Bozzolo and Brock designed such an experiment utilizing a standard persuasion paradigm (see Petty & Cacioppo, 1986). In their study, participants were given a persuasive message that contained either weak or strong arguments. The message was in favor of comprehensive exams at a "distant university." Some participants were led to believe the message was unavailable to others (low availability), whereas others were led to believe that it was readily available (high availability). Analysis indicated increased message processing in the unavailability conditions for those participants who were low in need for cognition. Increased processing was shown by more attitudinal differentiation (message-consistent attitude change) in response to the strong and weak arguments in the unavailability conditions. Low need-for-cognition participants in the available condition did not seem to be processing the message to reflect differential argument strength, whereas high need-for-cognition participants did so. Bozzolo and Brock conjectured that high need for cognition participants may have perceived message unavailability as an indicator of the likelihood of comprehensive exams actually being instituted at their school and that, consequently, they may have been somewhat distracted from message processing in this condition. In sum, this experiment showed that people's perceptions of scarcity can be related to increases in the motivation to process information.

Two recent studies by Brannon and Brock (2001a, 2001b) have further examined the hypothesis that scarcity acts to increase elaboration. In Study 1 of Brannon and Brock (2001b), college participants were informed that they tested high for a psychological trait called picture-mindedness (PM). Half of the participants were told this was a rare trait and half were told it was a common trait. Participants then read a message about picture-mindedness. For half of the participants within each scarcity condition, PM was described as a positive characteristic, for the other half PM was described as a negative characteristic. Participants then rated their attitudes toward PM, and completed a thought-listing measure concerning the message they had read. Analysis revealed the predicted Scarcity × Valence interaction. When PM was defined as a positive trait, scarcity made it seem more positive. When PM was defined as a negative trait, scarcity made it seem more negative. Furthermore, a main effect of scarcity was found with respect to the thought-listing measure. For both positive and negative messages, scarcity was associated with increased message-consistent thinking. A path analysis indicated that the Scarcity × Valence effect on attitudes was in fact mediated by message-consistent thoughts. In sum, there was strong evidence in favor of the increased-elaboration hypothesis as opposed to the heuristic-cue hypothesis. Study 2 was similar to Study 1 except that situation-mindedness (SM) was substituted for picture-mindedness, and a well-known manipulation of cognitive load (Gilbert & Hixon, 1991) was instituted. According to a heuristic-cue account, a load manipulation should not diminish scarcity effects. The increased-elaboration view, however, would argue that a load manipulation should decrease thoughtful processes, and, thus, also scarcity effects. The Scarcity × Valence interaction found in Study 1 was replicated, and path analytic procedures again showed mediation of the obtained interaction by message-consistent thoughts. However, this was only the case in the no-load condition. In the load condition, no interaction was obtained.

Taken together, these two studies provide strong evidence for the SEP model (scarcity-elaboration-polarization). The cognitive load manipulation in Study 2 was especially important in helping to eliminate an alternative account of the main findings in Study 1 and Study 2. It could be assumed that participants used a simple scarcity heuristic to valuate their newly discovered traits, and then ruminated about the attributes of the trait to the extent that their valuations were extreme. This sequence might explain the thought-listing mediation results in that attitudes would have mediated rumination, rather than the reverse. According to this account, however, a cognitive load manipulation should not have had any effect on attitude ratings. It should only have affected rumination-based mediation. This was not found to be the case as the load manipulation did reduce the effects on attitudes.

Brannon and Brock (2001a) again tested SEP in a pair of field settings. In Study 1, experimenters placed calls to telephone operators and requested that they be connected to an out-of-state number. This number was rigged so that there would never be an answer. After one failed try, the operators were asked to attempt again. In one condition, the experimenter mentioned that it was the only time this month that the call could be made (high restriction). In another condition, the experimenter mentioned that it was the only time that day the call could be made (low restriction). Thus, differences in restriction functioned as a scarcity manipulation (few vs. many opportunities to make the call). After mentioning information about calling constraints, experimenters gave one of two reasons for the urgency of the call. In the strong argument condition, experimenters said that they wanted to contact the person to "talk to him about matters that affect his job, his family, and his health." In a weak argument condition, this reason was changed to, "talk to him about matters that may not make any difference at all." This argument strength manipulation was intended to be used in the same way as in the previous series of Brock and Brannon (2001b) experiments—as a diagnostic measure of the degree of elaborative thinking. The dependent measure was the actual number of times the operator was willing to ring; operator ringing was taken as a measure of compliance with the wishes of the caller. Results showed that strong arguments were always associated with an increased number of rings relative to weak arguments, but that, consistent with SEP, this difference was pronounced under the high restriction condition.

In a conceptually similar study (Study 3), participants were drive-thru customers at a local Mexican fast-food restaurant. Experimental manipulations were delivered by order takers who were supervised by experimenters. Regardless of the actual order, order takers were asked to suggest a cinnamon twist to customers. Restriction was manipulated by having the order-takers point out that the twists were "made with our special recipe avail ble today only" (high restriction), or were "made with our usual recipe for this year" (low restriction). Argument strength was also manipulated. The high quality argument was as follows: "The cinnamon twist goes great with Mexican food, you know." The low quality argument read: "The cinnamon twist is not really Mexican food, you know." Similarly to Study 1, argument quality affected cinnamon twist sales only when restrictions were high.

In sum, there is now ample evidence to support the increased-elaboration hypothesis over the heuristic-cue hypothesis. In light of the reinterpretation of Verhallen's results mentioned earlier, a systematic review of empirical tests of the scarcity-valuation relationship that have used a motivational account of scarcity effects is needed to determine if obtained patterns of results could also be explained by the increased-processing perspective. In any case, it is safe to say that the increased-elaboration hypothesis has breathed new theoretical life into commodity theory.

FUTURE DIRECTIONS

Cross-Cultural Applications

A portion of the future work related to commodity theory will be related to disentangling the heuristic-cue from the increased-elaboration accounts. In addition, interesting connections can be discerned between commodity theory and several cognate avenues of research. For example, recent work by Cialdini, Wosinska, Barrett, Butner, and Gornik-Durose (1999) on differences in susceptibility to compliance techniques in individualistic versus collectivist cultures has shown that culture can moderate the efficacy of certain techniques. They found that social proof techniques, which are externally motivated, tend to produce more compliance in collectivist societies (Poland) than in individualistic societies (The United States) whereas commitment/consistency techniques, which are internally motivated, were more influential in individualistic than in collectivist societies. It seems plausible to speculate that people in collectivist cultures may have an aversion to scarce attributes and objects because they avoid distinctiveness (Triandis, 1989).

Other Applications

Research on attraction and relationships may benefit from conceptualizing potential partners as commodities that can be "owned" in some sense. For example, Petty and Mirels (1981) showed that individuals would be liked more to the extent that they self-disclosed information that was perceived as scarce. More recently, Madey et al. (1996) examined the closing time phenomena whereby target individuals are perceived to be more attractive just near closing time in bars (cf. Pennebaker et al., 1979). They found that people do indeed become more attractive near closing time (as opportunities to meet become more scarce), but only for people not in committed relationships, and only for opposite sex patrons. Wegner, Lane, and Dimitri (1994) found that relationships with a degree of secrecy tend to be more tantalizing than open relationships. Finally, one of the central tenets of the social exchange theory of stability of relationships is that stability will be greater to the extent that fewer alternative options are available (see Rusbult, 1983). In other words, to the extent that the present partner is perceived as a personally scarce commodity in some way, stability is increased. In confirmation of commodity theory predictions, Jemmott, Ashby, and Lindenfeld (1989) found that college students who believed that there were a small number of members of the opposite sex on campus reported being more committed to their current romantic partner. Aside from these established lines of research, it would also be interesting to examine the general effects of scarce characteristics on attraction. It would be expected that rare, as compared to common, positive traits would make a person more attractive, and rare unusual negative traits would make a person less attractive.

There are undoubtedly other areas that could benefit from the commodity theory perspective. A final example is research on inadmissible evidence in court cases. Inadmissible evidence is, ironically, weighted more heavily than admissible evidence in subsequent juror judgments (e.g., Sommers & Kassin, 2001; Sue, Smith, & Caldwell, 1973). Commodity theory explains this finding readily: Information on which restrictions are placed will be weighted more heavily than similar information on which no restrictions are placed. The increased-elaboration account is a good candidate for mediation of the relationship.

Extending commodity theory to domains in which core factors (Table 9.1) play an important role would not only be useful for understanding those domains, but would also be likely to clarify the boundary conditions of commodity theory.

ACKNOWLEDGMENTS

Timothy C. Brock and Philip J. Mazzocco, Department of Psychology, The Ohio State University.

This research was supported in part by National Institute of Mental Health predoctoral traineeship (Grant No. T32-MH 19728), the inaugural Gatskill Fellowship, and an Alumni Grant for Graduate Research and Scholarship to the second author.

We appreciate the comments of Rex Wright, Jeff Greenberg, and Geoff Kaufman on an earlier version of this chapter.

REFERENCES

Alchian, A. A., & Allen, W. R. (1967). *University economics.* Belmont, CA: Wadsworth.

Bozzolo, A. M., & Brock, T. C. (1992). Unavailability effects on message processing: A theoretical analysis and an empirical test. *Basic and Applied Social Psychology, 13,* 93–101.

Brannon, L. A., & Brock, T. C. (2001a). Limiting time for responding enhances behavior corresponding to the merits of compliance appeals: Refutations of heuristic-cue theory in service and consumer settings. *Journal of Consumer Psychology, 10,* 135–146.

Brannon, L. A., & Brock, T. C. (2001b). Scarcity claims elicit extreme responding to persuasive messages: Role of cognitive elaboration. *Personality and Social Psychology Bulletin, 27,* 365–375.

Brehm, J. W. (1966). *A theory of psychological reactance.* New York: Academic Press.

Brehm, S. S., & Brehm, J. W. (1981). *Psychological reactance: A theory of freedom and control.* New York: Academic Press.

Brehm, J. W., Stires, L. K., Sensenig, J., & Shaban, J. (1966). The attractiveness of an eliminated choice alternative. *Journal of Experimental and Social Psychology, 2,* 301–313.

Brehm, J. W., Wright, R. A., Solomon, S., Silka, L., & Greenberg, J. (1983). Perceived difficulty, energization, and the magnitude of goal valence. *Journal of Experimental Social Psychology, 19,* 21–48.

Brewer, M. B. (1991). The social self: On being the same and different at the same time. *Psychological Bulletin, 86,* 475–482.

Brock, T. C. (1968). Implications of commodity theory for value change. In A. G. Greenwald, T. C. Brock, & T. M. Ostrom (Eds.), *Psychological foundations of attitudes* (pp. 243–275). New York: Academic Press.

Brock, T. C., & Becker, L. A. (1965). Ineffectiveness of "overheard" counterpropaganda. *Journal of Personality and Social Psychology, 2,* 654–660.

Brock, T. C., & Brannon, L. A. (1992). Liberalization of commodity theory. *Basic and Applied Social Psychology, 13,* 135–144.

Cialdini, R. B. (1985). *Influence: Science and practice* (1st ed.). Glenview, IL: Scott, Foresman.

Cialdini, R. B. (2001). *Influence: Science and practice* (4th ed.). Boston: Allyn & Bacon.

Cialdini, R. B., Wosinska, W., Barrett, D. W., Butner, J., & Gornik-Durose, M. (1999). Compliance with a request in two cultures: The differential influence of social proof and commitment/consistency on collectivists and individualists. *Personality and Social Psychology Bulletin, 25,* 1242–1253.

Ditto, P. H., & Jemmott, J. B. (1989). From rarity to evaluative extremity: Effects of prevalence information on evaluations of positive and negative characteristics. *Journal of Personality and Social Psychology, 57,* 16–26.

Emerson, R. M. (1962). Power-dependence relations. *American Sociological Review, 27,* 31–41.

Folger, R. (1992). On wanting what we do not have. *Basic and Applied Social Psychology, 13,* 123–133.

Fromkin, H. L. (1968). *Affective and valuation consequences of self-perceived uniqueness deprivation.* Unpublished doctoral dissertation, Ohio State University.

Fromkin, H. L. (1970a). Effects of experimentally aroused feelings of indistinctiveness upon valuation of scarce and novel experiences. *Journal of Personality and Social Psychology, 16,* 521–529.

Fromkin, H. L. (1970b). Uniqueness deprivation and valuation of unavailable and novel experiences. *Proceedings of the 78th Annual Convention of the American Psychological Association, 7,* 479–480.

Fromkin, H. L., & Brock, T. C. (1973). Erotic materials: A commodity theory analysis of the enhanced desirability that may accompany their unavailability. *Journal of Applied Social Psychology, 3,* 219–231.

Fromkin, H. L., & Snyder, C. R. (1980). The search for uniqueness and valuation of scarcity: A neglected dimension of value in exchange theory. In K. Gergen, M. S. Greenberg, & R. H. Willis (Eds.), *Social exchange: Advances in theory and research* (pp. 57–75). New York: Plenum.

Gilbert, D. T., & Hixon, J. G. (1991). The trouble of thinking: Activation and application of stereotypic beliefs. *Journal of Personality and Social Psychology, 60,* 509–517.

Hasher, L., & Zacks, R. T. (1984). Automatic processing of fundamental information: The case of frequency of occurrence. *American Psychologist, 39,* 1372–1388.

Jenkins, P. (2001). *Beyond tolerance: Child pornography on the Internet.* New York: New York University Press.

Jenkins, P. (2002). Bringing the loathsome to light. *Chronicle of Higher Education, March 1,* B16–B17.

Jemmott, J. B., Ashby, K. L., & Lindenfeld, K. L. (1989). Romantic commitment and the perceived availability of opposite-sex persons: On loving the one you're with. *Journal of Applied Social Psychology, 19,* 1198–1211.

Lynn, M. (1989). Scarcity effects on desirability: Mediated by assumed expensiveness. *Journal of Economic Psychology, 10,* 257–274.

Lynn, M. (1991). Scarcity effects on value: A quantitative review of the commodity theory literature. *Psychology and Marketing, 8,* 43–57.

Lynn, M. (1992a). Scarcity's enhancement of desirability: The role of naive economic theories. *Basic and Applied Social Psychology, 13,* 67–78.

Lynn, M. (1992b). The psychology of unavailability: Explaining scarcity and cost effects on value. *Basic and Applied Social Psychology, 13,* 3–7.

Lynn, M., & Snyder, C. R. (2002). Uniqueness seeking. In C. R. Snyder & S. J. Lopez (Eds.), *Handbook of positive psychology* (pp. 395–410). New York: Oxford University Press.

Madey, S. F., Simo, M., Dillworth, D., Kemper, D., Toczynski, A., & Perella, A. (1996). They do get more attractive at closing time, but only when you are not in a relationship. *Basic and Applied Social Psychology, 18,* 387–393.

Pennebaker, J. W., Dyer, M. A., Caulkins, R. S., Litowitz, D. L., Ackerman, P. L., Anderson, D. B., & McGraw, K. M. (1979). Don't all the girls get prettier at closing time: A country and western application to psychology. *Personality and Social Psychology Bulletin, 5,* 122–125.

Petty, R. E., & Cacioppo, J. T. (1986). The elaboration likelihood model of persuasion. In L. Berkowitz (Ed.), *Advances in experimental social psychology* (Vol. 19, pp. 123–205). San Diego, CA: Academic Press.

Petty, R. E., & Mirels, H. L. (1981). Intimacy and self-disclosure: Effects on interpersonal attraction for males and females. *Personality and Social Psychology Bulletin, 7,* 493–503.

Pincus, S., & Waters, L. K. (1976). Effect of age restrictions and pornographic content on desirability of reading material. *Psychological Reports, 38,* 943–947.

Rusbult, C. E. (1983). A longitudinal test of the investment model: The development (and deterioration) of satisfaction and commitment in heterosexual involvements. *Journal of Personality and Social Psychology, 45,* 101–117.

Seta, J. J., & Seta, C. E. (1992). Personal equity-comparison theory: An analysis of value and the generation of compensatory and noncompensatory expectancies. *Basic and Applied Social Psychology, 13,* 47–66.

Shippee, G., Mowen, J., & Gregory, W. L. (1981). "Scarcity" of behavioral evidence for commodity theory. *Replications in Social Psychology, 1,* 15–20.

Snyder, C. R. (1992). Product scarcity by need for uniqueness interaction: A consumer Catch-22. *Basic and Applied Social Psychology, 13,* 9–24.

Sommers, S. R., & Kassin, S. M. (2001). On the many impacts of inadmissible testimony: Selective compliance, need for cognition, and the overcorrection bias. *Personality and Social Psychology Bulletin, 27,* 1368–1377.

Sue, S., Smith, R. E., & Caldwell, C. (1973). Effects of inadmissible evidence on the decisions of simulated jurors: A moral dilemma. *Journal of Applied Social Psychology, 3,* 345–353.

Triandis, H. C. (1989). The self and social behavior in differing cultural contexts. *Psychological Review, 96,* 506–520.

Veblen, T. (1965). *The theory of the leisure class.* New York: Kelly.

Verhallen, T. M. M. (1982). Scarcity and consumer choice behavior. *Journal of Economic Psychology, 2,* 299–322.

Verhallen, T. M. M., & Robben, H. S. J. (1995). Unavailability and the evaluation of goods. *Kyklos, 48,* 369–387.

Wegner, D. M., Lane, J. D., & Dimitri, S. (1994). The allure of secret relationships. *Journal of Personality and Social Psychology, 66,* 287–300.

Wills, T. A. (1981). Downward comparison principles in social psychology. *Psychological Bulletin, 90,* 245–271.

Worchel, S. (1992). Beyond a commodity theory analysis of censorship: When abundance and personalism enhance scarcity effects. *Basic and Applied Social Psychology, 13,* 79–92.

Worchel, S., & Arnold, S. (1973). The effects of censorship and attractiveness of the censor on attitude change. *Journal of Experimental Social Psychology, 9,* 365–377.

Worchel, S., Arnold, S., & Baker, M. (1975). The effects of censorship on attitude change: The influence of censor and communication characteristics. *Journal of Applied Social Psychology, 5,* 227–239.

Worchel, S., Lee, J., & Adewole, A. (1975). Effects of supply and demand on ratings of object value. *Journal of Personality and Social Psychology, 32,* 906–914.

Wright, R. A. (1992). Desire for outcomes that are more and less difficult to attain: Analysis in terms of energization theory. *Basic and Applied Social Psychology, 13,* 25–45.

Zellinger, D. A., Fromkin, H. L., Speller, D. E., & Kohn, C. A. (1975). Commodity theory analysis of the effects of age restrictions upon pornographic materials. *Journal of Applied Psychology, 60,* 94–99.

10

Risk and Reactance: Applying Social-Psychological Theory to the Study of Health Behavior

Frederick X. Gibbons
Meg Gerrard
Elizabeth A. Pomery
Iowa State University

Before we began working on this chapter, we conducted a computer search of the psychology literature, using the key terms *health* and *reactance*. We didn't find much—only 10 or 11 references in the last 25 years—which might lead to the conclusion that reactance theory (Brehm, 1966; Brehm & Brehm, 1981) has not had much of an impact in this area. That's definitely not the case. In fact, this kind of search seriously underestimates the influence that Brehm and his theory have had on health behavior research. That influence is indirect, and it takes a little digging to uncover, but it is real and significant. Brehm's work has played an important role in the development of a relatively new subarea of health psychology usually referred to as health–social. This is the area in which most of our own research has been conducted over the last 10 years. It is also an area that we believe will continue to expand in popularity and impact in the next decade, not only because the application of social psychology theory and principles to the study of health has demonstrated utility, but also because the study of health behavior provides an excellent opportunity for testing basic social psychology theories—such as reactance.

We describe some of our own research in this chapter. More generally, our goal is to present a brief general summary of the role that reactance theory has played in the study of health and health behavior. We focus on this (sub)area of health–social and use various research examples to illustrate the kinds of questions that psychologists interested in the topic have considered. We conclude with a brief discussion of a model of health risk behavior that we have been working on that has borrowed some of Brehm's ideas and concepts.

HEALTH AND CONTROL

Health–social psychology is the study of social-psychological factors that affect health. It involves the application of social psychological theories to further the understanding of health-promoting and health-impairing behaviors, including substance use, risky sexual behavior, exercise, health screening, and sun protection. Exactly when this hybrid area began is hard to say, but it is clear that Howard Leventhal's work on reactions to fear-arousing communications, conducted in the 1960s (Leventhal, Singer, & Jones, 1965; Leventhal & Watts, 1966), was instrumental. Leventhal demonstrated convincingly that social psychology theory could be applied effectively to the study of health and health behavior, and in so doing, further understanding of both the theory and the behavior. His work was followed by a number of important developments in the 1970s, which were directly related to some of Brehm's (1966) basic ideas. These developments included research on reactance and the Type A coronary-prone behavior pattern (Carver, 1980; Glass, 1977), and reactance as a factor influencing compliance with medical regimens (Taylor, 1979; see Fogarty, 1997, for a recent review). The most significant application of the theory, however, had to do with reactance as a response to perceived loss of control.

Loss of Control and Illness

Among the most innovative research to come out of that time period (1970s) was the work done in David Glass's labs at NYU and then at the University of Texas. Using Glass and Singer's (1972) urban stress work as a model, Glass and his students, including David Krantz, Jamie Pennebaker, Chuck Carver, Mike Scheier, and Karen Matthews, conducted a number of laboratory experiments aimed at exploring the *physical* manifestations of the psychological experience of loss of control. Typical of this work is a study by a group of Glass's students. Pennebaker, Burnam, Schaeffer, and Harper (1977) exposed college students to aversive noise and varied the amount of control that the students thought they had over the stimulus. As expected, the students who thought they had less control were more likely to report experiencing physical symptoms, such as dizziness, upset stomach, and nasal congestion. Other studies documented similar types of effects, perhaps the most notable being the work of Langer and Rodin (1976; Rodin & Langer, 1977) showing that minor interventions intended to increase nursing home residents' perceptions of control over their lives (e.g., having a say in determining their recreational activities or their room arrangement) was associated with increased longevity—arguably the ultimate health DV.

Learned Helplessness. These were not reactance studies, per se, and perceived loss of control is not the same thing as reactance. As Brehm and Brehm (1981) pointed out, however, having control is akin to having behavioral freedom(s): "Hence, reduction in control arouses reactance, and reactance impels the individual to try to restore control" (p. 6). This general theme had been developed earlier in Wortman and Brehm's (1975) *Advances* chapter in which they proposed a reconciliation and integration of reactance theory with the growing body of literature on learned helplessness. The argument, essentially, was that the first step in response to perceived loss of control is typically an attempt to restore the freedoms that are thought to be threatened. If these efforts are unsuccessful, they will be curtailed. If the perception of uncontrollability continues, efforts to restore freedom will cease altogether. Eventually, the person (or animal) will decline into a state of learned helplessness, which has been linked with significant mental and physical health problems (see Lovallo, 1997).

A convincing demonstration of this progression/integrative model can be seen in a study by Baum, Fleming, and Reddy (1986) that examined the perceived loss of control associated with unemployment. They had employed, recently unemployed, and chronically (long-term) unemployed persons work on a series of embedded figures tasks that were solvable but required persistence (i.e., some frustration tolerance). Baum et al. found, as expected, that employed and recently unemployed persons responded to the challenging task by increasing their efforts, exactly as reactance theory would predict. In contrast, those who had been unemployed for a while—and therefore were most stressed and experiencing the greatest loss of control—responded by cutting back their efforts, which is typical of learned helplessness. Moreover, these responses were accompanied by physiological changes: The high reactance group had higher levels of urinary epinephrine and norepinephrine (indicators of arousal) than did the long-term unemployed group.

In short, this research indicated that reactance is the first step toward the mental and physical decline that can accompany the significant loss (or surrender) of perceived psychological control. Moreover, because it involved application of social psychology theory to the study of health issues, this early work on reactance and control had an important impact on the development of health–social psychology (Krantz, Grunberg, & Baum, 1985; Rodin & Salovey, 1989; Salovey, Rothman, & Rodin, 1998). The theory continues to influence the area of health–social through its significant involvement in research on health and persuasion.

HEALTH COMMUNICATION

Message Framing

The impact of reactance theory can be seen clearly in the literature on health communication, specifically, reactions to different components of health messages. A prime example is the recent work by Rothman and Salovey (1997) indicating that health messages elicit a kind of reactance that can lead to healthy behavior change. Using some of Tversky and Kahneman's (1981) ideas on message framing, Rothman and Salovey have argued that health messages that are *loss* framed—that is, that warn recipients of the consequences they will face if they fail to engage in a particular protective behavior (e.g., "If you don't floss, you will lose those teeth")—can be very effective (cf. Heilman & Garner, 1975). The freedoms at stake here have to do with health status rather than behavior, and yet, they are very basic—the freedom to smile, for example, or even to have teeth, or more generally, the freedom that comes with being healthy. As a result, this type of reactance can be very motivating and apparently very constructive (Kalichman & Coley, 1995; Meyerowitz & Chaiken, 1987).

Fear

Another important issue in the area of health communication that involves reactance (again indirectly) has to do with the role that fear plays in health persuasion. Early research in this area was based on an assumption that messages that induced high levels of fear arousal are most effective, because (it was assumed) message recipients will change their behavior in an attempt to reduce the aversiveness associated with the fear. That assumption proved to be too simple, however, as subsequent research suggested that the fear/behavior change relation is not linear and, in fact, is much more complex than first thought (Leventhal & Singer, 1966; Mewborn & Rogers, 1979). Too much fear, for example, can elicit a "boomerang effect" in which recipients react against the anxiety produced by the message (Witte & Allen, 2000). Thus, recipients can demonstrate reactance to high fear communications on two dimensions: (a) in response to the fear that they are experiencing, which can lead to avoidance of the message, and (b) in response to the content of the message, which can produce the boomerang reaction.

Building on Leventhal's early health communication research, Witte developed a revised model of fear and persuasion, called the extended parallel process model (Witte, 1992, 1994, 1999), that outlines criteria for effective fear-based appeals. The model suggests that fear can motivate significant behavior change as long as it is accompanied by high perceived efficacy for the recommended actions. The combination of high fear and low efficacy is counterproductive, however, as it is likely to lead to message rejection, which is considered to be a type of reactance.

Consistent with the communication literature (e.g., Buller, Borland, & Burgoon, 1998), Witte's model includes audience characteristics as an important moderator of response to the communication (Witte & Morrison, 1995). A message that may seem quite reasonable to one group may come across as threatening to another (Austin, 1995). One key factor, in terms of health risk, is whether the risky behavior has already been initiated. Telling a young adult who is already smoking to stop doing it is likely to elicit a different response than admonishing an adolescent not to start. Thus, an important factor that determines health communication effectiveness is also an important issue in reactance theory: prior exercise of the freedom (cf. Snyder & Wicklund, 1976). In other words, is the message being presented part of an *intervention* program intended to stop a behavior, or a *prevention* program trying to delay or prevent onset of the behavior?

Intervention

Using the fear communication work as a basis, several experimental intervention studies have looked at reactance as a mediator of the relation between message strength, or message threat, and compliance. Bensley and Wu (1991), for example, presented college-age drinkers and nondrinkers with antidrinking messages that were either high or low in behavioral threat (e.g., "... any reasonable person must acknowledge these conclusions ..." vs. "We believe that these conclusions are reasonable."). Those exposed to the high-threat message demonstrated a boomerang effect: They reported more intention to drink in the future. In a second study, male heavy drinkers who had been exposed to a high-threat message responded by drinking more than those in a low-threat condition in a (supposedly unrelated) subsequent alcohol "taste test."

In a similar study, Buller et al. (1998) looked at the effect of message strength on parents' plans to protect their children from sun exposure. They used what they called "inductive" and "deductive" communications, meaning the message either suggested reasons to change behavior or more or less mandated a change, and had either low or high language "intensity" or forcefulness. What they found, as expected, was that the deductive, forceful message did elicit reactance from those parents who had already indicated that they had no specific intentions to protect their children. Buller et al. concluded that more forceful messages should be avoided when the audience includes a significant number of individuals who are not convinced of the need for change, but that such messages can be effective (up to a point) among those who believe change is necessary.

They also suggested that the issue is more complex when it comes to reaching audiences that have not yet made a decision about whether to engage or not to engage; such is the case with younger adolescents prior to initiation of substance use.

Prevention

The best known substance abuse prevention model in this country is DARE (Drug Abuse Resistance Education), a classroom-based prevention program that uses a "just say no" approach. DARE has been very well funded (Brown, 2001), in spite of a track record that has been described in terms ranging from "unimpressive" to "mixed," depending on who is providing the description (Lynam et al., 1999). Scientific assessments of its effectiveness (e.g., using meta-analytic techniques) have generally fallen into the former category, however (Ennett, Tobler, Ringwalt, & Flewelling, 1994). The program is based on a very fundamental assumption about adolescent behavior, which is that substance use is almost always a reaction to some kind of peer pressure. In other words, kids don't want to use drugs or drink, but other (usually older) kids want them to, which means that if an adolescent can be empowered to decline offers and resist pressure, it's very unlikely that he or she will use.

The program is derived, more or less, from two theoretical perspectives. The first is the expectancy-value model of attitude–behavior consistency (Bruvold & Rundall, 1988), a prime example being the theory of reasoned action (Fishbein & Ajzen, 1975). This approach assumes that behavioral decisions are deliberative and are based on an assessment of the costs and benefits associated with different courses of action, for example, (positive) alcohol expectancies vis-à-vis perceived alcohol risk. This decision process is thought to be a reasoned (although not necessarily rational) one that ultimately will lead to behavior that is thought to maximize the perceived benefit:cost ratio. The second theoretical approach that DARE borrows from is inoculation theory (McGuire, 1964; see Chassin, Presson, & Sherman, 1990), which argued that presenting an audience (e.g., children) with an example of the type of persuasive messages they are likely to hear (e.g., from older children) allows them to develop more effective counterarguments ("They will try to convince you that drugs are . . . This is what you should say to them: . . .").

The kind of approach that DARE uses has intuitive appeal, especially for parents ("if my child is doing something wrong it's because others have coerced him/her into doing it"; Donnermeyer, 2000). It also has its critics, however, who perceive a significant discrepancy between program popularity (viz. funding) and program efficacy (Brown, 2001). At a theoretical level, there are two primary points of contention. One is a belief that adolescent behavior is not only not rational (expectancy-value theories would not necessarily claim that it is), but, it is often not even reasoned (Kippax & Crawford, 1993; discussed later). The second is the belief that adolescents have different assessments of both costs and benefits than adults have or think that they (adolescents) have. Although interesting, this debate is not entirely pertinent to the focus of this chapter. Some of the criticisms of this program and the model it is based on are quite relevant, however.

A Boomerang Effect. In a series of studies, Donaldson and his colleagues presented a cogent argument as to why resistance education is often not effective with regard to curtailing substance use (Donaldson, Graham, & Hansen, 1994; Donaldson, Graham, Piccinin, & Hansen, 1995; Donaldson et al., 1996; Donaldson, Thomas, Graham, Au, & Hansen, 2000). Once again, the argument involves audience characteristics. They suggest that resistance messages can be quite effective for those adolescents who have already made a decision not to use substances. In this case, effective means that the programs can increase refusal skills—adolescents apparently do learn new and more creative ways to refuse offers to do behaviors that they probably didn't want to do in the first place. On the other hand, the program is less effective, and may even backfire, among those adolescents who have not yet made up their minds to avoid using (i.e., *non*abstainers) *and* who have an opportunity to use—for example, those attending schools in which substances are perceived to be readily available. In Donaldson's research (Donaldson et al., 1995; Donaldson et al., 2000), this latter group actually increased in their use.

Altering Cognitions. This increase in usage among nonabstainers was mediated by a change in their perceptions about substances and substance use. These adolescents apparently concluded from the (extensive) efforts put into this program that substance use was more common than they had previously thought. As a number of studies have shown, such increases in adolescents' perceptions of prevalence among their peers is often associated with an increase in their own use (Gerrard, Gibbons, Benthin, & Hessling, 1996). Donaldson et al. (1995) argued that normative-based programs that try to change adolescents' social cognitions about use—prevalence being a primary example of such a cognition—tend to be more effective with nonabstainers, and there is some support for this contention (Donaldson et al., 1996; Graham, Marks, & Hansen, 1991; MacKinnon et al., 1991). In other words, peers influence adolescents' substance use both directly (through provision of substances—i.e., "availability") *and* indirectly (through cognitions about use and about users). This social cognition approach is consistent with our own research and the theoretical basis behind it. We return to this issue later.

Refusal Education and Reactance

Implicit Threat. Although it is possible to present refusal training in a low-key manner that does not threaten most adolescents, there is an implicit message in these programs that many young people will not accept. Basically, the message is that their behavior is determined to a large extent by others. Most social psychologists would have little trouble with this claim, but adolescents don't see it that way. When asked why they chose to use substances or engage in other kinds of risky behaviors, adolescents will often provide reasons that are quite similar to those their parents or other adults would give—curiosity, stress reduction, pleasure seeking, and so forth (Beyth-Marom, Austin, Fischhoff, Palmgren, & Jacobs-Quadrel, 1993). They do not buy the notion that their forays into risky behavior are influenced, let alone dictated, by others. Our own data illustrate this point. We asked members of one of our adolescent panels (N = 400; M = 17 years old) if they feel pressured to drink whenever they do so; 63% said that is not at all the case, and only 2% reported that was definitely true (see Table 10.1). A year later we asked them a similar question: Whose idea was it the first time you had sex; 82% said it was a joint decision, only 16% said it was mostly or entirely their partner's idea.

Interestingly, many adolescents have no difficulty acknowledging the possibility that the substance use of others is strongly influenced by their peers (Sussman et al., 1995), even though they don't acknowledge that social influence plays much of a role in their own decision making. In fact, when we describe coercion or influence situations to them, they typically respond by claiming that refusal efficacy is not a significant issue for them. For example, when members of the panel mentioned earlier (M = 18 years old) were asked how they would respond if a group of their friends were trying to get them to take a drink when they didn't really want to, 71% said they definitely or probably would not take it (see Table 10.1); 86% (90% of the females) said they would not give in to a boy-/girlfriend's pressure to have sex if they were not ready for sex.

Implicit Versus Explicit Threat. How adolescents respond to these messages, then, will be determined to a large extent by what they are currently doing, together with the threat they perceive from the message. Those who have already made a decision not to engage will respond favorably, in part, because the message does not arouse any reactance in them, either explicitly or implicitly. There is no *explicit* threat because they

TABLE 10.1
Adolescents' Perceptions of Social Influence on Risky Behaviors

1) Do you feel pressured when you drink?[a]				
Not at all	A little	Somewhat	Yes	
63	27	7	2	
2) Whose idea was your first sexual encounter?				
All partner's	Mostly partner's	Both	Mostly yours	All yours
6	10	82	0	3
3) Would you take a drink from a friend even if you didn't want to?				
Definitely not	Probably not	Maybe	Probably	Definitely
41	30	11	11	7
4) Would you have sex in response to boy/girlfriend pressure even if you didn't want to?				
Definitely not	Probably not	Maybe	Probably	Definitely
63	23	8	5	1

Note. Reflects percentage choosing each option.
[a]M = 17 years old; all others M = 18 years old.

are being advised to do something they have already decided to do. There is no *implicit* threat because the message that they are hearing is not suggesting that their behavior is determined by others; they have effectively "assumed control" of their substance use by making a decision not to use. In contrast, those who have already made a decision to use are likely to experience reactance on both accounts: the more obvious threat to their freedom to do what they want, and the implicit message that their decision to use was really not entirely their own.

Finally, there is a large group of adolescents who are undecided about use (the size of this group diminishes with age, as more of them make decisions one way or the other; Reis-Bergan, Gibbons, & Gerrard, 2003). The explicit message may not be threatening to them—especially if it is presented in a low-key manner—but the implicit message, once again, does not resonate. For one thing, they are not so sure that they don't want to try the substance. In addition, they don't like the suggestion that the decision—yes or no—is being made partly by others. We have found in the focus groups we have run for our intervention studies that adolescents react almost as negatively to the idea that they are being manipulated by their peers as they do to the suggestion that they need to do what their parents and other adults tell them to do. For this reason, we have changed the message that we present to them so that it acknowledges the fact that they may very well have some interest in participating in some of these behaviors—even if they have no specific plans to do so at this time.

Reasoned Action Versus Social Reaction

When we ask adolescents in our studies if they are intending to use substances any time in the next year, the vast majority (up to about age 16 or 17) will say no. Nonetheless, a significant percentage of those "non-intenders" will report a year later that they have, in fact, used. For example, 1/3 of the members of the panel mentioned earlier ($M = 16$ years old) indicated they had never drunk alcohol and had never even considered doing it (i.e., they responded with a 1 on a 7-pt. consideration scale); a year later, 20% of this group indicated they had done it. Similarly, 44% indicated they had no intention *or* expectation at all of driving after drinking in the next year (i.e., they provided a 1 on each of three separate intention and expectation questions), and yet a year later, 28% of those non-intenders reported that they had done it. Most of these young people were not lying; they were not even responding in a socially desirable manner. The fact is they had no intention of engaging, quite possibly right up until the time they actually did engage (and for some of them even after they had engaged more than once). Their risky behavior was not planned or intentional; instead, it was a reaction to a social situation in which there was an *opportunity* to engage in the risky behavior. This distinction between behavior that is reasoned or planned and behavior that is reactive is at the heart of our prototype/willingness (P/W) model of adolescent health risk behavior. We present a brief description of the model (see Gibbons & Gerrard, 1995, 1997; Gibbons, Lane, et al., 2003, for further description), and then discuss the implications of the model and reactance theory for preventive–intervention programs.

A PROTOTYPE/WILLINGNESS MODEL OF ADOLESCENT HEALTH BEHAVIOR

We view health risk behaviors among adolescents as primarily social "events;" they are almost always done in the presence of, and sometimes for the benefit of, friends and peers. Consequently, the P/W model uses social-psychological theory and principles in an effort to understand, predict, and eventually alter these behaviors. A basic assumption of the model is that there are two paths to risk behavior. One is the reasoned path; it reflects the fact that for some adolescents, risk behavior is planned or intentional. These young people have thought about the behavior and made a conscious decision one way or the other—either to do it or not to do it. There is evidence of this reasoning process, which fits well with the expectancy-value perspective, even among very young adolescents (as young as 10 or 11; Gibbons et al., 2002).

The second path to risk is the social reaction path. Adolescents who follow this route have not thought much about risky behavior or its consequences, and indeed may have *avoided* such consideration (Gerrard et al., 2002; Gibbons, Gerrard, Ouellette, & Burzette, 1998). In addition, a fair number of them had no intention at all to engage prior to the time they ended up doing so—but they had not made a decision not to do so, either. When asked to articulate what their thoughts are about engaging, they will reveal considerable ambivalence; they're not planning on doing it, but they haven't ruled it out. In other words, they suggest they might be *willing* to use (or have unprotected sex) under some circumstances, even though they have no intentions to do so. This willingness is a focal construct in the model.

Behavioral Willingness

We define behavioral willingness (BW) as an openness to risk opportunity, an inclination to respond to risk situations if and when they occur. BW is distinguished from behavioral intention (which is the only proximal antecedent to behavior in expectancy-value theories) in a number of ways, including the amount of contemplation or consideration associated with each, the attributions of responsibility that are involved (much more internal for intentions than BW), and the focus of attention associated with each (more external or environmental for BW). Both of these proximal antecedents predict adolescent health risk behavior, and they do so independently, as well as in concert. In a series of studies, BW has been shown to add significantly to the variance in substance use and risky sex that is explained by intentions (see Gibbons & Gerrard, 1997; Gibbons et al., 2003, for reviews). Among younger adolescents—age 11 through 15 or 16—BW has been shown to be a better predictor of risky behavior than intentions, largely because use at this age is more often a reaction to social situations than a planned or premeditated action (Gibbons et al., 2002; Reis-Bergan et al., 2003).

Images

The second unique element of the P/W model is the image or prototype that adolescents have of the type of person *their age* who engages in the behavior. Young people have clear images of the type of adolescent who smokes, for example (Chassin, Tetzloff, & Hershey, 1985), or drinks (Burton, Sussman, Hansen, Johnson, & Flay, 1989), or has casual sex (Thornton, Gibbons, & Gerrard, 2002). There is some consensus about these images, which means that young people realize that if they were to engage in the behaviors, they would become associated with the image—others would label them as "smokers" or "druggies." Thus, the images are social consequences of the behavior. For the most part, the images are negative and therefore tend to have an inhibitory impact on decisions to engage in the behavior ("Do I want to be seen as a drinker?"). The more negative the adolescent's image, the less willing he or she is to engage in the behavior (and accept these social consequences). In short, images have an important influence on risk behavior, and that influence is mediated by BW.

Prototypes, Willingness, and Preventive Interventions

We have incorporated several elements of the P/W model in a preventive–intervention program being conducted with African American children (*M* = age 10 at wave 1) in rural Georgia (Brody, Murry, Gerrard, Gibbons, & Wills, 2001). Aspects of other prevention programs, both normative based (Donaldson et al., 1996; Graham et al., 1991) and family based (Spoth, Redmond, & Shin, 2001) are included, as well, in an attempt to delay or prevent onset of alcohol consumption and risky sexual behavior. We use this program as an example of our theoretical approach to preventing substance use.

Unlike most refusal or reasoned approaches, we neither assume nor suggest to the adolescents that their behavior is mostly a reaction to influence attempts from others. Instead, an effort is made to get them to acknowledge a normal level of curiosity and interest in the behaviors. We tell them that most people their age don't have any intentions or plans to use substances or have sex, and they probably fall into that category. Nonetheless, as they are well aware, a fair number of young people will end up doing so anyway. One reason for this is that they don't spend time before they get in these situations thinking about the behavior and its consequences, or what they might do when the situation does occur. As suggested earlier, BW is partly a result of an avoidance of consideration of risky behaviors (Gerrard et al., 2002; Gibbons et al., 1998); getting young people to think ahead of time what might happen should reduce their willingness.

Social Consequences. There are a number of possible consequences that the adolescents are asked to consider, some of which have to do with health and health risk, of course. Risk considerations don't always affect their behavior, however (Gerrard, Gibbons, & Bushman, 1996). Part of the problem is that adolescents who are not intending to engage in a particular risky behavior do not feel vulnerable to the potential consequences associated with that behavior ("I'm not planning on doing it, so I really don't need to worry about what might happen"). Other less obvious but potentially more impactful consequences of risky behavior that we point out are the social consequences associated with a given risk behavior. As in most normative-based programs (e.g., the Adolescent Alcohol Prevention Trial; Donaldson et al., 1994), we inform the adolescents about their normal tendency to overestimate the prevalence of the behaviors among their peers. Related to this tendency to inflate perceptions of prevalence is a corresponding tendency to overestimate the favorability of peers' risk images. Thus, adolescents learn in the intervention sessions that substance use or risky sex is not as common as they thought. They also learn that people who do these behaviors are not admired by a majority of their peers; in fact, these images tend to be quite negative. They realize, then, that if they were to engage in the behaviors, they will acquire some of these unfavorable image characteristics themselves. In short, the program takes one possible motivation for engaging—to look cool or sophisticated—and turns it around completely. Many ambivalent adolescents are not willing to pay this (social) price in order to satisfy their curiosity about the experience.

Internal Attributions. Finally, we focus a fair amount on attributions. Our belief is that encouraging external attributions for risk behavior (others cause you to do it) not only arouses some reactance, it also may facilitate willingness. Consequently, internal attributions are emphasized. Basically, the message is that risky behaviors are very tempting and interest in them is normal for people this age; at the same time, engaging in the behaviors is not an accident and it's not someone else's fault. If they do the behaviors, it's usually because they had some interest in them and didn't have a plan for avoiding the situation or for resisting the temptation (not just the offer). The goal, then, and again focus groups suggest that this can be effective, is to present a message that arouses minimal reactance in the audience. If anything, they are told to assume more control over their behavior, as well as more responsibility for its outcomes.

Admittedly, this kind of approach will not have much of an impact on those adolescents who are "intenders," the small but significant group who have made a decision to engage. It's not likely that we will arouse much reactance in these young people either, however. The only thing they are being told to do is to consider the behavior and its consequences, but because intentions involve some premeditation and planning (Ajzen, 1996), they have probably already done some of that. So, a boomerang effect is not likely to be a concern. Those who have decided not to use may not relate well to the program, mostly because they find it irrelevant. However, once again, there is little that is objectionable in the program for them, so they shouldn't react negatively. The group that we are most likely to have an impact on is those in the middle, the adolescents who have little or no intention to engage but have some willingness to do so (typically about 20% to 30% of the population, depending on age and the behavior involved; Gibbons, Lane, Gerrard, Eggleston, & Reis-Bergan, 2003). They are aware of this willingness and will acknowledge it when asked appropriately; evidence of this comes from the discriminant predictive validity of the construct in various studies. But they still maintain that they have no plans or intentions, or even expectations (cf. Warshaw & Davis, 1985) to do the behavior.

These willing but not intending adolescents are a logical (and efficient) group to target. On the one hand, they are clearly at risk. Precautions, such as carrying condoms or taking effective contraception such as the pill, assigning a designated driver, or even avoiding certain risk opportunities, require some acknowledgment of a tendency toward engaging in the behavior (Weinstein, 1988) and they aren't doing that ("I have no intention of getting drunk, so why should I ask someone to stay sober enough to drive me home?"). On the other hand, their "commitment" to the behavior is far from firm, and it is based, at least to some extent, on normative misperceptions that can be corrected or at least altered. It is possible to educate young people with regard to what their peers are actually doing and what they are thinking vis-à-vis risky behavior. Moreover, lab studies have shown that correcting overestimations of the prevalence of risky behaviors reduces willingness to engage in the behavior and that reduction is mediated by a change in prototypes (Eggleston, 1996). Direct attempts to alter risk images in the lab (i.e., make them more negative) have also been shown to lead to a reduced willingness to engage in the associated risk behavior (Gibbons, Lane, et al., 2003).

Summary

Adolescents do not respond well to the suggestion that their behavior is, will be, or was determined by others. Oftentimes, prevention or intervention communications that do not appear to be threatening may elicit a kind of reactance in adolescents due to their implicit message: You are being manipulated. Acknowledging that they are likely to be interested in many of the behaviors that they see others engaging in encourages young people to accept responsibility for their actions and reduces the likelihood that they will tune out the message. In addition, helping them to consider what freedoms they will likely surrender by engaging in risky behavior—that is, both the health *and* the social consequences that often accompany these actions—should help promote compliance rather than reactance. In short, this social–cognitive approach appears to be a potentially effective means of altering adolescent risk behavior.

CONCLUSION

There is an important relation between psychological reactance and both physical and mental health. That relation is not straightforward, however. Instead, it is indirect or "mediated," and it can be seen in several different domains. Reactance theory has had a significant influence on the study of how individuals respond to a perception that they are losing control; this perception, in turn, can have important mental and physical health consequences. The impact of reactance theory can be seen most clearly in its application to the area of health communication. A number of studies over the last 30 years have suggested that health communications can arouse reactance in two ways: (a) explicitly, by threatening the freedom to engage in certain behaviors that are quite common and, by their very nature, enticing and exciting; and (b) implicitly, by suggesting that individuals—especially young people—are not really in control of these behaviors. Using basic principles of reactance theory, psychologists have been able to develop prevention and intervention programs that can reduce the likelihood of this kind of response and, therefore, stand a better chance of succeeding. More generally, research in these two areas has demonstrated the utility of social psychological theory in understanding and perhaps improving health behavior. In this sense, reactance theory has been instrumental in the development of a new area of study with considerable potential: health–social psychology.

REFERENCES

Ajzen, I. (1996). Dual-mode processing in the pursuit of insight is no vice. *Psychological Inquiry, 10,* 110–112.

Austin, E. W. (1995). Reaching young audiences: Developmental considerations in designing health messages. In E. Maibach & R. L. Parrott (Eds.), *Designing health messages: Approaches from communication theory and public health practice* (pp. 114–144). Thousand Oaks, CA: Sage.

Baum, A., Fleming, R., & Reddy, D. M. (1986). Unemployment stress: Loss of control, reactance and learned helplessness. *Social Science and Medicine, 22,* 509–516.

Bensley, L. S., & Wu, R. (1991). The role of psychological reactance in drinking following alcohol prevention messages. *Journal of Applied Social Psychology, 21,* 1111–1124.

Beyth-Marom, R., Austin, L., Fischhoff, B., Palmgren, C., & Jacobs-Quadrel, M. (1993). Perceived consequences of risky behaviors: Adults and adolescents. *Developmental Psychology, 29,* 549–563.

Brehm, J. W. (1966). *A theory of psychological reactance.* New York: Academic Press.

Brehm, S. S., & Brehm, J. W. (1981). *Psychological reactance: A theory of freedom and control.* New York: Academic Press.

Brody, G. H., Murry, V. M., Gerrard, M., Gibbons, F. X., & Wills, T. A. (2001). [Preventing alcohol use among African American youth]. Unpublished raw data.

Brown, J. H. (2001). Youth, drugs, and resilience education. *Journal of Drug Education, 31,* 83–122.

Bruvold, W. H., & Rundall, T. G. (1988). A meta-analysis and theoretical review of school based tobacco and alcohol intervention programs. *Psychology and Health, 2,* 53–78.

Buller, D. B., Borland, R., & Burgoon, M. (1998). Impact of behavioral intention on effectiveness of message features: Evidence from the family sun safety project. *Human Communications Research, 24,* 433–453.

Burton, D., Sussman, S., Hansen, W. B., Johnson, C. A., & Flay, B. R. (1989). Image attributions and smoking intentions among seventh grade students. *Journal of Applied Social Psychology, 19,* 656–664.

Carver, C. S. (1980). Perceived coercion, resistance to persuasion, and the Type A behavior pattern. *Journal of Research in Personality, 14,* 467–481.

Chassin, L., Presson, C. C., & Sherman, S. J. (1990). Social psychological contributions to the understanding and prevention of adolescent cigarette smoking. *Personality and Social Psychology Bulletin, 16,* 820–822.

Chassin, L., Tetzloff, C., & Hershey, M. (1985). Self-image and social-image factors in adolescent alcohol use. *Journal of Studies on Alcohol, 46,* 39–47.

Donaldson, S. I., Graham, J. W., & Hansen, W. B. (1994). Testing the generalizability of intervening mechanism theories: Understanding the effects of adolescent drug use prevention interventions. *Journal of Behavioral Medicine, 17,* 195–216.

Donaldson, S. I., Graham, J. W., Piccinin, A. M., & Hansen, W. B. (1995). Resistance-skills training and onset of alcohol use: Evidence for beneficial and potentially harmful effects in public school and in private Catholic schools. *Health Psychology, 14,* 291–300.

Donaldson, S. I., Sussman, S., MacKinnon, D. P., Severson, H. H., Glynn, T., Murray, D. M., et al. (1996). Drug abuse prevention programming: Do we know what content works? *American Behavioral Scientist, 39,* 868–883.

Donaldson, S. I., Thomas, C. W., Graham, J. W., Au, J. G., & Hansen, W. B. (2000). Verifying drug abuse prevention program effects using reciprocal best friend reports. *Journal of Behavioral Medicine, 23,* 585–601.

Donnermeyer, J. F. (2000). Parents' perceptions of a school-based prevention education program. *Journal of Drug Education, 30,* 325–342.

Eggleston, T. J. H. (1996). *Altering sexual prototypes via prevalence information: An experimental analogue to a sexual intervention program.* Unpublished doctoral dissertation, Iowa State University.

Ennett, S. T., Tobler, N. S., Ringwalt, C. L., & Flewelling, R. L. (1994). How effective is drug abuse resistance education? A meta-analysis of Project DARE outcome evaluations. *American Journal of Public Health, 84,* 1394–1401.

Fishbein, M., & Ajzen, L. (1975). *Belief, attitude, intention, and behavior: An introduction to theory and research.* Reading, MA: Addison-Wesley.

Fogarty, J. S. (1997). Reactance theory and patient noncompliance. *Social Science Medicine, 45,* 1277–1288.

Gerrard, M., Gibbons, F. X., Benthin, A. C., & Hessling, R. M. (1996). A longitudinal study of the reciprocal nature of risk behaviors and cognitions in adolescents: What you do shapes what you think, and vice versa. *Health Psychology, 16,* 344–354.

Gerrard, M., Gibbons, F. X., & Bushman, B. J. (1996). Relation between perceived vulnerability to HIV and precautionary sexual behavior. *Psychological Bulletin, 119,* 390–409.

Gerrard, M., Gibbons, F. X., Reis-Bergan, M., Trudeau, L., Vande Lune, L., & Buunk, B. P. (2002). Inhibitory effects of drinker and nondrinker prototypes on adolescent alcohol consumption. *Health Psychology, 21,* 601–609.

Gibbons, F. X., & Gerrard, M. (1995). Predicting young adults' health-risk behavior. *Journal of Personality and Social Psychology, 69,* 505–517.

Gibbons, F. X., & Gerrard, M. (1997). Health images and their effects on health behavior. In B. P. Buunk & F. X. Gibbons (Eds.), *Health, coping, and well-being: Perspectives from social comparison theory* (pp. 63–94). Mahwah, NJ: Lawrence Erlbaum Associates.

Gibbons, F. X., Gerrard, M., & Lane, D. J. (2003). A social reaction model of adolescent health risk. In J. M. Suls & K. Wallston (Eds.), *Social psychological foundations of health and illness* (pp. 107–136). Oxford, UK: Blackwell.

Gibbons, F. X., Gerrard, M., Ouellette, J. A., & Burzette, R. (1998). Cognitive antecedents to adolescent health risk: Discriminating between behavioral intention and behavioral willingness. *Psychology and Health, 13,* 319–339.

Gibbons, F. X., Gerrard, M., Vande Lune, L., Wills, T. A., Brody, G. H., & Conger, R. D. (2002). *Risk cognitions mediate the effects of context on African American adolescents' substance use.* Manuscript submitted for publication.

Gibbons, F. X., Lane, D. J., Gerrard, M., Eggleston, T. J., & Reis-Bergan, M. (2003). *Image manipulation as a means of reducing risk willingness.* Manuscript in preparation.

Glass, D. C. (1977). *Behavior patterns, stress, and coronary disease.* Hillsdale, NJ: Lawrence Erlbaum Associates.

Glass, D. C., & Singer, J. E. (1972). *Urban stress.* New York: Academic Press.

Graham, J. W., Marks, G., & Hansen, W. B. (1991). Social influence processes affecting adolescent substance use. *Journal of Applied Psychology, 76,* 291–298.

Heilman, M. D., & Garner, K. A. (1975). Counteracting the boomerang: The effects of choice on compliance to threats and promises. *Journal of Personality and Social Psychology, 31,* 911–917.

Kalichman, S. C., & Coley, B. (1995). Context framing to enhance HIV-antibody-testing messages targeted to African American women. *Health Psychology, 14,* 247–254.

Kippax, S., & Crawford, J. (1993). Flaws in the theory of reasoned action. In D. J. Terry, C. Gallois, & M. McCamish (Eds.), *The theory of reasoned action: Its application to AIDS-preventive behaviour* (pp. 253–269). Oxford, UK: Pergamon Press.

Krantz, D. S., Grunberg, N. E., & Baum, A. (1985). Health psychology. *Annual Review of Psychology, 36,* 349–383.

Langer, E. J., & Rodin, J. (1976). The effects of choice and enhanced personal responsibility for the aged: A field experiment in an institutional setting. *Journal of Personality and Social Psychology, 34,* 191–198.

Leventhal, H., & Singer, R. P. (1966). Affect arousal and positioning of recommendations in persuasive communications. *Journal of Personality and Social Psychology, 4,* 137–146.

Leventhal, H., Singer, R. P., & Jones, S. (1965). Effects of fear and specificity of recommendation upon attitudes and behavior. *Journal of Personality and Social Psychology, 2,* 20–29.

Leventhal, H., & Watts, J. C. (1966). Sources of resistance to fear-arousing communications on smoking and lung cancer. *Journal of Personality, 34,* 155–175.

Lovallo, W. R. (1997). *Stress & health: Biological and psychological interactions.* Thousand Oaks, CA: Sage.

Lynam, D. R., Milich, R., Zimmerman, R., Novak, S. P., Logan, T. K., Martin, C., Leukefeld, C., & Clayton, R. (1999). Project DARE: No effects at 10-year follow-up. *Journal of Consulting and Clinical Psychology, 67,* 590–593.

MacKinnon, D. P., Johnson, C. A., Pentz, M. A., Dwyer, J. H., Hansen, W. B., Flay, B. R., & Wang, E. Y. (1991). Mediating mechanisms in a school-based drug prevention program: First-year effects of the Midwestern Prevention Project. *Health Psychology, 10,* 164–172.

McGuire, W. (1964). Inducing resistance to persuasion: Some contemporary approaches. In L. Berkowitz (Ed.), *Advances in experimental social psychology* (Vol. 1, pp. 191–229). New York: Academic Press.

Mewborn, C. R., & Rogers, R. W. (1979). Effects of threatening and reassuring components of fear appeals on physiological and verbal measures of emotion and attitudes. *Journal of Experimental Social Psychology, 15,* 242–253.

Meyerowitz, B. E., & Chaiken, S. (1987). The effect of message framing on breast self-examination attitudes, intentions, and behavior. *Journal of Personality and Social Psychology, 52*, 500–510.

Pennebaker, J. W., Burnam, M. A., Schaeffer, M. A., & Harper, D. C. (1977). Lack of control as a determinant of perceived physical symptoms. *Journal of Personality and Social Psychology, 35*, 167–174.

Reis-Bergan, M., Gibbons, F. X., & Gerrard, M. (2003). *From willingness to intention: Experience as a moderator of the shift from reactive to reasoned behavior.* Manuscript in preparation.

Rodin, J., & Langer, E. J. (1977). Long-term effects of a control-relevant intervention with the institutionalized aged. *Journal of Personality and Social Psychology, 35*, 897–902.

Rodin, J., & Salovey, P. (1989). Health psychology. *Annual Review of Psychology, 40*, 533–579.

Rothman, A. J., & Salovey, P. (1997). Shaping perceptions to motivate health behavior: The role of message framing. *Psychological Bulletin, 121*, 3–19.

Salovey, P., Rothman, A. J., & Rodin, J. (1998). Health behavior. In D. T. Gilbert, S. T. Fiske, & G. Lindzey (Eds.), *The handbook of social psychology* (4th ed., Vol. 2, pp. 633–683). New York: McGraw-Hill.

Snyder, M. L., & Wicklund, R. A. (1976). Prior exercise of freedom and reactance. *Journal of Experimental Social Psychology, 12*, 120–130.

Spoth, R. L., Redmond, C., & Shin, C. (2001). Randomized trial of brief family interventions for general populations: Adolescent substance use outcomes 4 years following baseline. *Journal of Consulting and Clinical Psychology, 69*, 627–642.

Sussman, S., Galaif, E. R., Stacy, A. W., Moss, M. A., Dent, C. W., Craig, S., Simon, T. R., & Anderson-Johnson, C. (1995). Continuation high schools: Youth at risk for drug abuse. *Journal of Drug Education, 25*, 191–200.

Taylor, S. E. (1979). Hospital patient behavior: Reactance, helplessness, or control. *Journal of Social Issues, 35*, 156–184.

Thornton, B., Gibbons, F. X., & Gerrard, M. (2002). Risk perception and prototype perception: Independent processes predicting risk behavior. *Personality and Social Psychology Bulletin, 28*, 986–999.

Tversky, A., & Kahneman, D. (1981). The framing of decisions and the psychology of choice. *Science, 211*, 453–458.

Warshaw, P. R., & Davis, F. D. (1985). Disentangling behavioral intention and behavioral expectation. *Journal of Experimental Social Psychology, 21*, 213–228.

Weinstein, N. D. (1988). The precaution adoption process. *Health Psychology, 7*, 355–386.

Witte, K. (1992). Putting the fear back into fear appeals: The extended parallel process model. *Communication Monographs, 59*, 329–349.

Witte, K. (1994). Fear control and danger control: A test of the extended parallel process model (EPPM). *Communication Monographs, 61*, 113–134.

Witte, K. (1999). Fear as motivator, fear as inhibitor: Using the extended parallel process model to explain fear appeal successes and failures. In P. Andersen & L. Guerrero (Eds.), *Handbook of communication and emotion: Research, theory, applications, and contexts* (pp. 423–450). New York: Academic Press.

Witte, K., & Allen, M. (2000). A meta-analysis of fear appeals: Implications for effective public health campaigns. *Health Education and Behavior, 27*, 591–615.

Witte, K., & Morrison, K. (1995). Using scare tactics to promote safer sex among juvenile detention and high school youths. *Journal of Applied Communication Research, 23*, 128–142.

Wortman, C. B., & Brehm, J. W. (1975). Responses to uncontrollable outcomes: An integration of reactance theory and the learned helplessness model. In L. Berkowitz (Ed.), *Advances in experimental social psychology* (pp. 277–336). New York: Academic Press.

11

From State to Trait and Back Again: Reactance Theory Goes Clinical

Varda Shoham
Sarah E. Trost
Michael J. Rohrbaugh
University of Arizona at Tucson

Good ideas sometimes have side effects. Back in 1966, Jack Brehm defined reactance as a motivational state aroused in response to threatened behavioral freedom that motivates a person to restore that freedom. As Sharon Brehm (1976) pointed out a quarter of a century ago, this construct has enormous implications for clinical psychology. It helps to explain how some people get stuck, why they don't change, and why some treatments don't work. Most clinical researchers, however, construed reactance as a trait with the hope that recognizing a client as "reactant" would guide clinicians to better tailor intervention strategies to client type and thereby increase treatment efficacy. As a result, the construct of reactance was recast from motivational state to personality trait and was most frequently investigated as a client attribute, hypothesized to interact with type of treatment within the framework of the attribute-by-treatment research paradigm (ATI; Beutler, 1991; Shoham-Salomon & Hannah, 1991; Snow, 1991). As this line of research turned highly problematic, we propose that clinical psychology has much to gain by restoring reactance to its original meaning as a motivational state.

In the first two parts of the chapter, we review research on reactance as a treatment moderator. With the exception of one study that investigated this moderator as an induced state (Shoham-Salomon, Avner, & Neeman, 1989), most investigators chose to treat reactance as a trait. In the second part of the chapter, we argue that conceptualizing reactance as a stable personality feature, a hypersensitivity to limitations on one's freedom (e.g., Beutler, Mohr, Grawe, Engle, & MacDonald, 1991; Dowd, Milne, & Wise, 1991), led investigators down a fruitless path, which we view as a detour. These efforts encountered serious problems of construct validity and distracted attention from Brehm's original conceptualization of reactance as a motivational state.

In the third part of the chapter, we go back to Brehm's (1966) conceptualization of reactance as a state and suggest that it is highly relevant to interpersonal processes of social influence involving clients, their relatives, and even their therapists. We describe situations where reactance is unintentionally induced by caring helpers (spouses, parents, therapists) who make well-intentioned attempts to restrict other people's freedom to engage in health-compromising behavior (e.g., drinking, smoking). These attempts often enter ironic, problem–solution loops, where more restrictions lead to more of the behavior and more of the behavior leads to further attempts to restrict it. We end the chapter by proposing the arousal of reactance as the mechanism that mediates such interpersonal ironic processes, and describe current implications for treatment development.

REACTANCE AS A TREATMENT MODERATOR: RESEARCH ON PARADOXICAL INTERVENTIONS

All psychological treatments involve a certain degree of social influence whereby therapists try to persuade clients to engage in new ways to behave, think, and feel (cf. Frank, 1973). In behavior therapy, therapists try to convince clients to engage in behaviors that are incompatible with the behavior targeted for change, thus restricting clients' freedom to continue engaging in the symptomatic behavior. Although one may think that such freedom is easy to give up, clients are often far less ready to change than is implied by the mere fact that they show up for the first session (Prochaska, DiClemente, & Norcross, 1992).

Informed by Brehm's (1966) reactance theory, Rohrbaugh and his colleagues (Rohrbaugh, Tennen, Press, & White, 1981; Tennen, Rohrbaugh, Press, & White, 1981) distinguished between problem behavior that clients experience as relatively free or volitional (e.g., procrastination, drinking, smoking) and behavior that clients experience as unfree or uncontrollable (e.g., panic, obsessive–compulsive disorders, erectile dysfunction). Reactance is more likely to be aroused when clients undergo pressure to give up a behavioral freedom, that is, to give up a behavior in which they choose to engage or, at least, feel that they are choosing. Drinkers and smokers, even those who are defined as "dependent," often report that they can quit any time ("I just haven't made up my mind yet"). Reactance can be triggered by pressure from concerned relatives as well as from paid helpers such as therapists. For that reason, Rohrbaugh et al. suggested that a class of intervention called "paradoxical" would work best in situations where clients' reactance potential is maximized.

The term *paradoxical interventions* refers to therapeutic tactics that have the common denominator of attempting to induce change by discouraging it. Thus, paradoxical interventions seem to contradict the goals they are designed to achieve. In the most common type of paradoxical intervention, the therapist prescribes the very symptoms that clients present as a complaint (e.g., "take time to procrastinate"). These techniques can be applied and explained apart from the theoretical model in which they were developed and can be found in virtually all schools of psychotherapy (Seltzer, 1986). Nevertheless, there are striking differences in how therapists of different theoretical orientations use paradoxical intervention. In comparing cognitive–behavioral and strategic–systemic approaches—the two frameworks most amenable to therapeutic paradox—one finds that behavior therapists use "paradoxical intention," a compliance-based paradox aimed at interrupting within-person exacerbation cycles. In contrast, strategic–systems therapists tend to use defiance-based paradoxical interventions where therapists limit clients' freedom *not* to engage in the symptomatic behavior and as such, expect clients to do the opposite of what is proposed. The former type of intervention maximizes clients' compliance by giving an explicit rationale for the prescription whereas the latter maximizes defiance by either giving a minimal rationale ("we need you to do this for diagnostic purposes") or by framing suggestions in a manner that is inconsistent with clients' views of themselves and the problem (Fisch, Weakland, & Segal, 1982).

Rohrbaugh et al.'s (1981) theoretical model suggested that some, but not all types of paradoxical interventions work because they mobilize clients' reactance in the service of change. They further proposed that compliance-based paradox would work better for clients who perceive the target behavior as unfree and when there is a low potential for reactance, whereas defiance-based paradoxical interventions would work best when clients perceive the target behavior as volitional (free), and when a situation is loaded with reactance potential.

Inspired by Rohrbaugh et al.'s model of therapeutic change, Shoham and her students at Tel Aviv University undertook a series of studies to test the hypothesis that clients who experience or exhibit psychological reactance would respond more favorably to a defiance-based paradoxical intervention than would low-reactance clients, whereas the opposite would be the case for a self-control intervention whereby clients receive straightforward compliance-based instructions on how to engage in more productive study habits. Following a preliminary analogue study that used paradoxical versus stress-management methods to reduce laboratory-induced stress (Shoham-Salomon & Jancourt, 1985), Shoham-Salomon et al. (1989) conducted two studies with clients complaining of procrastination. An experimental study was followed by a correlational study and both hypothesized that level of client (induced or exhibited) reactance would serve as a moderator of clients' response to paradoxical versus self-control interventions. The investigators chose to treat the problem of academic procrastination because one can safely assume that college students think they can exercise freedom of choice regarding when (and even if) to study.

The experimental study is the only ATI study thus far that has treated reactance as a state. The investigators manipulated client reactance by using a procedure grounded in Brehm's (1966) theory and research paradigm. Prior to the beginning of treatment, each participant had a 5-minute meeting with an experimenter and read two single-paragraph descriptions of treatments for procrastination. The two descriptions were pilot tested to differ in level of attractiveness and were fairly general so that each of them could suit either the paradoxical or the self-control interventions. Prior to reading the descriptions, participants were told they would be free to choose between the two treatments. As predicted, all clients chose the more attractive treatment. Clients were randomly assigned to the low-reactance condition in which they were told they would receive their treatment of choice or to the high-reactance condition in which they were told their treatment of choice was not available. No further explanation was given by the experimenter. Clients were then escorted to the therapy room, where they met their therapist.

Each of the four therapists conducted either the paradoxical or the self-control treatment according to a preplanned randomized schedule. Therapists were informed that the nature of the design was aimed at finding which intervention was better for whom rather than the overall superiority of one intervention over another, but they did not know that clients' reactance was the hypothesized moderator of treatment efficacy or, for that matter, that clients were randomly exposed to either high- or low-reactance conditions. A check on the manipulation confirmed that therapists believed that both treatments would yield an equivalent overall outcome and that they thought of differential predictors of treatment outcome in terms of general personality traits (e.g., level of emotional awareness, neuroticism, agreeableness, and problem severity) rather than as reactance potential or evoked reactance.

Both treatments followed manualized guidelines and entailed two 30-minute individual sessions in which the client's problem of procrastination was discussed and condition-appropriate directives were presented. Under paradoxical interventions, therapists emphasized the puzzling nature of procrastination and established it as "something worth exploring in order to reach a better awareness . . ." (p. 593). Clients were asked to deliberately engage in procrastination behavior so that they and their therapists would have a better chance to understand it. To do so, they were instructed to spread out the course materials that they were supposed to work on but not to engage in active study. Instead, they were to have half an hour of purposeful procrastination each day, in which they sat away from the desk, spending their time daydreaming or doing whatever else they usually did when they procrastinated and "concentrate on producing the procrastination for diagnostic purposes" (p. 593). Therapists underscored that studying at these times was prohibited but allowed that if clients succeeded in the therapeutic task for 6 days, they could take the seventh day off and study or not study, as they wished.[1]

The self-control interventions were designed to be comparable with the paradoxical interventions by including all the nonparadoxical elements of the intervention and by replicating, as closely as possible, the procedures described by Lopez and Wambach (1982). Therapists referred to procrastination as a "learned habit" and emphasized that the clients needed to "develop new behaviors that were incompatible with procrastination" (p. 593). They instructed clients to select a place where they could study effectively and to "study daily, as much as possible" at that location under improved stimulus-control conditions.

In essence, whereas the paradoxical intervention restricted client freedom to embark on behavior change, the self-control intervention restricted client freedom to engage in the problem. Specifically, studying during designated times was prohibited by the paradoxical intervention and prescribed in the self-control intervention. In more general terms, therapists' stance toward immediate behavior change was to discourage it in the former and encourage it in the latter. Clients' reported improvement was met with empathic caution, in addition to some skepticism in the paradoxical intervention and congratulations in the self-control condition.

In Shoham-Salomon et al.'s (1989) first study, clients low and high on induced reactance were randomly assigned to paradoxical versus self-control treatments. Results yielded the expected Reactance × Treatment interaction: Clients in the high-reactance condition benefited more from the paradoxical than from the self-control treatment. There was no significant difference in effective study time in the low-reactance condition.

Shoham-Salomon et al. (1989) then conducted a second, correlational study to examine whether clients who exhibit higher levels of reactance in

[1]A more detailed description of both treatments appears in Shoham-Salomon et al. (1989), as well as in Lopez and Wambach's (1982) study, after which these interventions were modeled.

response to a provocation at the onset of treatment would benefit more from paradoxical intervention relative to clients who start treatment with lower levels of reactance. Thus, rather than manipulating reactance, the investigators measured it. They reasoned, however, that due to the nature of the construct, reactance is not easy to measure, especially via a paper-and-pencil questionnaire. (In fact, the level of reactance of a client who would openly admit to this state of mind might be questioned.) As such, Shoham-Salomon et al. used a naturalistic measure of expressed reactance based on ratings of the client's content-filtered voice when responding to a reactance-provoking question. Voice tone was chosen as the least controllable channel of communication that "leaks" uncensored affective states of mind (Zucerman, DePaulo, & Rosenthal, 1986). At the beginning of the first session, therapists asked clients to describe their procrastination problem and, more specifically, to address the following question: "To what extent do you think you can overcome and control your procrastination problem on your own, without my help?" The first 20 seconds of clients' responses to this question were rated by four naïve female judges for the amount of spitefulness in clients' tone of voice after the content had been filtered (Rogers, Scherer, & Rosenthal, 1971). Clients were considered to be more "reactant" the more spiteful, uninhibited, and active their content-filtered tone of voice sounded. The results of Study 2 replicated the results obtained in Study 1, with client reactance predicting greater therapeutic benefit under paradoxical, but not self-control interventions.

More recently, Shoham, Bootzin, Rohrbaugh, and Urry (1996) used a similar voice-based measure of client reactance as clients entered a treatment for sleep-onset insomnia and answered the same reactance-provoking question as in the procrastination studies. Whereas the symptom of insomnia itself is often perceived as less controllable (or "free") than procrastination, one can safely assume that clients feel free to choose the behavior in which they engage when they go to bed. The defiance-based paradoxical intervention applied in this study targeted client attempts to fall asleep by asking them to try to stay awake in order to preserve a positive meaning that insomnia may have in the client's life (e.g., ruminating on the events of the day so that they can better understand their relationships with others or better plan for future activities). The comparison of paradoxical versus skill-oriented progressive muscle relaxation (PMR) interventions yielded a similar Reactance × Treatment interaction effect. Both interventions outperformed a measurement-only control group, but insomniacs high and low on the voice measure of reactance responded differentially—and in the predicted directions—to treatments. This differential "effect" of reactance was most pronounced at 6-month follow-up: Highly reactant PMR clients experienced longer sleep latencies than did their low-reactance counterparts whereas high-reactance clients continued to fare better than low-reactance clients under paradoxical intervention.

While corroborating the role of reactance as a treatment moderator, the findings of Shoham-Salomon et al.'s (1989) Study 2 and Shoham et al.'s (1996) insomnia study raise questions regarding the construct of reactance and the validity of its measurement. Although Shoham and her colleagues intended to treat reactance as a provoked state, their findings could easily be interpreted as lending support to the formulation of reactance as a trait: When provoked, some people may react more strongly than others against anything they perceive as a threat to their freedom, and when they do so, they are better candidates for the technique of prescribing the symptom; when therapists recommend that they continue to be symptomatic, these people improve out of defiance. Even though there was no evidence that these people were likely to behave "reactantly" in other freedom-challenging situations, high-reactance clients in Shoham's studies behaved in a predictable way, compatible with the notion that they possess a trait of reactance.

Taking a Detour: The Search for Reactant Clients

We have serious doubts regarding the validity of existing measures as indicators of trait reactance. These doubts include the voice measure used by Shoham and colleagues. Clients high on this measure responded to therapists' provocation with voice tones that sounded to naïve listeners as spiteful, uninhibited, and active. Yet, the construct validity of the voice tone as a measure of reactance was not established independently from the mere fact that the measure yielded the hypothesized prediction and did so repeatedly across samples—procrastination and insomnia—and across languages/cultural contexts—Hebrew and English. To complicate things even further, when Shoham et al. (1996) used the voice measure and a self-report trait measure (the Therapeutic Reactance Scale [TRS]; Dowd et al., 1991) in the same study, these two measures of (allegedly) the same construct did not correlate.

The TRS is one of several attempts at capturing trait reactance that can be measured via self report. This 28-item questionnaire was developed by Dowd, Milne, and Wise (1984, 1991) to assess clients' tendencies to experience psychological reactance. It includes items such as "if I am told what to do, I often do the opposite" and "I have a strong desire to maintain my personal freedom," and consists of two correlated subscales that assess verbal and behavioral reactance. The TRS yields acceptable levels of internal consistency (ranging from .75 to .84) and moderate levels of stability over a 3-week period, with test–retest reliabilities ranging from .57 to .60 (Dowd et al., 1991). Individuals who score highly on the TRS also score highly on a variety of personality characteristics such as dominance, internal locus of control, autonomy, defensiveness, aggressiveness, and minimal concern for making a good impression on others (Dowd et al., 1991; Dowd & Wallbrown, 1993; Dowd, Wallbrown, Sanders, & Yesenosky, 1994).

The use of the TRS has been extended to research designed to test the role of reactance as a treatment moderator. In one such study, Dowd et al. (1988) examined a defiance-based paradoxical intervention among clients with problems of procrastination or test anxiety. Clients were divided into high and low reactant groups as identified by the TRS, and were randomly assigned to paradoxical and nonparadoxical treatments. Although it was predicted that high-reactant subjects would show more symptom reduction when receiving a defiance-based intervention, there was no difference in treatment effectiveness for high- and low-reactant clients.

A review of studies across investigators and laboratories suggests that the TRS yields equivocal results as a treatment moderator. Whereas two studies by the investigators who developed the TRS (Dowd et al., 1988; Swoboda, Dowd, & Wise, 1990) failed to establish reactance as a moderator, or even to show that within the paradoxical intervention group, more reactant clients fared better, other investigators replicated findings by Shoham and colleagues when using the TRS to measure reactance. Two such studies found reactance to moderate response to paradoxical versus nonparadoxical interventions. Paradoxical interventions reduced sleep latencies among insomnia clients (Horvath & Goheen, 1990) and somatic anxiety among athletes (Carter & Kelly, 1997). In both studies, clients higher on the TRS responded better to the paradoxical versus the nonparadoxical intervention, which was not the case for low-reactance clients. Another study by Kelly and Nauta (1997) found a similar pattern of differential effect of instruction to express versus suppress intrusive thoughts among individuals low or high on the TRS. Subjects high on the TRS fared better when they were instructed to have their intrusive thoughts, and even to engage in having them by expressing them freely. These (highly reactant?) subjects reported feeling more out of control and disturbed by their intrusive thoughts when they were instructed to suppress them.

But does the TRS measure reactance? As with the voice tone measure, the construct validity of the TRS is questionable. Both measures may capture an oppositional style or defensiveness that responds better to (or is "tricked" by) the strategic or indirect nature of paradoxical interventions. Yet, this oppositional style may have little to do with the individual's "consistent tendency to perceive and react to situations as if one's *freedom* [italics added] were being threatened" (Kelly & Nauta, 1997, p. 1124). In fact, Dowd et al. (1988) found that although the TRS did not appear to moderate response to the two treatments, results suggested that high-scoring clients were generally less satisfied with either treatment *regardless* of the level of threat that the treatment posed to clients' behavioral freedom.

An indirect way to examine construct validity of a measure is to apply it to an extreme population that, by definition, should be high on the measure. Our ongoing study of change-resistant smokers provides such an opportunity (Rohrbaugh et al., 2001). Our participants are smokers who continue to smoke despite having heart or lung disease. When people continue to engage in a behavior that is highly restricted by societal norms and doctors' orders one could reason that they would be high on a measure such as the TRS. Our preliminary data indicate, however, that our sample's TRS scores are not elevated above those of the general population (e.g., a median score of 70 reported by Kelly & Nauta, 1997).

Another Reactance × Treatment interaction was reported by Beutler and colleagues (Beutler et al., 1991), who attempted to capture clients' reactance potential by using a less direct index. To compose a reactance score, they used an arithmetic combination of MMPI indices of manifest anxiety (Taylor Manifest Anxiety Scale) and social defensiveness (Edwards Social Desirability Scale). Interestingly, this composite score went through several name changes without any alterations to the actual scoring system. It was originally labeled as "defensive high-anxious" by Asendorpf and Scherer (1983). Beutler et al. (1991) referred to it first as "defensive-anxious," then as "defensive-resistant," then as a "resistance potential measure," and finally—as "reactance." Although Beutler et al. (1991) acknowledged the shaky ground upon which the construct validity of the measure stands, they nevertheless reported that reactant clients benefited less from two authoritative treatments for depression (cognitive group therapy and focused expressive psychotherapy) than from a non-authoritative self-paced (supportive/self-directed) therapy. Beutler et al. (1991) reported that this pattern of findings was replicated cross-culturally, in Germany. Once again, reactance was inferred from *what a measure can do* rather than from *what a measure stands for*.

A recent study by Baker, Sullivan, and Marszalek (2001) reported that the TRS and Beutler et al.'s reactance potential measure did not correlate. Similar to the samples used by Beutler and colleagues, Baker et al.'s participants were older than the college students participating in Dowd et al.'s studies (average age was mid-40s) and were treatment seekers diagnosed with Major Depression.

The disconnect between the two measures of the same construct can be better understood by examining the components of Beutler et al.'s measure. Conceptually, it is not clear why people who are high on measures of anxiety and social desirability should also be high on reactance. In fact, Dowd and colleagues reasoned that anxiety should be used to establish divergent validity and that highly reactant people should be low on social desirability. Indeed, Lukin, Dowd, Plake, and Kraft (1985) reported that the TRS and the State-Trait Anxiety Inventory (Spielberger, Gorsuch, & Lushene, 1970) did not correlate. Moreover, Dowd et al. (1994) predicted, and found, that people high on the TRS pay little attention to impressions they make on others, a trait that should correlate negatively with social desirability. In sum, using the same label of "reactance," Dowd and colleagues and Beutler and colleagues referred to different traits. Although Beutler's reactant client is anxious and defensive, Dowd's reactant client is oppositional, intolerant, likely to express feelings, aggressive, high on internal locus of control, dominant, autonomous, and nonaffiliative (Dowd & Wallbrown, 1993; Dowd et al., 1994; Morgan, 1986). The picture portrayed by the correlates of the TRS bear some similarity to the dimensions rated in Shoham's voice measure (spiteful, uninhibited, and active), although, as found by Shoham et al. (1996), the TRS and the voice measures did not correlate either.

Beyond the question of construct validity of the measure, the TRS seems to be a useful predictor of who would be a "difficult client." Clients who score higher on self-reported reactance also report a history of noncompliance with medication regimen (Moore, Sellwood, & Stirling, 2000). Moreover, they miss more appointments, terminate therapy sooner, and are less satisfied with treatment (Dowd et al., 1991).

Do people higher on a trait measure of reactance also show higher determination to restore thwarted freedom in situations where the level of threat to freedom is experimentally manipulated? No study to date has shown that. An unpublished study that tested this hypothesis (Baker & Sullivan, 2001) failed to support it. In the absence of such findings, the questions of whether reactance can be (a) conceptualized and (b) measured as a trait remain open. In the next and final section of the chapter, we return to the concept of reactance as a motivational *state* aroused when people are faced with a threat to their behavioral freedom, directing them to reestablish the threatened or eliminated freedom.

Reactance and Interpersonal Ironic Processes

In real-world relationships reactance is often inadvertently induced, prompting a vicious cycle that is difficult to break. Substance abuse provides a private case and a fertile context for such cycles. People are most likely to try to restrict other people's behavioral freedom when they perceive the behavior (e.g., smoking, drinking) as counterproductive or destructive, even though the very same behavior may be experienced by the behaving individual (e.g., smoker, drinker) as a legitimate choice. When such a perceived freedom to behave is threatened, an aroused state of reactance may lead the individual to protect and restore freedom by doing more of the restricted behavior, which, in turn, may lead others to intensify their attempts to further restrict the behavior in question and so on. The following case vignette and interpretation demonstrate an ironic maintenance of substance abuse.

> While conducting an assessment study of physician-referred smokers who continued to smoke despite having multiple risk factors for heart or lung disease, we encountered the following couple. Jake, a 56-year-old semi-retired electrician and NRA member, had had a stroke, was diabetic, and had high blood pressure. Not surprisingly, both his family physician and his wife, Janet, very much wanted him to quit smoking—but Jake himself wasn't much interested. He agreed to participate in our research project because "the wife and doctor wanted me to" (and perhaps also because we were to pay the couple $250).
>
> In the laboratory, we interviewed Jake and Janet at some length about a variety of matters related to smoking, their health, and their relationship. We also observed and videotaped their interaction, both when Jake was smoking and when he was not. In a nutshell, Jake and Janet showed many features of demand-withdraw interaction. Janet would frequently urge him not to smoke; for example, she would comment on how bad it smells and wave her hand to fan away the smoke. For his part, Jake showed no inclination to be influenced by this. In fact, his characteristic response was to speak less (withdraw) and smoke more. At one point in the interview he said simply, "The more she pushes me, the more I'll smoke!" Later, when Janet reflected on their interaction, she said "I don't know if Jake can control his smoking or not, but I think he *chooses* to smoke around me—and I find that very frustrating." Although Janet tried not to nag, she found it difficult not to urge Jake "to give it [quitting] a try." Interestingly, she had done this when Jake temporarily cut back his cigarette consumption during a bout with bronchitis—and he promptly resumed full-blown smoking.
>
> Our inquiries also revealed that, 10 years earlier, Jake had recovered from alcoholism. He said he did so only after Janet stopped saying, "If you loved me enough, you'd give up the booze": When she gave up on him and said instead, "I don't care what you do any more," Jake enrolled in a treatment program.
>
> From our perspective, Janet and Jake's dance illustrates the ironic maintenance of substance abuse. Despite their conflicts, it seemed to us that this couple truly loved each other—and that Janet's attempts to influence Jake's smoking and drinking were motivated by genuine concern for his (and their) welfare. It was also apparent that the more Janet pushed Jake to change, the less inclined he was to do so—and that the more he reacted against her attempts to restrict his behavior by withdrawing, the more she demanded change. We also suspect that had we (or any other well-intentioned helper) attempted to "treat" this couple with a direct, high-

demand approach that pushed Jake to change, the result would have been a very short-lived therapy.

By definition, an irony is an outcome of events contrary to what was, or might have been intended (*Webster's New World Dictionary*, 1982). Thus, well-intentioned attempts to reduce a behavioral freedom to smoke may turn ironic if they motivate the smoker to keep the behavior going or even increase its frequency. Moreover, albeit understandable attempts by a smoker to stave off threats to his or her behavioral freedom may turn ironic if they are perceived by the well-intentioned helper as a restriction of his or her behavioral freedom (to express frustration or demand change), thus arousing reactance and fueling further attempts at eliminating the (smoking) behavior. In the next section, we describe our research on drinking and smoking, in which reactance was not directly manipulated or even measured. We conceptualize reactance as a hypothetical mediator involved in ironic processes of problem maintenance and change.

We borrowed the term "ironic process" from Dan Wegner (1994, 1997), whose ingenious lab experiments showed how trying to exert mental control—by attempting thought suppression (e.g., trying not to think of a white bear)—often backfires, and actually leads to more thought intrusion. Wegner's theoretical formulations focused solely on within-person ironic processes. Yet, in our view, ironic processes occur *between* as well as within people and it is within the context of interpersonal influence attempts that reactance may play a more important role. Social contexts ranging from courtship and family interaction to the war on drug use provide countless examples of how persistent attempts to influence someone else's behavior can have consequences opposite those intended. (This broader view of problem-maintaining solutions has been a central theme in the work of Weakland, Fisch, Watzlawick, and their family-oriented clinical colleagues for nearly three decades; Watzlawick, Weakland, & Fisch, 1974.)

The idea of ironic process reflects a parsimonious principle: Many problems persist precisely because people continue in unsuccessful attempts to solve them. This is a simple but powerful idea because it (a) tells us where to look to understand what keeps problems going (look for "more of the same" solution), (b) suggests what needs to happen for a problem to get unstuck (someone must do "less of the same"), and (c) sheds some light on iatrogenic treatment processes.[2]

What keeps problems going? At the interpersonal level, diverse lines of research exemplify ironic processes between parents and children, hus-

[2]In this chapter we address the first and third points. For details on interrupting ironic processes, see Shoham and Rohrbaugh (1997) and Rohrbaugh and Shoham (2001).

bands and wives, and even caregivers and care receivers. Although not designed to document ironic processes per se, clinical studies suggest that escalating interpersonal cycles, based on family members' miscarried solution efforts, inadvertently help to maintain behavioral manifestations of such disparate problems as child conduct disorder (Patterson, 1982), schizophrenia (Rosenfarb, Goldstein, Mintz, & Nuechterlein, 1995), and depression (Coyne, Kahn, & Gotlib, 1987). Theory and research on "social control" similarly suggest that attempts by social-network members to influence health-compromising behavior such as smoking and drinking can actually exacerbate those behaviors (Lewis & Rook, 1999). Studies of helping behavior demonstrate that well-intentioned caregiving efforts sometimes elicit negative reactions from the care recipients (Newsom, 1999), and from the social-development literature comes documentation of an ironic "Romeo and Juliet effect" (Driscoll, Davis, & Lipetz, 1972), wherein parental interference fans the flames of adolescents' romantic love.

In our own research with alcohol-involved couples, we have examined factors contributing to the maintenance of alcoholism. One such factor, demand–withdraw interaction (DWI), is a common yet potentially devastating ironic cycle in which the more one person pursues, nags, or demands change, the more the other distances, defends, avoids, or withdraws (Christensen & Heavey, 1993). A common scenario is that a nondrinking spouse makes well-intentioned demands that the drinker change, but these lead only to withdrawal (and more drinking), which leads to more demands from the frustrated spouse, more withdrawal by the drinker, and so on.

In a study of male alcoholics and their spouses (Shoham, Rohrbaugh, Stickle, & Jacob, 1998), we asked couples to conduct two 10-minute interaction tasks in which the two partners discussed (a) a marital disagreement (conflict), and (b) the husband's drinking. Observational ratings of each interaction task produced measures of two patterns for each couple: wife-demand/husband-withdraw (Wd/Hw), and husband-demand/wife-withdraw (Hd/Ww). Ratings of demand behavior included "demands," "nags," "criticizes," "pressures partner to change"; ratings of withdrawal behavior included items such as "withdraws," "avoids," "defends," "changes topic," "diverts discussion" (Christensen & Heavey, 1993). As expected, when the couples discussed the husband's drinking, there were higher levels of Wd/Hw than the opposite pattern of Hd/Ww. (This was not the case for interactions in which couples discussed a relationship conflict not related to drinking; in these interactions, the husband was as often in the demand role as the wife.) In other words, wives' attempts to engage husbands with requests for change in drinking were met with further withdrawal—and if, by withdrawing, the drinker hoped to get the wife off his back, that was not successful either.

Although we have no direct evidence that each partner's behavior aroused a motivational state of reactance in the other partner, one can argue that each partner's behavior posed a threat to the behavioral freedom of the other. One can further argue that the recipient of such a threat experiences an elevated level of reactance (of the "don't tell me what not to do" type), which motivates him or her to restore behavioral freedom by intensifying the behavior that got this ironic process going in the first place. Figure 11.1 portrays such a cycle whereby a partner's demand for sobriety arouses a drinker's reactance, which motivates the drinker to withdraw and drink more. The drinker's behavior poses a threat to partner's freedom to demand ("don't nag or I'll drink more"), thus arousing reactance and elevating the attractiveness of the demanding behavior, which, ironically, exacerbates drinking. In the absence of direct measurement of both partners' level of reactance within the various phases of the DWI sequence, however, the mediating role of reactance remains theoretical.

Perhaps the strongest evidence of ironic process in Shoham et al.'s (1998) study was the finding that higher levels of Wd/Hw (but not Hd/Ww) correlated with lower levels of readiness to change reported by the alcoholic, both concurrently and after the acute phase of treatment (Rohrbaugh, 1999). Although we cannot say whether high wife demand resulted in low readiness to change or vice versa, the couple pattern this correlation implies is consistent with an ironic problem-solution loop.

If ironic processes are as universal as we think they are, it should not be surprising that therapists, too, can become entrapped in ironic processes by applying solutions that feed back to maintain the very problems they are trying to ameliorate. Our study comparing cognitive–behavioral and family-systems treatments for male alcoholics (Shoham et al., 1998) illustrates how high-demand interventions can drive alcoholics out of treat-

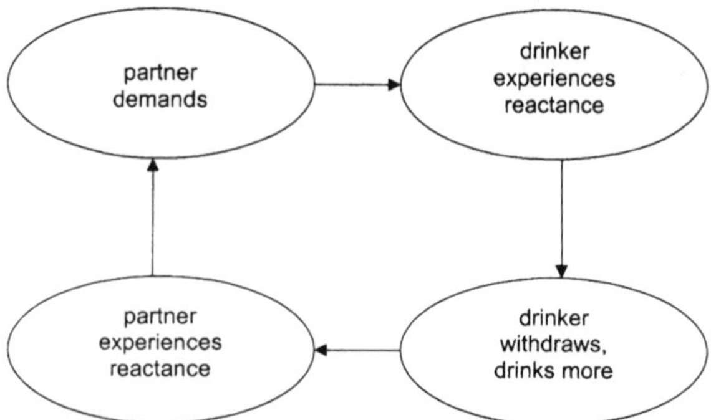

FIG. 11.1. The mediating role of reactance in the ironic maintenance of substance abuse.

ment, especially when the intervention recapitulates ironic influence processes occurring between the drinker and his spouse. The two couple treatments in this study—cognitive–behavior therapy (CBT) and family-systems therapy (FST)—differed in the level of demand they placed on the drinker for abstinence and change and in the way each intervention dealt with reluctance to change. CBT took a firm stance about expected abstinence from alcohol, confronted reluctance, and used adjunctive breathalyzer tests to ensure compliance, whereas FST used less direct strategies, although drinking was a primary target for change in both treatments. FST assumed that an external demand for sobriety would elevate the drinker's reactance and motivate him to protect his freedom to drink. Thus, therapists were trained to join with client reluctance to change and speak the "language of reactance" by presenting the pros and cons of quitting and emphasizing that it is the drinker's choice whether or not to quit (e.g., "nobody can do it for you, and I am not going to pressure you to quit: It is entirely your decision").

Based on the ironic-process model, we hypothesized that high-demand CBT would be less suited than low-demand FST for couples engaged in DWI because CBT replicates the couple's problem pattern by providing "more of the same" ineffective solution: An alcoholic husband may thus withdraw from a demanding therapy in the same way he withdraws from a demanding wife. The retention and abstinence results generally supported this prediction: We found significant DWI × Treatment interactions indicating that, when couples higher on pretreatment DWI were assigned to CBT, they attended fewer sessions, were more likely to drop out, and tended to have poorer drinking outcomes, whereas DWI levels made little difference in FST. Also as predicted, statistical moderation of response to the two treatments was stronger for the Wd/Hw pattern than for the Hd/Ww pattern, especially when DWI was rated during the couple's discussion of the husband's drinking.

These couple-level relational-moderator results parallel findings from the individual-level studies reported earlier, indicating that clients high on psychological reactance tend to benefit more from strategic, paradoxical interventions than from straightforward education and skill training (Shoham-Salomon et al., 1989). In both of these clinical contexts—one where an individual client resists persistent influence from a therapist and the other where a male drinker resists influence from his spouse—treatments that exert different levels of direct pressure for change appear to yield different results to the extent that they elevate or reduce clients' reactance and activate (or avoid) interpersonal ironic processes. The heuristic value of this work lies in predicting who will benefit most and least from different treatments, based on the match (or mismatch) between how a treatment attempts to exert influence and the extent to which clients participate in reactance-laden ironic influence processes in their own lives.

SUMMARY, CHALLENGES, TREATMENT IMPLICATIONS, AND FUTURE DIRECTIONS

The construct of reactance is highly relevant to theories of problems and to theories of change—the two pillars of clinical science. As a mediator, reactance can explain how repeated attempts to solve a problem turn ironic by keeping the problem going or making it worse. Moreover, various levels of reactance aroused in contexts within which change is expected to occur (e.g., more or less coercive treatment) can yield differential predictions as to the likelihood that such change will take place. Reactance can also serve as a treatment moderator when settings (e.g., mandatory vs. voluntary treatments) vary in the level to which they offer client choice or threaten client behavioral freedom.

We argue, however, that the search for treatment moderators in the form of traits led reactance researchers to take a detour we view as fruitless for two reasons: (a) Reactance may not be a stable trait, and (b) what is currently measured as a trait may not reflect the construct of reactance. Thus far, we are not convinced by evidence that there are people who are more or less reactant across the board. (Incidentally, smokers labeled as "change resistant" because they smoke despite having a heart or lung disease—thus consistently resisting other people's attempts to limit their freedom to smoke—do not seem to have sufficient levels of reactance "in them" to react against nicotine, a substance that a vast majority of them view as limiting their options to free themselves of its controlling grip; Rohrbaugh et al., 2001.) Moreover, we have serious doubts that the various measures of reactance as a trait necessarily reflect a struggle to retain freedom, let alone agree with each other regarding what a reactant person would look like.

Whether conceptualized as a mediator or a moderator, the main challenge facing clinical scientists interested in reactance is how to measure it or, at least, document its existence beyond the hypothetical formulations suggested earlier. If reactance is a mediator fueling ironic problem-solution loops, clinicians may intervene to change this problem-maintaining process. This can be done by offering choices at each point of the treatment and emphasizing clients' freedom to retain the problem behavior (Miller & Rollnick, 1991, 2002; Watzlawick et al., 1974). This can also be done by helping a concerned partner to back off from his or her attempts to limit the other's behavioral freedom (Rohrbaugh & Shoham, 2001; Shoham & Rohrbaugh, 1997). A documented change in the level of reactance should, by theory, relate to *subsequent* reduction in the target behavior and, ultimately, to a positive treatment outcome.

ACKNOWLEDGMENTS

Correspondence regarding this article should be addressed to Varda Shoham, Department of Psychology, University of Arizona, Tucson, AZ 85721-0068.

The work reported in this chapter was partially supported by grants from NIMH (RO1-MH47451), NIAAA (RO1-1108486), and NIDA (R21-DA13121).

REFERENCES

Asendorpf, J. S., & Scherer, K. R. (1983). The discrepant repressor: Differentiation between low anxiety, high anxiety, and repression of anxiety by autonomic-facial-verbal patterns of behavior. *Journal of Personality and Social Psychology, 45,* 1334–1346.

Baker, K., & Sullivan, H. (2001, November). *Green eggs and ham: A test of the construct validity of two measures of psychological reactance.* Paper presented at the meeting of the North American Chapter of the Society for Psychotherapy Research, Puerto Vallarta, Mexico.

Baker, K., Sullivan, H., & Marszalek, T. (2001, November). *Therapeutic reactance in a depressed client sample: A comparison of two measures.* Paper presented at the meeting of the North American Chapter of the Society for Psychotherapy Research, Puerto Vallarta, Mexico.

Beutler, L. E. (1991). Have all won and must all have prizes? Revisiting Luborsky et al.'s verdict. *Journal of Consulting and Clinical Psychology, 59,* 226–232.

Beutler, L. E., Mohr, D. C., Grawe, K., Engle, D., & MacDonald, R. (1991). Looking for differential treatment effects: Cross-cultural predictors of differential psychotherapy efficacy. *Journal of Psychotherapy Integration, 1,* 121–141.

Brehm, J. W. (1966). *A theory of psychological reactance.* New York: Academic Press.

Brehm, S. S. (1976). *The application of social psychology to clinical practice.* New York: Halsted Press.

Carter, J. E., & Kelly, A. E. (1997). Using traditional and paradoxical imagery interventions with reactant intramural athletes. *Sport Psychologist, 11,* 175–189.

Christensen, A., & Heavey, C. L. (1993). Gender differences in marital conflict: The demand/withdraw interaction pattern. In S. Oskamp & M. Costanzo (Eds.), *Gender issues in contemporary society* (pp. 113–141). Newbury Park, CA: Sage.

Coyne, J. C., Kahn, J., & Gotlib, I. H. (1987). Depression. In T. Jacob (Ed.), *Family interaction and psychopathology* (pp. 509–534). New York: Plenum.

Dowd, E. T., Hughes, S. L., Brockbank, L., Halpain, D., Seibel, C., & Seibel, P. (1988). Compliance-based and defiance-based intervention strategies and psychological reactance in the treatment of free and unfree behavior. *Journal of Counseling Psychology, 35,* 370–376.

Dowd, E. T., Milne, C. R., & Wise, S. L. (1984, August). *The therapeutic reactance scale: Development and reliability.* Paper presented at the American Psychological Association Convention, Toronto.

Dowd, E. T., Milne, C. R., & Wise, S. L. (1991). The Therapeutic Reactance Scale: A measure of psychological reactance. *Journal of Counseling and Development, 69,* 541–545.

Dowd, E. T., & Wallbrown, F. (1993). Motivational components of client reactance. *Journal of Counseling & Development, 71*, 533–538.

Dowd, E. T., Wallbrown, F., Sanders, D., & Yesenosky, J. M. (1994). Psychological reactance and its relationship to normal personality variables. *Cognitive Therapy & Research, 18*, 601–612.

Driscoll, R., Davis, K. E., & Lipetz, M. E. (1972). Parental interference and romantic love: The Romeo and Juliet effect. *Journal of Personality and Social Psychology, 24*, 1–10.

Fisch, R., Weakland, J. H., & Segal, L. (1982). *The tactics of change*. San Francisco: Jossey-Bass.

Frank, J. D. (1973). *Persuasion and healing* (2nd ed.). Baltimore: Johns Hopkins University Press.

Horvath, A. O., & Goheen, M. D. (1990). Factors mediating the success of defiance- and compliance-based interventions. *Journal of Counseling Psychology, 37*, 363–371.

Kelly, A. E., & Nauta, M. M. (1997). Reactance and thought suppression. *Personality and Social Psychology Bulletin, 23*, 1123–1132.

Lewis, M. A., & Rook, K. S. (1999). Social control in personal relationships: Impact on health behaviors and psychological distress. *Health Psychology, 18*, 63–71.

Lopez, F. G., & Wambach, C. A. (1982). Effects of paradoxical and self-control directives in counseling. *Journal of Counseling Psychology, 29*, 115–124.

Lukin, M., Dowd, E. T., Plake, B. S., & Kraft, R. G. (1985). Comparing computerized versus traditional psychological assessment in counseling. *Computers in Human Behavior, 1*, 49–58.

Miller, W. R., & Rollnick, S. (1991). *Motivational interviewing: Preparing people to change addictive behavior*. New York: Guilford.

Miller, W. R., & Rollnick, S. (2002). *Motivational interviewing: Preparing people for change* (2nd ed.). New York: Guilford.

Moore, A., Sellwood, W., & Stirling, J. (2000). Compliance and psychological reactance in schizophrenia. *British Journal of Clinical Psychology, 39*, 287–295.

Morgan, R. D. (1986). *Individual differences in the occurrence of psychological reactance and therapeutic outcome*. Unpublished doctoral dissertation, University of Nebraska, Lincoln.

Newsom, J. T. (1999). Another side to caregiving: Negative reactions to being helped. *Current Directions in Psychological Science, 8*, 183–187.

Patterson, G. R. (1982). *A social learning approach: Coercive family process*. Eugene, OR: Castalia.

Prochaska, J. O., DiClemente, C. C., & Norcross, J. C. (1992). In search of how people change: Applications to addictive behavior. *American Psychologist, 47*, 1102–1114.

Rogers, P. L., Scherer, K. R., & Rosenthal, R. (1971). Content filtering human speech. *Behavioral Research Methods and Instrumentation, 3*, 16–18.

Rohrbaugh, M. (1999, June). Demand-withdraw interaction and the ironic maintenance of alcoholism. In V. Shoham (Chair), *Demand-Withdraw Couple Interaction: Contextual Perspectives on Problems and Change*. Symposium conducted at the meeting of the American Psychological Society, Denver, CO.

Rohrbaugh, M. J., & Shoham, V. (2001). Brief therapy based on interrupting ironic processes: The Palo Alto model. *Clinical Psychology: Science and Practice, 8*, 66–81.

Rohrbaugh, M. J., Shoham, V., Trost, S., Muramoto, M., Cate, R. M., & Leischow, S. (2001). Couple dynamics of change-resistant smoking: Toward a family consultation model. *Family Process, 40*, 15–31.

Rohrbaugh, M., Tennen, H., Press, S., & White, L. (1981). Compliance, defiance, and therapeutic paradox: Guidelines for strategic use of paradoxical interventions. *American Journal of Orthopsychiatry, 51*, 454–467.

Rosenfarb, I. S., Goldstein, M. J., Mintz, J., & Nuechterlein, K. H. (1995). Expressed emotion and subclinical psychopathology observable within the transactions between schizophrenic patients and their family members. *Journal of Abnormal Psychology, 104*, 259–267.

Seltzer, L. F. (1986). *Paradoxical strategies in psychotherapy: A comprehensive overview and guidebook.* New York: Wiley.

Shoham, V., Bootzin, R. R., Rohrbaugh, M. J., & Urry, H. (1996). Paradoxical versus relaxation treatment for insomnia: The moderating role of reactance. *Sleep Research, 24a,* 365.

Shoham, V., & Rohrbaugh, M. J. (1997). Interrupting ironic processes. *Psychological Science, 8,* 151–153.

Shoham, V., Rohrbaugh, M., Stickle, T., & Jacob, T. (1998). Demand-withdraw interaction moderates response to cognitive-behavioral vs. family-systems therapy for alcoholism. *Journal of Family Psychology, 12,* 557–577.

Shoham-Salomon, V., Avner, R., & Neeman, R. (1989). You are changed if you do and changed if you don't: Mechanisms underlying paradoxical interventions. *Journal of Consulting and Clinical Psychology, 57,* 590–598.

Shoham-Salomon, V., & Hannah, M. T. (1991). Client-treatment interaction in the study of differential change processes. *Journal of Consulting and Clinical Psychology, 59,* 217–225.

Shoham-Salomon, V., & Jancourt, A. (1985). Differential effectiveness of paradoxical interventions for more versus less stress-prone individuals. *Journal of Counseling Psychology, 32,* 443–447.

Snow, R. E. (1980). Aptitude processes. In R. E. Snow, P. Federico, & W. E. Montague (Eds.), *Aptitude, learning, and instruction: Vol. 1. Cognitive processes analyses of aptitude.* Hillsdale, NJ: Lawrence Erlbaum Associates.

Spielberger, C. D., Gorsuch, R. L., & Lushene, R. E. (1970). *STAI: Manual for the State-Trait Anxiety Inventory.* Palo Alto, CA: Consulting Psychologists Press.

Swoboda, J. S., Dowd, E. T., & Wise, S. L. (1990). Reframing and restraining directives in the treatment of clinical depression. *Journal of Counseling Psychology, 37,* 254–260.

Tennen, H., Rohrbaugh, M., Press, S. E., & White, L. (1981). Reactance theory and therapeutic paradox: A compliance-defiance model. *Psychotherapy: Theory, Research & Practice, 18,* 14–22.

Watzlawick, P., Weakland, J. H., & Fisch, R. (1974). *Change: Principles of problem formation and problem resolution.* New York: Norton.

Webster's New World Dictionary of the American Language (2nd ed.). (1982). New York: Simon & Schuster.

Wegner, D. M. (1994). Ironic processes of mental control. *Psychological Review, 101,* 34–52.

Wegner, D. M. (1997). When the antidote is the poison: Ironic mental control processes. *Psychological Science, 8,* 148–150.

Zucerman, M., DePaulo, B. M., & Rosenthal, R. (1986). Humans as deceivers and lie detectors. In P. D. Blanck, R. Buck, & R. Rosenthal (Eds.), *Nonverbal communication in the clinical context* (pp. 13–35). University Park: Pennsylvania State University Press.

12

Ability Perception Determinants of Effort-Related Cardiovascular Response: Mood, Optimism, and Performance Resources

Rex A. Wright
Jason Franklin
University of Alabama at Birmingham

One of the wonderful things about well-formulated theories is that they can lead you conceptually and empirically to places that you never intended to go. No theory illustrates this better than Jack Brehm's theory of motivational intensity (Brehm, 1975; Brehm & Self, 1989). Brehm's theory was conceived with subjective aspects of motivation in mind. More specifically, it was conceived with the goal of improving the prediction and understanding of approach and avoidant desire (e.g., Brehm, Wright, Solomon, Silka, & Greenberg, 1983). However, much of the research inspired by the theory has been physiological in nature. Furthermore, much has involved predictor variables that Brehm surely did not envision when he began considering motivational intensity issues.

In this chapter, we discuss one line of investigation that has come about unexpectedly as a result of Brehm's motivational intensity theory. We do so with several purposes in mind. One is to raise the profile of this body of work among investigators interested in social motivation. Although the work has potential for telling us a great deal about the operation of motives in social situations, it is likely to be unfamiliar to some social motivation investigators because it has been reported largely in publications outside the mainstream of social psychology. Further purposes for our discussion are to update other reviews of this work (Wright, 1998; Wright & Kirby, 2001) and illustrate something that Brehm has devoted much of his academic life helping people to appreciate: just how practical theories can be.

We begin the chapter by outlining the analysis that has guided this work and by describing fundamental research findings. We then review new studies that provide evidence relevant to the guiding analysis, comment on them, and consider what this line of research may tell us about social motivation. We conclude by commenting briefly on the practicality of theories and Brehm as "a scientist's scientist."

CARDIOVASCULAR RESPONSES TO BEHAVIORAL CHALLENGE

A major focus of studies in our laboratory over the past 15 years has been cardiovascular (CV) responses in people confronted with mental and physical tasks. Within the relevant research literature, mental and physical tasks are commonly referred to as "behavioral challenges." Therefore, that is how we refer to them here. We have been interested in people's CV responses to behavioral challenges in part because the responses have been tied empirically to certain health risks (e.g., that for hypertension), with stronger responses conferring greater risk than weaker ones (Blascovich & Katkin, 1993; Dembroski, Schmidt, & Blümchen, 1983). We also have been interested in the responses because CV adjustment is widely understood to be a part of the energy mobilization process (Brener, 1987) and therefore potentially informative with respect to people's motivational states, including their social motivational states.

Ability Perception Influence

One aspect of our CV response research has concerned the CV effects of *ability perception* in the behavioral challenge situation. Ability study designs and predictions have been guided by three fundamental ideas.

1. Sympathetic nervous system influence on the heart varies as a function of effort, or task engagement. This is the so-called "active coping" hypothesis advanced by the late psychophysiologist, Paul Obrist (Obrist, 1976, 1981; see also Light, 1981). In theory, the greater the effort, the more pronounced should be the sympathetic effect.

2. Effort on a task will be proportional to the difficulty of that task when success appears possible and worthwhile, given the importance of success, and low irrespective of task difficulty when success appears impossible or excessively difficult, given the importance of success. This derives from Brehm's motivational intensity theory. It implies that so long as people believe they can do what needs to be done, and that success is worth the effort, they should try harder the more difficult the task. When

people see effort as futile, or believe a task calls for more effort than it is worth, they should do nothing.

3. People who view themselves as incapable with respect to a task (low-ability people) will perceive the task as more difficult than will people who view themselves as capable with respect to the task (high-ability people). This has been suggested by a variety of writers, including Brehm (Ford & Brehm, 1987; Kukla, 1972; Meyer & Hallermann, 1977; Smith & Pope, 1992). It implies, for example, that an inexperienced carpenter should find it harder to build a storage shed than should an experienced carpenter.

Together, these ideas have a number of important implications. One is that low-ability people should evince stronger sympathetic CV responses to behavioral challenges than should high-ability people so long as they view success as possible and worthwhile. The reason is because low-ability people should exert greater effort than should high-ability people when they view success as possible and worthwhile.

A second implication is that low-ability people should sometimes evince weaker sympathetic CV responses to behavioral challenges than should high-ability people. The reason in this case is because low-ability people should withhold effort at a lower level of challenge difficulty than should high-ability people, concluding at a lower difficulty level that success is impossible or excessively difficult for them. To be precise, low-ability people should show less CV responsiveness than high-ability people when success appears impossible or excessively difficult to them, but possible and worthwhile to the high-ability group.

Still another implication of the propositions is that sympathetic CV responsiveness to behavioral challenges should sometimes be minimal regardless of ability perception. This is because even high-ability people should withhold effort if challenge difficulty is great enough. Once this difficulty level has been reached, effort should be low and equivalent for low- and high-ability groups.

Speaking broadly, these ideas imply that the relationship between ability perception and sympathetic CV response to behavioral challenges should be complex, depending on the difficulty of the challenges and the importance of success. The implied complexity is illustrated in Fig. 12.1, which plots effort (and, hence, sympathetic CV responsiveness) against difficulty for people low and high in ability perception.

Evidence

Recent reviews (Wright, 1996, 1998; Wright & Kirby, 2001) have revealed that there is a good deal of empirical support for the first two perceived ability implications previously mentioned, and some empirical support

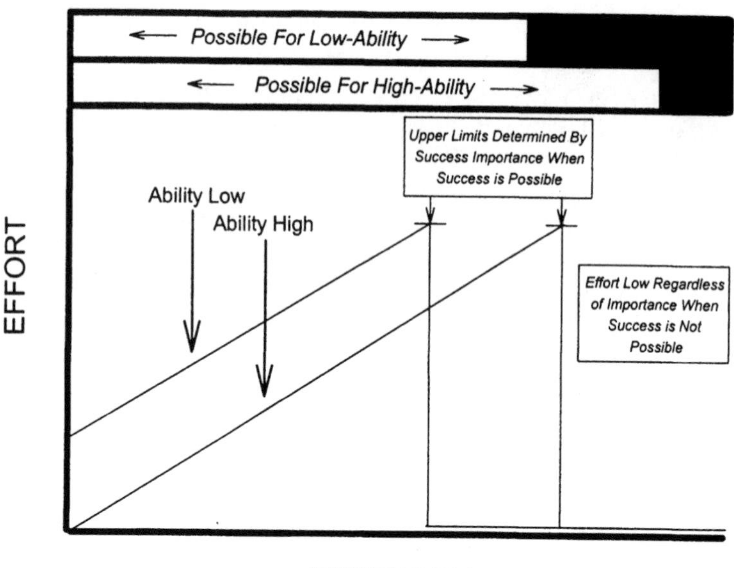

FIG. 12.1. Effort as a function of task difficulty for people with low and high perceived ability.

for the third. Typical of studies supporting the first two implications is a study by Wright and Dill (1993), which examined ability perception effects at two levels of challenge difficulty. Participants first were urged to do their best on a scanning task and then told that they had performed well in comparison to others (87th percentile) or poorly in comparison to others (12th percentile). Later, participants were presented a second scanning task and told they could earn a prize by attaining a high standard (85th percentile of other performances) or low standard (15th percentile of other performances).

Systolic blood pressure (SBP) responses assessed just before and during the second performance period were in a crossover pattern, reflecting relatively greater responsiveness for low-ability participants than for high-ability participants when the standard was low, but the reverse of that when the standard was high. The interaction was expected for SBP responses because they are partially determined by how forcefully the heart contracts, and this is determined chiefly (if not solely) by sympathetic nervous system arousal (Brownley, Hurwitz, & Schneiderman, 2000; Papillo & Shapiro, 1990). Analysis of diastolic blood pressure (DBP) responses yielded the same interaction and means in a similar crossover pattern.

Empirical support for the third implication comes from a study by Wright, Murray, Storey, and Williams (1997, Experiment 2). It began with instructions leading male and female participants to believe that one sex had greater ability than the other with respect to a certain memory task. Half of the participants were led to believe that men had greater ability (masculine task conditions) and half were led to believe women had greater ability (feminine task conditions). Once participants read the instructions, they performed the memory task with the understanding that they could earn a prize if they attained a high or extremely high performance standard. As expected, SBP responses during performance were greater for the high-ability participants (that is, men in the masculine task conditions and women in the feminine task conditions) than for the low-ability participants (that is, men in the feminine task conditions and women in the masculine task conditions) when the standard was high, but were low for both ability groups when the standard was extreme.

Although recent reviews have revealed support for the perceived ability implications we have identified, it is noteworthy that the reviews either did not consider or considered only partially three new programs of ability perception research. The new programs directly concern the impact of *mood, dispositional (i.e., trait) optimism,* and *performance resource depletion* on CV responsiveness. However, at a deeper level, they concern ability perception influence on CV response, because investigators involved in the research assume that mood, optimism, and performance resources affect CV responses by affecting ability appraisals. Conceptually, studies in the programs are similar to the Wright et al. (1997) study. In the Wright et al. study, sex served as a proxy for ability perception once the experimental instructions were delivered. In these studies, mood, optimism, and performance resources can be viewed as ability perception proxies.

The new programs of ability perception research provide important additional data relevant to the question of how ability perception influences CV responses to behavioral challenge. Moreover, they provide fresh clues about the manner in which ability perceptions are determined, an issue that is important theoretically and practically. Therefore, we consider these programs in the following sections.

Cardiovascular Influence of Mood

The most developed of the new research programs is the program concerned with CV mood effects. It has been carried out by Guido Gendolla and his colleagues in Germany. The main idea guiding studies in the program is that mood impacts CV responses not directly, but rather indirectly, by influencing appraisals of ability and difficulty, and thus ultimately task engagement. Gendolla argues that ability appraisals should tend to be lower in negative moods than in positive moods. Accordingly, difficulty appraisals should tend to be higher in negative moods than in positive moods, and mood/CV-response relations should be the same as the perceived-ability/effort relations indicated in Fig. 12.1.

Gendolla's mood analysis has been tested in studies that have assessed CV responses in two periods, one in which participants have had a positive or negative mood induced, and another in which participants have been presented a task. The general expectation has been that mood will not affect sympathetic CV responses during the first period, but will affect those responses during the second. However, precise predictions with respect to CV responsiveness during performance have depended on the nature of the assigned task and task-relevant instructions.

Simple Mood Effects. In one set of studies, participants were presented a task in the performance period with instructions to do their best (Gendolla, Abele, & Krüsken, 2001; Gendolla & Krüsken, 2001a; Gendolla & Krüsken, 2002a, Experiment 2). The investigators assumed that the task would appear more difficult to negative mood participants than to positive mood participants, but not so difficult that success would be viewed as impossible or excessively difficult, given the reasons to do well. Accordingly, they predicted that sympathetic CV responses during performance would be greater for negative mood participants than for positive mood participants.

Results consistently confirmed predictions. Consider, for example, findings obtained in the study by Gendolla et al. (2001). This study induced mood by having participants listen to (happy or sad) music or recall (happy or sad) life events, and involved letter cancellation. During mood induction, neither blood pressure nor HR responses were affected by mood. By contrast, during performance, SBP responses were inversely proportional to mood valence.

Mood × Difficulty Interactions. Two studies varied the difficulty of the task presented in the performance period. One induced mood with (happy or sad) music and involved an easy or difficult letter-cancellation task (Gendolla & Krüsken, 2001b). Difficulty was manipulated by telling participants that they would have to attain a performance standard 20% slower (easy condition) or 20% faster (difficult condition) than one they had attained in practice. As in the previous studies, there were no CV effects of mood during the induction period. However, during performance there were Mood × Difficulty interaction patterns for SBP and DBP responsiveness. When difficulty was low, pressure elevations were relatively greater for the negative mood group than for the positive mood group. On the other hand, when difficulty was high, pressure elevations were relatively greater among positive mood participants, presumably because the negative mood participants viewed the difficult task as impossible or excessively difficult.

The other mood study of this type induced mood with (happy or sad) memory recollection and involved an easy, difficult, or very difficult memorization task (Gendolla & Krüsken, 2002a, Experiment 1). The memory tasks required participants to memorize four, seven, or 20 groups of four randomized letters in 5 minutes. Again, there were no mood effects during mood induction. During performance, though, mood combined with difficulty to predict SBP responsiveness. When difficulty was low, SBP responses were relatively greater for negative mood participants than for positive mood participants. When difficulty was high, the reverse was true. And when difficulty was very high, SBP responses were relatively low for both mood groups. The latter effect was anticipated on the grounds that the very difficult task would exceed what positive and negative mood participants would or could do.

More Complex Interactions. A final pair of studies from Gendolla's laboratory (Gendolla & Krüsken, 2002b, Experiments 1 & 2) tested an implication of the ability analysis described earlier that not only had been untested in other mood studies, but also had been untested in ability studies not involving mood. The implication is that when success appears possible to both low- and high-ability groups, success importance should determine the difficulty level at which each group withholds effort and, hence, shows a relatively reduced sympathetic CV response. These studies had the same design and produced nearly identical results. Therefore, we describe only the first of the two.

CV assessments were made while participants went through a mood induction procedure, and then again later while participants performed an easy or difficult memory task. The induction technique involved watching an excerpt from a (funny or sad) film; the task was to memorize either four or seven groups of four randomized letters in 5 minutes. Success importance was manipulated by telling some participants (importance low) that a relaxation period would follow the performance period, and other participants (importance high) that a relaxation period would follow the performance period only if they did well. The latter participants were told that if they did poorly they would have to perform the memory task again.

There were four major predictions:

1. CV responses should be unaffected by the experimental variables during induction.

2. Performance period CV responses under *easy* conditions should be modest overall and stronger for negative mood participants than for posi-

tive mood participants irrespective of success importance. In making this prediction, the investigators observed that the easy task called for little effort. They also made two assumptions, that difficulty appraisals would be higher for negative than for positive mood participants, and that both negative and positive mood participants would view success as worthwhile even when importance was low.

3. Performance period CV responses under *difficult* conditions should be strong for positive mood participants irrespective of success importance. This was founded on the idea that positive mood participants would view success on the difficult task as relatively effortful, but worthwhile even when importance was low.

4. Performance period CV responses under difficult conditions should be weak for negative mood participants when importance is low, but especially strong for these participants when importance is high. The assumption here was that negative mood participants would view success on the difficult task as especially effortful, and therefore worthwhile only when importance was high.

Analysis of SBP responses yielded the predicted four-way (Mood × Difficulty × Importance × Period) interaction, with SBP means in the expected pattern (Fig. 12.2).

Summary. To summarize, Gendolla and his colleagues have collected an impressive amount of data documenting CV mood effects. The data indicate that mood does not affect CV responses directly, but can affect them by determining how much effort people exert in meeting a challenge. Patterns of CV response observed are consistent with the ideas that have guided ability perception studies in our laboratory if one assumes that ability appraisals are lower in a negative mood than in a positive mood.

Optimism Influence on CV Response

Only a step removed from Gendolla's mood research is the new program of research concerned with the influence of dispositional optimism on CV response. This research program has been carried out by Leslie Kirby and her colleagues here in the United States. Kirby assumes that just as mood should impact ability appraisals, so should dispositional optimism. Specifically, people low in dispositional optimism should tend to have lower ability appraisals than people high in dispositional optimism. If they do, then dispositional optimism should combine with difficulty to determine effort-related CV responses in the same way that mood appears to do so.

To date, Kirby has examined the CV effects of optimism in two studies (Kirby, Vaga, Penacerrada, & Wright, 2003, Studies 1 & 2). Both studies

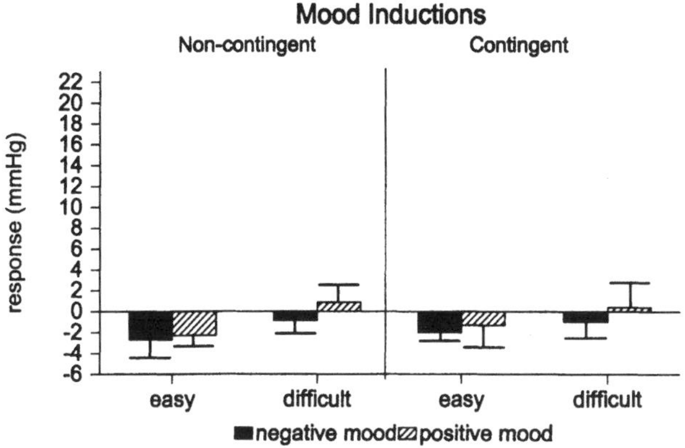

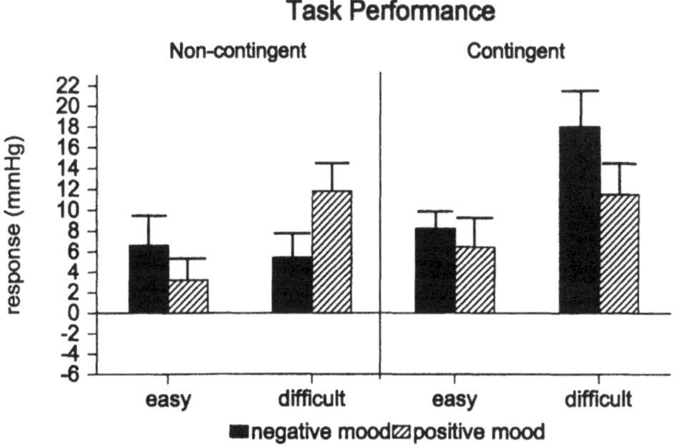

FIG. 12.2. Systolic blood pressure response (i.e., change) and standard errors during the mood induction (upper panel) and task performance (lower panel) periods for participants assigned easy and difficult tasks under conditions of low success importance (noncontingent) and high success importance (contingent). Change is measured in millimeters of mercury. From "The Joint Effect of Informational Mood Impact and Performance-Contingent Consequences of Effort-Related Cardiovascular Response," by G. H. E. Gendolla and J. Krüsken, 2002b, *Journal of Personality and Social Psychology, 83,* Figure 2. Reprinted with permission.

measured optimism by means of (college) student scores on Scheier and Carver's (1985) Life Orientation Test (LOT). The first study identified optimists as students whose LOT score fell above the median for a large group and pessimists as students whose LOT score fell below the median of the group. The second study identified optimists as students whose LOT score fell in the upper quartile of scores for a large group and pessimists as students whose LOT score fell in the lower quartile of scores for the group. Each study presented a subset of students from each LOT-defined group a

TABLE 12.1
Systolic Blood Pressure Responses of Participants Low and High in Optimism, Under Easy and Difficult Task Conditions

Optimism	*Low*		*High*	
Difficulty	*Easy*	*Difficult*	*Easy*	*Difficult*
Study 1	4.57	2.07	3.31	5.37
Study 2	6.61	–.76	1.90	3.81

Note. Responses reflect change from baseline in millimeters of mercury. Means are covariance adjusted for baseline.

series of easy or difficult anagrams, telling the students that they could avoid an unpleasant noise if they solved half.

Systolic blood pressure responses measured during anagram performance were in the expected crossover pattern, with the Optimism × Difficulty interaction approaching significance in the first study (p = .11) and attaining significance in the second (p = .006, see Table 12.1). Whereas optimistic participants showed a relative increase in responsiveness from the easy condition to the difficult condition, pessimistic participants showed the reverse. Further, whereas optimistic participants showed relatively weaker responses than pessimistic participants when the anagrams were easy, they showed relatively stronger responses than pessimistic participants when the anagrams were difficult.

Analysis of DBP responses measured during performance yielded an Optimism × Difficulty interaction (p < .05) in the first optimism study, but no effects in the second. Where the interaction was obtained, it reflected the same crossover response pattern as was observed for SBP.

Performance Resource Effects

The remaining new program of research is the one concerned with the effect of performance resource depletion on CV responsiveness. Work in it takes the view that ability perception should be diminished (and difficulty appraisals should be enhanced) to the degree that performance resources are depleted. The work also assumes that performance resource effects on ability perception should tend to be task specific, in other words, that the depletion of resources in one performance system (e.g., that involved in vocal production) should tend to affect ability perception with respect to tasks relevant to that system (e.g., singing), but not ability perception with respect to tasks irrelevant to the system (e.g., listening).

Like Kirby's optimism reasoning, the performance resource reasoning has been examined in two studies to date. The first (Wright & Penacerrada, 2002) initially required participants to make a series of easy or difficult grips on a hand dynamometer with either their right or left hand. It then required participants to make and hold with their right hand a moderately difficult dynamometer grip while CV responses were measured. Initial performance of the difficult grips with the right hand was expected to reduce participants' perceived ability to carry out the second task (right handedly), but not so much that success would appear impossible or excessively difficult. By contrast, initial performance of the difficult grips with the left hand was expected to have little, if any, impact on participants' perceived ability to carry out the second task. Therefore, it was predicted that effort-related CV responses during the second grip would be greater when the initial grips were difficult than when they were easy if the initial grips were performed right handedly, but not if the initial grips were performed left handedly.

Results for SBP supported the hypothesis. For participants who gripped initially with their right hand, responses were greater when the initial grips were difficult than when they were easy. For participants who gripped initially with their left hand, responses were unrelated to the difficulty of the initial grips.

The second performance resource study (Wright, Martin, & Bland, 2003) had two main purposes: (a) to partially replicate CV findings from the original resource study using a cognitive task, and (b) to extend the original study by examining CV depletion effects at low and high levels of challenge difficulty. The latter purpose was deemed especially important because the ability analysis implies that resource effects should vary depending on the difficulty of the challenge with which people are confronted. So long as success appears possible and worthwhile to groups who are more and less resource depleted, effort and associated CV responses should be greater for the more depleted group. However, when success appears possible and worthwhile to the less depleted group, but not to the more depleted group, effort and associated CV responses should be greater for the less depleted group.

Participants initially performed an easy counting task (resource depletion low) or a hard counting task (resource depletion high) for 5 minutes. The easy task was to count forward from zero in increments of one at 5 sec intervals; the difficult task was to count backward from 375 in increments of 3 at the same time intervals. Shortly after counting, the participants were presented a series of mental arithmetic problems (task B) and told they could earn a modest prize by attaining a low performance standard (30th percentile of other performances) or a high performance standard (80th percentile of other performances).

Analysis indicated that the depletion factor interacted with the task B difficulty factor to determine SBP and DBP responses during the second performance period. Among participants for whom depletion was low, the responses were relatively stronger when task B was difficult than when task B was easy. Presumably, these participants saw success as possible and worthwhile in both difficulty conditions. Among participants for whom depletion was high, the opposite response pattern was in evidence: Responses were relatively stronger when task B was easy than when it was difficult. Presumably, these participants saw success as more difficult overall than the other participants, and both possible and worthwhile only in the easy condition.

Comments on the New Studies

Studies in the new research programs strengthen considerably the empirical case for the ability analysis outlined at the beginning of this chapter. One way they do so is by providing multiple conceptual replications of CV effects that were observed in the perceived ability studies that preceded them, using different tasks and means of establishing low and high ability groups. Effects replicated most often have been those related to the ability analysis implications described earlier that sympathetically mediated CV responses should be (1) greater for low ability people than for high ability people when challenges are relatively easy, and (2) greater for high ability people than for low ability people when challenges are relatively difficult. These have been replicated at least once within each new research program.

Also replicated was the effect observed by Wright et al. (1995, Experiment 2), pertaining to the implication that sympathetic CV responses should be low for both ability groups when challenges are very difficult to meet. This was reproduced in the mood study that presented participants an easy, difficult, or very difficult memorization task (Gendolla & Krüsken, 2002a, Experiment 1). Consistent with expectations, SBP responses were found to be low for both mood (i.e., perceived ability) groups when difficulty was very high.

A second way studies in the new programs strengthen the case for the ability analysis is by providing two tests of a fourth analysis implication, one that was not tested in prior ability perception research. The fourth implication is that success importance should determine the difficulty level at which low and high ability groups withhold effort and, hence, show a reduced sympathetic CV response when success appears possible to both groups. This was tested in the studies that crossed a mood manipulation with difficulty and success importance factors (Gendolla & Krüsken, 2002b, Experiments 1 & 2). Once again, CV findings comported with expectations, with both studies producing the predicted interaction for SBP responsiveness.

In addition to confirming and extending findings from previous ability perception studies, studies in the new research programs also provide fresh clues about the manner in which ability perceptions are determined. Specifically, the studies provide evidence that mood, dispositional optimism, and performance resources can affect ability perceptions. In doing so, they suggest that the ability perception process is likely to be complex and to involve factors that may appear superficially to be well removed from it.

The Ability Perception Process. Concerning the ability perception process, some may be tempted to conclude that mood, optimism, and performance resource factors play similar roles in it. However, we would suggest that they play somewhat different roles because they belong to different classes of factors involved in the process. One class of factors involved is factors that affect people's actual ability to perform, such as natural endowments (e.g., talents) and training (i.e., acquired skill). In theory, factors in this class should affect ability perception only to the degree that people detect their ability level. If conditions are such that people either cannot detect their ability level, or lack the will to do so, then factors in this class should have no impact on ability perception.

A separate class of factors involved in the ability perception process is factors that can affect ability judgments, but have no influence on actual ability. Examples of factors in this class are group identification (e.g., identification with men or women) and perceptual contrast. It may be argued that whereas factors in the first class should affect ability perception only to the degree that people detect their ability level, factors in this second class should affect ability perception only to the degree that people do *not* detect their ability level. When people have a firm grasp of their ability with respect to some type of activity—based, for example, on years of experience comparing their performance to the performance of others—they should be relatively or completely immune to the influence of these factors.

Performance resources affect ability directly, and therefore belong in the first class of factors above. Mood and optimism do not affect ability and therefore belong in the second class of factors. An implication is that performance resources, on the one hand, and mood and optimism, on the other, should have different potencies with respect to their influence on ability appraisals under different task conditions. Performance resources should have their strongest influence on ability appraisals under conditions conducive to ability detection. By contrast, mood and optimism should have their strongest influence on the appraisals under conditions not conducive to ability detection.

Point of Caution. Although there is good reason to believe that the mood, optimism, and resource studies ultimately demonstrate ability perception and ensuing difficulty effects, we should note that the studies did not consistently document this empirically. Not all of the studies included ability and difficulty measures. Moreover, the studies that did include these measures did not always produce the anticipated ability and difficulty appraisal effects.

The best evidence for ability and difficulty mediation of CV responses comes from Gendolla's mood experiments, which in five cases assessed and found expected differences between mood groups in ability or difficulty perception (Gendolla, Abele, & Krüsken, 2001; Gendolla & Krüsken, 2001b; Gendolla & Krüsken, 2002a, Experiment 2; Gendolla & Krüsken, 2002b, Experiments 1 & 2). The optimism and resource studies included assessments of ability or difficulty perception. However, they produced no effects of optimism or resources on those measures.

At present, we can only speculate as to why anticipated ability and difficulty effects have not been obtained consistently. It could be that perceived ability and difficulty effects are sometimes subtle and thus difficult to detect empirically (Strube, 1989). It also could be that the effects sometimes have a different phenomenology than one might first suppose. For example, diminished cognitive ability could sometimes be manifested subjectively as muddled thought instead of as a reduced capacity to perform. A worthy goal for future investigation would be to clarify this important and difficult issue.

SOCIAL MOTIVATIONAL LESSONS

This volume is concerned thematically with motivational analyses of social behavior. Therefore, it is appropriate to consider social motivational lessons that can be taken from the full body of work that we have discussed. The most obvious lesson is that ability perception should play a pivotal and varied role in determining effort and CV responsiveness (presumably indicative of energy mobilization) in people confronted with social challenges. This role becomes apparent when one considers the example of a man provided the chance to retaliate against someone who has offended him. In theory, the man's engagement and CV response levels should be a function of (1) his ability perception with respect to the specific activity that must be executed, in combination with (2) the difficulty of that activity, and (3) the importance of success. Under some conditions, increased ability perception should be associated with lower effort and CV responsiveness; under other conditions, it should be associated with higher effort and CV responsiveness; and under still other conditions, it should have no impact on effort and CV responsiveness.

It is noteworthy that the complex relationship between ability perception and CV responsiveness indicated by this work is unique in social science. Traditionally, social scientists have assumed that autonomic arousal is linearly related to ability perception, with the relation being positive when attractive contingencies are involved, and negative when aversive contingencies are involved (for elaboration, see Wright, 1998).

It is also noteworthy that the effort effects indicated by the work contrast markedly with ones assumed in some prominent social psychological theories. For example, contemporary theories of persuasive message processing assume that there is a simple relationship between ability and effort. That is, they assume that message recipients process more carefully (i.e., effortfully) when their ability to comprehend is high than when their ability to comprehend is low (Petty & Wegener, 1998). If the present reasoning is correct, message processing should sometimes be more intense for low ability people than for high ability people, and sometimes low for both groups.

Further social motivational lessons that can be taken from the work discussed are (1) that social events (e.g., an argument, which could deplete cognitive resources, or loss of a companion, which could induce sadness) can alter motivation by altering ability perception, and (2) that social motivation can be tracked physiologically. The latter lesson seems especially important because investigators interested in social behavior historically have had great difficulty verifying their motivational assumptions. Most often, social investigators have verified the assumptions by way of self-report and performance. However, self-report and performance are suspect as motivational indices for a variety of reasons. Inclusion of CV measures in social research protocols could provide convergent information that would markedly improve researchers' ability to grasp the underpinnings of effects being studied.

FINAL THOUGHTS

Students who train with Jack Brehm are exposed to an enormous amount of wisdom. Surely among the most important pieces of wisdom passed on during training is that theory is invaluable in science. Theories not only integrate seemingly disparate phenomena, they are just plain practical in the sense that they allow people to anticipate the conditions under which different effects should occur. Jack came to possess this wisdom honestly, of course. It was passed to him by his academic advisor, Leon Festinger, and passed to Festinger by Kurt Lewin.

The line of investigation that we have described here illustrates, we hope, the practicality of theory. Note that the reasoning behind the work involves two fundamental components: (1) a proposition linking effort to CV adjustment, and (2) a conceptual framework for predicting effort. The first component is of great value, indeed indispensable to the work. However, it could not be taken far without the second component. Knowledge that variable A impacts variable B is of use only insofar as one can anticipate the value of A.

Another piece of wisdom passed on during training with Jack is that science is about ideas and understanding, as opposed to the trappings of academic success. Although this may seem like a simple lesson, one does not have to look far to see that more than a few people have missed it. And even those of us who understand the lesson and have taken it to heart sometimes find ourselves pursuing goals that are out of line with it.

Jack not only absorbed and embraced the preceding lesson, he has conducted himself consistently in accord with it. Jack is famous in informal social psychology circles for his willingness *not* to publish if he believes it would be premature to do so. He also is well known for his intellectual independence, his willingness to conduct research on a shoestring budget, and his penchant for running his own study participants if he sees a need for it. Standing back, what one sees in Jack is a scientist's scientist, an investigator of great competence engaged in investigation for the sheer joy of it. Would that there were more people in the world of science like him, and that more people in that world understood the value of his kind.

ACKNOWLEDGMENTS

Preparation of this chapter was facilitated by Grant SBR97-27707 from the NSF to the first author. Portions were written while Jason Franklin was at the University of Utah. Correspondence should be sent to Rex Wright, Department of Psychology, University of Alabama at Birmingham (UAB), Birmingham AL 35294. Internet correspondence should be directed to rwright@uab.edu.

REFERENCES

Blascovich, J., & Katkin, E. S. (Eds.). (1993). *Cardiovascular reactivity to psychological stress and disease.* Washington, DC: American Psychological Association.

Brehm, J. W. (1975). *A theory of motivational suppression.* Unpublished manuscript, University of Kansas.

Brehm, J. W., & Self, E. (1989). The intensity of motivation. In M. R. Rozenweig & L. W. Porter (Eds.), *Annual review of psychology* (pp. 109–131). Palo Alto: Annual Reviews.

Brehm, J. W., Wright, R. A., Solomon, S., Silka, L., & Greenberg, J. (1983). Perceived difficulty, energization, and the magnitude of goal valence. *Journal of Experimental Social Psychology, 19*, 21–48.

Brener, J. (1987). Behavioral energetics: Some effects of uncertainty on the mobilization and distribution of energy. *Psychophysiology, 24*, 499–412.

Brownley, K. A., Hurwitz, B. E., & Schneiderman, N. (2000). Cardiovascular psychophysiology. In J. T. Cacioppo, L. G. Tassinary, & G. G. Berntson (Eds.), *Handbook of psychophysiology* (pp. 224–264). New York: Cambridge University Press.

Dembroski, T. M., Schmidt, T. H., & Blümchen, G. (1983). *Biobehavioral bases of behavior*. Basel, Switzerland: Karger.

Ford, C. E., & Brehm, J. W. (1987). Effort expenditure following failure. In C. R. Snyder & C. E. Ford (Eds.), *Coping with negative life events: Clinical and social psychological perspectives* (pp. 51–79). New York: Plenum.

Gendolla, G. H. E., Abele, A. E., & Krüsken, J. (2001). On the role of mood in the energization process. *Emotion, 1*, 12–24.

Gendolla, G. H. E., & Krüsken, J. (2001a). Mood state and cardiovascular response in active coping with an affective-regulative challenge. *International Journal of Psychophysiology, 41*, 169–180.

Gendolla, G. H. E., & Krüsken, J. (2001b). The joint impact of mood state and task difficulty on cardiovascular and electrodermal reactivity in active coping. *Psychophysiology, 38*, 548–556.

Gendolla, G. H. E., & Krüsken, J. (2002a). Mood state, task demand, and effort-related cardiovascular response. *Cognition and Emotion, 16*, 577–603.

Gendolla, G. H. E., & Krüsken, J. (2002b). The joint effect of informational mood impact and performance-contingent consequences on effort-related cardiovascular response. *Journal of Personality and Social Psychology, 83*, 271–283.

Kirby, L. D., Vaga, A., Penacerrada, D. K., & Wright, R. A. (2003). *Personality, physiology, and performance: The effects of optimism on task engagement*. Unpublished manuscript.

Kukla, A. (1972). Foundations of an attributional theory of performance. *Psychological Review, 79*, 454–470.

Light, K. C. (1981). Cardiovascular responses to effortful active coping: Implications for the role of stress in hypertension development. *Psychophysiology, 18*, 216–225.

Meyer, W. U., & Hallermann, R. (1977). Intended effort and informational value of task outcome. *Archives of Psychology, 129*, 131–140.

Obrist, P. A. (1976). The cardiovascular-behavioral interaction as it appears today. *Psychophysiology, 13*, 95–107.

Obrist, P. A. (1981). *Cardiovascular psychophysiology: A perspective*. New York: Plenum Press.

Papillo, J. F., & Shapiro, D. (1990). The cardiovascular system. In J. T. Cacioppo & L. G. Tassinary (Eds.), *Principles of psychophysiology: Physical, social, and inferential elements* (pp. 456–512). New York: Cambridge University Press.

Petty, R. E., & Wegener, D. T. (1998). Attitude change: Multiple roles for persuasion variables. In D. T. Gilbert, S. T. Fisk, & G. Lindzey (Eds.), *The handbook of social psychology* (4th ed., pp. 323–390). New York: McGraw-Hill.

Smith, C. A., & Pope, L. K. (1992). Appraisal and emotion: The interactional contributions of situational and dispositional factors. In M. S. Clark (Ed.), *Review of personality and social psychology. Vol. 14: Emotion and social behavior* (pp. 32–62). Newbury Park, CA: Sage.

Strube, M. J. (1989). Assessing subjects' construal of the laboratory situation. In N. Schneiderman, S. M. Weiss, & P. G. Kaufman (Eds.), *Handbook of research methods in cardiovascular behavioral medicine* (pp. 527–542). New York: Plenum.

Wright, R. A. (1996). Brehm's theory of motivation as a model of effort and cardiovascular response. In P. M. Gollwitzer & J. A. Bargh (Eds.), *The psychology of action: Linking cognition and motivation to behavior* (pp. 424–453). New York: Guilford.

Wright, R. A. (1998). Ability perception and cardiovascular response to behavioral challenge. In M. Kofka, G. Weary, & G. Sedek (Eds.), *Personal control in action: Cognitive and motivational mechanisms* (pp. 197–232). New York: Guilford.

Wright, R. A., & Dill, J. C. (1993). Blood pressure responses and incentive appraisals as a function of perceived ability and objective task demand. *Psychophysiology, 30,* 152–160.

Wright, R. A., & Kirby, L. D. (2001). Effort determination of cardiovascular response: An integrative analysis with applications in social psychology. In M. Zanna (Ed.), *Advances in experimental social psychology* (Vol. 33, pp. 255–307). San Diego, CA: Academic Press.

Wright, R. A., Martin, R. E., & Bland, J. L. (2003). Energy resource depletion, task difficulty, and cardiovascular response to a mental arithmetic challenge. *Psychophysiology, 40,* 98–105.

Wright, R. A., Murray, J. B., Storey, P., & Williams, B. J. (1997). Ability analysis of gender relevance and sex differences in cardiovascular response to behavioral challenge. *Journal of Personality and Social Psychology, 73,* 405–417.

Wright, R. A., & Penacerrada, D. K. (2002). Energy resource depletion, ability perception, and cardiovascular response to a behavioral challenge. *Psychophysiology, 39,* 182–187.

13

The Intensity of Motivation When the Self Is Involved: An Application of Brehm's Theory of Motivation to Effort-Related Cardiovascular Response

Guido H. E. Gendolla
University of Geneva

What determines the intensity of motivation when people are personally involved in a performance setting? Do people automatically mobilize maximal effort when their achievements have direct implications for their self-esteem, self-definition, or personal interests? Intuitively, this appears to be reasonable, because performing well is highly important under such conditions. On the other hand, there is replicated evidence that effort mobilization follows a conservation principle, at least when people pursue material goals, such as money or other valuable goods (Wright, 1996). Accordingly, people do not mobilize more effort than necessary in the goal pursuit process. Rather, effort is mobilized proportionally to the extent of demand, as was posited in the early "difficulty law of motivation" (Ach, 1935; Hillgruber, 1912).

Brehm has formulated a comprehensive theory that makes predictions about the intensity of motivation (e.g., Brehm & Self, 1989; Brehm, Wright, Solomon, Silka, & Greenberg, 1983). Regarding effort mobilization for attaining material goals, this theory has received clear and ample empirical support. However, little is known about effort mobilization in the pursuit of more abstract goals like maintaining self-esteem and trying to attain a self-definition. This lack of research is surprising because motivation has played a major role in several prominent self-theories. Relevant processes are for example self-awareness (Carver & Scheier, 1996; Duval & Wicklund, 1972), social evaluation (Cottrell, 1968; Geen & Bushman, 1989), self-esteem maintenance (Tesser, 1988), self-definition (Baumeister, 1986; Wicklund &

Gollwitzer, 1982), and terror management (Solomon, Greenberg, & Pyszczynski, 1990). But the research these approaches instigated was concerned more with the direction of motivation (i.e., what people do) than with the intensity of motivation (i.e., how vigorously they do it).

In this chapter, I argue that Brehm's motivation intensity theory is a practical and suitable framework for studying effort mobilization when the self is involved. I present and discuss preliminary research that demonstrates that effort mobilization under this performance condition in fact follows the principles outlined in Brehm's theory. Finally, I discuss alternative, although less appropriate, models of effort mobilization. The analysis starts with a definition of two central concepts—self-involvement and effort.

SELF-INVOLVEMENT

Self-involvement describes performance settings in which instrumental behavior has consequences and implications for people's self-definition, self-esteem, and personal interests. Self-involvement is very similar to ego-involvement—a concept that was introduced to psychology far earlier (e.g., Klein & Schoenfeld, 1941). There is, however, an important reason why I prefer the term self-involvement in the present analysis: Since Nicholls (1984) introduced his theory of motivation, ego-involvement has usually been reduced to only one performance condition—the external evaluation of abilities. However, according to Greenwald (1982), there are more performance settings than this one in which people become personally involved. These settings include people's personal interest in performing a task. Personal interest—a strong motivational variable (Izard, 1977; Silvia, 2001)—has nothing to do with ego-involvement in Nicholls' (1984) theory.

Self-involving performance conditions can be distinguished from conditions under which people strive for the *proximal* goal to attain concrete material (e.g., money) or physical (e.g., avoidance of pain) incentives, which have *no* direct implications for their self-definition, self-esteem, or personal interests. It has, however, also been argued that virtually any sort of goal striving has some sort of *distal* relevance for the self, because it refers to high-ranking, abstract self-related goals like subjective well-being (Geen, 1995). This is, of course, a maintainable position. But performance settings differ in the degree to which people's proximal goals are concrete physical incentives versus more abstract entirely self-related goals like experiencing competence (White, 1959) or satisfying personal interests (Deci & Ryan, 1985). Referring to proximal self-relevance, Greenwald (1982) has proposed three performance settings under which the self is involved. These are (1) *social evaluation* of one's abilities, (2) *self-evaluation* under self-awareness, and (3) personal importance or attraction of behaviors by means of their relation to personal *interests and values.*

EFFORT

Effort is defined as the mobilization of resources to carry out instrumental behavior (Brehm & Self, 1989). It primarily refers to the intensity aspect of motivation. In the goal striving process, effort is necessary to overcome obstacles and deterrents, which represent barriers between the person and the pursued goal. According to the "difficulty law of motivation" (Ach, 1935; Hillgruber, 1912), effort is thus mobilized proportionally to the difficulty of instrumental behavior—the more effort is necessary the more difficult it is to perform. Effort has been considered as a central aspect of goal-directed behavior in virtually all comprehensive models of human goal striving (e.g., Ach, 1935; Bandura, 1986; Carver & Scheier, 1996; Dewey, 1897; Gollwitzer, 1993; Heckhausen, 1977; Kuhl, 1985; Locke & Latham, 1990; McClelland, 1985). In such comprehensive models, effort needs to be mobilized for attaining goals once people have decided or agreed to pursue them. Brehm's motivation intensity theory explains how this takes place.

MOTIVATION INTENSITY THEORY

According to Brehm (e.g., Brehm et al., 1983; Brehm & Self, 1989), effort has the function to facilitate instrumental behavior. Consequently, the intensity of effort is determined by the difficulty of instrumental behavior, because effort is mobilized to overcome obstacles in the goal striving process. Difficulty levels can vary from very low to very high, actually impossible, levels; and difficulty can be unspecified, especially when people are confronted with unfamiliar demands. The model is built on the important premise that the organism follows a conservation principle, according to which only the necessary effort is mobilized. Drawing on the "difficulty law of motivation" (Ach, 1935; Hillgruber, 1912), it follows that effort is mobilized proportionally to the extent of difficulty up to the point where task difficulty is so high that goal attainment is impossible. When this point is accomplished, no more effort is mobilized and the person disengages.

Later, I discuss that other models have also been built on the "difficulty law of motivation" (e.g., Heider, 1958; Kukla, 1972; Locke & Latham, 1990). Compared with these approaches, Brehm's model makes more comprehensive predictions: It considers the role of incentive (or the importance of goal attainment) and also makes predictions for effort mobilization under conditions of unclear task difficulty.

Incentive defines the level of *potential motivation*, which reflects the maximum of energy a person is willing to expend for goal attainment. Potential motivation is defined by variables that traditional motivation research has posited as direct determinants of the intensity of motivation (see Heckhausen, 1991). When task difficulty is unclear, the level of potential motivation determines effort mobilization. But this is the only condition under which incentive directly governs the intensity of motivation. When task difficulty is clear, engagement rises proportionally to task difficulty up to a point where (a) deterrents are so high that goal attainment is actually impossible or (b) the magnitude of necessary energy is no longer justified by an outcome's importance.

Applying Motivation Intensity Theory to Self-Involving Performance Conditions

Brehm's model is well supported for performance conditions that promise concrete or physical incentives (see Brehm & Self, 1989; Wright, 1996; Wright & Brehm, 1989; Wright & Kirby, 2001). However, relatively little is known about performance conditions that include social evaluation of one's abilities, self-evaluation under self-awareness, or personal importance of behaviors by means of their relation to personal interests and values—the conditions that lead to self-involvement (cf. Greenwald, 1982).

According to the present analysis, self-involvement refers to the level of potential motivation in Brehm's model. Thus, with regard to effort mobilization, there is no qualitative difference between self-involving and non-self-involving performance conditions. In either case, effort mobilization will be determined by the interplay between potential motivation (defined by the extent of self-involvement) and task difficulty. As presented in Fig. 13.1, individuals are willing to expend more effort when self-involvement is high than when self-involvement is low. However, whether they do so depends on the level of subjective task difficulty. Consequently, individuals should generally only mobilize low effort when self-involvement is low, because high effort is not justified under this condition. People should also mobilize only low effort when task difficulty is low, because performing easy tasks requires only low effort regardless of the magnitude of self-involvement. When task difficulty is unclear, the

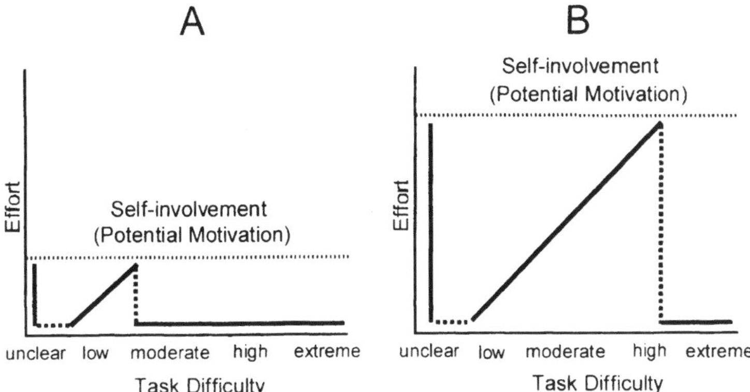

FIG. 13.1. Theoretical predictions of the joint impact of task difficulty and self-involvement on effort mobilization. Panel A shows predictions for effort mobilization when self-involvement is low. Panel B shows predictions for the condition that self-involvement is high.

level of potential motivation determines effort directly. Thus, high effort should only be mobilized when task difficulty is high or unclear under self-involving performance conditions.

Measuring Effort

Researchers have applied several methods to measure effort. Unfortunately, most of these are problematic. *Self-report measures* of effort expenditure (e.g., Meyer & Hallermann, 1977) are especially vulnerable for self-presentational influence. Research on self-handicapping has found that people report intentions to withdraw effort when it is possible to fail an important challenge (e.g., Pyszczynski & Greenberg, 1983; Rhodewalt & Fairfield, 1991). In addition to the general validity problems of self-reports (Nisbett & Wilson, 1977; Silvia & Gendolla, 2001), this is particularly problematic for self-reported effort for difficult tasks. *Persistence*, another potential indicator (e.g., Feather, 1961), is also ambiguous, because it raises the question of whether a person who works persistently with low intensity should be considered expending more effort than another person who works briefly but intensively. Moreover, persistence provides no information about the intensity of motivation in one specific moment.

Still another potential indicator of effort that has been used by researchers is *achievement*. At first glance, this may seem to be an appropriate measure—several models of motivation have linked achievement directly to the intensity of motivation (e.g., Ach, 1910; Atkinson, 1957; Eisenberger, 1992; Kukla, 1972; Locke & Latham, 1990). Effort and achievement are, however, not interchangeable concepts. Effort refers to the mobilization of resources to carry out instrumental behavior; achievement describes (only) the outcome of instrumental behavior. As demonstrated in experiments by Wright (1998), persons with high task-related abilities will expend only little effort but will nevertheless perform well, whereas persons with lower abilities have to expend high effort without any guarantee that this will bring return. The same effects occur when people perform in negative (higher subjective difficulty) or positive (lower subjective difficulty) moods (e.g., Gendolla, Abele, & Krüsken, 2001; Gendolla & Krüsken, 2001, 2002). Thus, effort expenditure does not automatically result in achievement. This is also evident in research on "overmotivation" (e.g., Heckhausen & Strang, 1988).

Cardiovascular Reactivity

In contrast to the approaches discussed so far, cardiovascular reactivity—changes in the activity of the cardiovascular system in the context of performance—is a more reliable and valid measure of the intensity of motivation. Drawing on pioneering work by Obrist (1976, 1981), there is now cumulative evidence that cardiovascular activity reflects not only physical effort (e.g., Wood & Hokanson, 1965) but also mental effort (see Wright, 1996, 1998; Wright & Kirby, 2001 for reviews).

Customary indices of cardiovascular activity are heart rate (HR, i.e., the frequency of pulse beats within a specific period of time), systolic blood pressure (SBP, i.e., the maximum pressure against the vessel walls following a heartbeat), and diastolic blood pressure (DBP, i.e., the minimum pressure between two heartbeats). As discussed by Wright (1996), these indices differ in their reliability as indicators of effort. SBP is determined by the contractility of the heart muscle and the resistance in the blood vessels (Obrist, 1981). Contractility is directly linked to the discharge of the sympathetic nervous system. Given that the sympathetic nervous system is responsible for activation and the mobilization of resources, SBP can be regarded as being systematically linked to effort mobilization. HR is affected by the independent impacts of both sympathetic and parasympathetic arousal (Berntson, Cacioppo, & Quigley, 1993). Because the parasympathetic nervous system is responsible for deactivation, HR can only reflect effort mobilization when the sympathetic impact is stronger than the parasympathetic impact—which is not always the case. Unlike SBP, DBP mainly depends on the total flow resistance in the blood vessels. DBP is not a reliable effort indictor because a sympathetic discharge increases resistance in some part of the vascular system, but decreases it in others. Thus, performance-related SBP reactivity is the most sensitive measure of effort mobilization among the cardiovascular indices discussed so far. Increases in sympathetic activity can, however, also result in simultaneous elevations of SBP, HR, and DBP (e.g., Smith, Baldwin, & Christensen, 1990).

Self-Involvement and Effort-Related Cardiovascular Response: Empirical Evidence

The theoretical predictions of Brehm's motivation intensity theory have been supported by numerous studies that have used cardiovascular reactivity as measure of the intensity of motivation (see Wright, 1996, 1998; Wright & Kirby, 2001 for reviews). However, the vast majority of these studies involved concrete material and physical operationalizations of potential motivation. Nevertheless, the research that has been conducted to date under self-involving performance conditions is supportive to the present argument that Brehm's model is well applicable to this behavioral realm.

Effects of Social Evaluation. Wright, Tunstall, Williams, Goodwin, and Harmon-Jones (1995) examined social evaluation of performance—a condition that leads to self-involvement (Greenwald, 1982). After habituation and assessment of cardiovascular baseline values, participants performed a memory task. Strings of three (easy condition) or eight (difficult condition) letters were presented on a computer screen. Each string was presented for 5 sec and followed by a blank screen lasting 2 sec. Then a target letter was presented and participants had to decide if the target letter occurred in the previously presented letter string or not. Participants were instructed to make at least 90% correct decisions. Feedback was given by the computer program after task completion.

In the social evaluation condition, participants learned that people in the control room would monitor their performance on a second computer screen and that they would consequently know if they succeeded or not. Participants in the no-evaluation condition believed that their performance would not be monitored—nobody would know if they attained the 90% criterion. The memory task was comprised of 40 trials. Cardiovascular measures were taken repeatedly in one-minute intervals during task performance. The results for SBP reactivity supported the predictions of the motivation intensity model: Reactivity in the social-evaluation/difficult condition was significantly stronger than in the other three cells, which did not differ from one another. Apparently, social evaluation defined the level of potential motivation and justified the high effort for the difficult task. In the no-evaluation conditions, potential motivation was lower and thus justified only low effort, regardless of task difficulty. However, these results were significant only for women.

Wright et al. (1995) conducted another experiment that investigated the effects of social evaluation during performance of an easy task versus a task without fixed performance standard. For the unfixed difficulty condition, it was expected that potential motivation would directly determine effort mobilization. The easy conditions were identical with Experiment 1—correctly identifying in 90% of 40 trials if a target letter had been presented in a string of three letters that was presented for 5 sec. Feedback was given after the 40 trials. In the unfixed difficulty condition, participants were also presented with three letter strings, but tried to attain 90% correct responses as fast as they could. That is, participants tried to "do-their-best" (Locke & Latham, 1990). Feedback was given after each trial. Social evaluation was manipulated in the same fashion as in Experiment 1: Participants were told that their responses could or could not be monitored by the experimenter. The pattern of performance-related SBP reactivity occurred as expected—this time for men as well as women: In the unfixed difficulty conditions, social evaluation increased reactivity. On the other hand, in the fixed (easy) conditions, evaluation had no impact—reactivity was low regardless of whether participants' responses could be monitored.

In summary, the Wright et al. (1995) studies supported the predictions of the motivation intensity model. High effort is mobilized when people perform tasks of high or unclear difficulty under the condition of social evaluation. A recent study by Wright, Killebrew, and Pimpalapure (2002) revealed corresponding results for social evaluation by high status observers. Note that social evaluation did not result in a general increase of cardiovascular arousal, as suggested by the social activation school of thought (e.g., Cottrell, 1968).

Another experiment by Wright, Dill, Geen, and Anderson (1998) involved five difficulty levels, ranging from very easy to extremely difficult. Specifically, participants performed the letter identification task and had to correctly identify at least 90% of 40 trials in which two, four, six, eight, and 10 letters were presented. Social evaluation was manipulated the same way as in the previous experiments by Wright et al. (1995). Results for SBP reactivity, which are presented in Table 13.1, supported the motivation intensity model: In the social evaluation conditions, systolic reactivity increased from the two-letter condition to the six-letters condition and then sharply decreased, describing the anticipated sawtooth-shaped curve. In the no-evaluation conditions, task difficulty had no significant impact on systolic reactivity, which was relatively low in all difficulty conditions.

The Identity–Effort Connection. An experiment by Gendolla (1998) examined another aspect of self-involvement—the extent of instrumentality of performance for accomplishing a personal identity-related goal. Ac-

TABLE 13.1
Systolic Blood Pressure Reactivity (in mmHg) During Task Performance

	Letters Per String				
Evaluation	*Two*	*Four*	*Six*	*Eight*	*Ten*
No evaluation	1.65	1.39	–0.66	0.69	–0.76
Social evaluation	0.43	3.31	4.91	1.48	0.91

Note. Task difficulty increases with the number of letters per strings. From "Social Evaluation Influence on Cardiovascular Response to a Fixed Behavioral Challenge: Effects Across a Range of Difficulty Levels," by R. A. Wright, J. C. Dill, R. G. Green, and C. A. Anderson, 1998, *Annals of Behavioral Medicine, 20,* p. 280.

cording to Baumeister (1986), people in modern Western societies have to create their identities actively on their own. Unlike previous epochs, in which an individual's place in society was automatically determined by factors like gender, social status, and the profession of the father, people nowadays (1) have to decide which identity goal they want to pursue, and (2) must invest effort to attain that goal. The experiment focused on the second process—effort mobilization.

Participants were freshmen in psychology who attended immediately before the beginning of their first term. All participants had already decided on a professional goal in the psychology realm (e.g., clinician, researcher etc.). After habituation and assessment of cardiovascular baselines, participants performed a memory task—they tried to correctly memorize a list of names within 5 minutes. For half of the participants, successful performance was relevant for attaining their pursued professional identity goal. In these conditions, participants learned that the list consisted of the names of prominent psychologists, which had to be learned in order to pass necessary examinations for a degree in psychology. That is, success brought participants closer to their identity goal—professional psychologist. The other participants were not informed about the names' connection to psychology. Additionally, task difficulty was manipulated on two levels. The list comprised eight names in the easy and 40 names in the difficult condition.

As expected and depicted in Fig. 13.2, the results supported the present application of the motivation intensity model to self-involving performance conditions: Performance-related responses of SBP and HR were high only when high identity relevance was bound up with high task difficulty. Thus, although success in the identity-relevant conditions had implications for an important life goal, participants did not mobilize more effort than necessary.

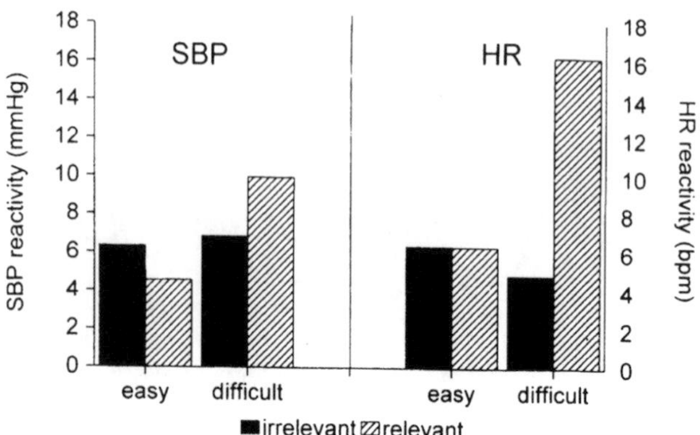

FIG. 13.2. Reactivity of systolic blood pressure (SBP) and heart rate (HR) during task performance in the experiment by Gendolla (1998).

The Classic Ego-Involvement Condition: Demonstrating a Valuable Ability. An experiment by Gendolla (1999) examined effort mobilization under another condition that leads to self-involvement: The demonstration of an important ability. After habituation and assessment of cardiovascular baselines, participants received written instructions to memorize within 5 minutes a list of random letter series, each consisting of four letters (e.g., A B C D). Furthermore, they were instructed to recall the letter series afterward and to tell the complete list to the experimenter. Thus, performance was evaluated. The level of task difficulty was manipulated through the number of letter series. These were four in the easy versus 20 in the very difficult conditions.

Providing participants with manipulated information about the task varied self-involvement. In the noninvolving conditions, participants read that the memory task was just run to bridge the time to the next experimental task. Participants in the self-involving conditions received, in contrast, the bogus information that the memory task would be conducted to test students' mnemonic abilities. Furthermore, participants in these conditions learned that numerous students would have to terminate their course of studies without a degree and that, according to recent research, the main reason for these failures would be their inability to learn under time pressure. Thus, success ostensibly indicated an ability that was important for academic mastery. During task performance, cardiovascular activity was assessed in intervals of 2 minutes, starting 30 sec after task onset.

As depicted in Fig. 13.3, the results for responses of SBP and HR supported the predictions: When task performance ostensibly reflected an important ability—effective learning under time pressure—reactivity was stronger in the difficult than in the easy condition. But when performance

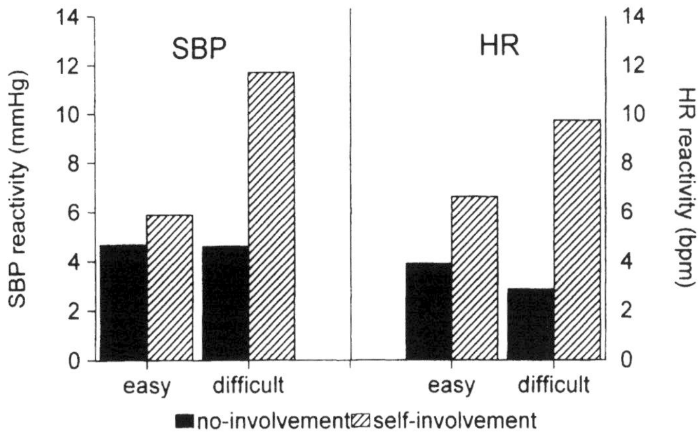

FIG. 13.3. Reactivity of systolic blood pressure (SBP) and heart rate (HR) during task performance in Experiment 1 by Gendolla (1999).

had no such diagnostic meaning, task difficulty had no impact and cardiovascular reactivity was relatively weak.

A second experiment by Gendolla (1999) was conducted to examine the task difficulty variable under self-involving performance conditions in more detail. The procedure was identical to that in the self-involving conditions of the first experiment. Task difficulty was, again, manipulated by the number of letter series (each consisting of four letters) participants tried to memorize within 5 minutes. These were two-letter series in the very easy condition, six-letter series in the moderate condition, and 20-letter series in the very difficult condition. As anticipated, performance-related reactivity of SBP, HR, and DBP increased from the easy to the moderate condition; however, reactivity on these measures dropped in the very difficult condition. This curvilinear shape of the effort function was unexpected and may suggest that the highest effort was mobilized on an intermediate difficulty level—as predicted in other approaches (e.g., Atkinson, 1957; Meyer, 1984). But the unexpected drop in effort-related cardiovascular reactivity in the difficult condition is also explicable by another process: In the very difficult condition, some of the participants learned while performing that is was impossible to succeed and consequently disengaged. This may have resulted, on average, in a slight drop in effort mobilization compared to the moderately difficult condition.

In order to test these possibilities, Gendolla and Richter (2002) conducted another experiment in which self-involvement was manipulated in the same fashion as in the first experiment by Gendolla (1999). Participants learned that the memory task was either a test that reflected an important ability—learning under time pressure—or believed that it was

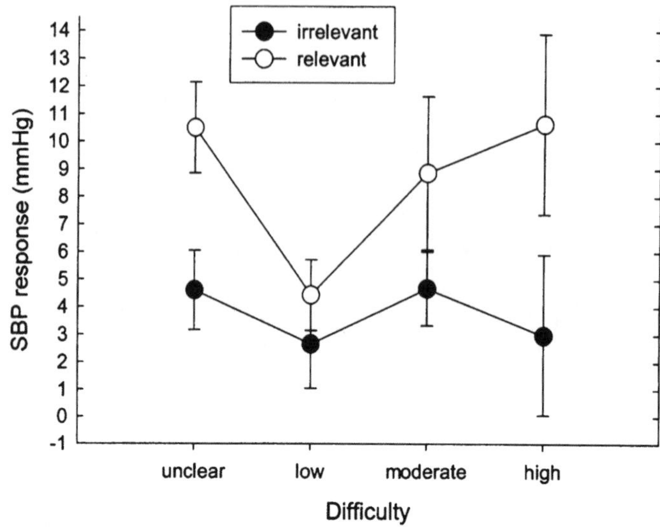

FIG. 13.4. Reactivity of systolic blood pressure (SBP) during task performance in the experiment by Gendolla and Richter (2002).

only a filler without diagnostic meaning. Task difficulty was manipulated on four levels. Participants were asked to memorize within 5 minutes two- (very easy), six- (moderately difficult), or 15- (very difficult) letter series, or were instructed to memorize as much as they could from the list of 15 series (unclear). As presented in Fig. 13.4, the results for SBP-reactivity during task performance clearly supported the predictions. In the non-self-involving conditions, no significant differences emerged between the four difficulty cells. But in the self-involving condition, SBP-reactivity was high in the unclear difficulty condition where participants were instructed to memorize as many items correctly as they could, and increased, as anticipated, from the very easy to the very difficult condition. The unclear and the very difficult conditions did not differ, suggesting that participants in these conditions mobilized effort up to the level of potential motivation, which was defined by the extent of self-involvement of performance. Thus, effort-related SBP reactivity exactly described the predicted nonlinear function.

Empirical Evidence: Summary

Drawing on Greenwald's (1982) analysis, I have proposed that three variables especially lead to self-involvement—social evaluation of own abilities, self-evaluation under self-awareness, and personal importance of performance through its relation to personal interests and values. Except for the effects of self-awareness on effort mobilization, there is evidence that the predictions of Brehm's motivation intensity theory (e.g., Brehm et al., 1983; Brehm & Self, 1989) apply to self-involving performance conditions. There is clear support for the assumptions that effort is mobilized proportionally to the extent of subjective task difficulty when performance is socially evaluated (Wright et al., 1995, 2002) and that social evaluation defines the level of potential motivation in this process. The same holds true when performance is relevant for accomplishing a personal identity goal (Gendolla, 1998), and when a personally important ability is evaluated (Gendolla, 1999; Gendolla & Richter, 2002). That is, the "difficulty law of motivation" (Ach, 1935; Hillgruber, 1912) applies also to self-involving performance conditions—an empirical fact that has been doubted in other approaches, as is now discussed.

SELF-INVOLVEMENT AND EFFORT: ALTERNATIVE MODELS

Direct Incentive Effects

Some authors have suggested that reward directly determines effort mobilization (e.g., Eisenberger, 1992; Fowles, 1983). Referring to self-involving performance conditions, this suggests that self-involvement directly determines effort because self-involvement makes success more important. However, as demonstrated in the studies previously discussed (Gendolla, 1998, 1999; Gendolla & Richter, 2002; Wright et al., 1995, 1998, 2002), this is not the case. As predicted by Brehm's motivation intensity model, a direct effect of incentive on the intensity of motivation occurred only when difficulty was unclear, rather than in general.

Attributional Theory of Performance. Several predictions of Kukla's (1972) model come close to Brehm's theory—especially in regard to its application to ability (Wright, 1998) and to mood effects (Gendolla & Krüsken, 2001). Both approaches are built on the "difficulty law of motivation" (Ach, 1935; Hillgruber, 1912) and share the idea that effort is proportionally mobilized to the extent of subjective task difficulty. Given that ability and effort have a compensational relationship (Heider, 1958), people with low ability need to mobilize more effort to accomplish a performance standard than people with high ability. If subjective difficulty is so high that goal attainment appears to be impossible, no more effort will be mobilized and the person will disengage. Due to the ability effect on subjective difficulty, people with low ability meet this point earlier than people with high ability.

Although Kukla's model and Brehm's theory share these basic ideas (see Wright, 1998), the predictions of the motivation intensity model are much more comprehensive: First, unlike the motivation intensity model, Kukla's model is silent on the effects of incentive in the process of effort mobilization. Consequently, Kukla's model cannot account for the demonstrated self-involvement effects discussed earlier. Second, Kukla's model makes no predictions about what happens when no clear performance standard is provided. Thus, the model cannot explain why people mobilize high effort when task difficulty is unclear, as has been previously demonstrated (e.g., Gendolla & Richter, 2002; Wright et al., 1995, 2002).

Goal-Setting Theory. Like the motivation intensity model, Locke and Latham's (1990) theory of goal setting and performance states that effort is mobilized proportional to subjective task difficulty, as posited in the "difficulty law of motivation" (Ach, 1935; Hillgruber, 1912). But in contrast to Brehm's model, goal-setting theory is silent about the role of incentive. This leads to a profound difference between the motivation intensity model and goal-setting theory in regard to the motivational effects of tasks without a clear performance standard. According to Locke and Latham, motivation is less intense if people perform tasks without a clear performance standard ("do-your-best") than when they perform a difficult task, that is, a task with a clear and high performance standard. But, as previously discussed, these conditions will produce the same effort effects (e.g., Gendolla & Richter, 2002; Wright et al., 1995). Consequently, goal-setting theory cannot account for the effects of self-involvement on effort mobilization.

Ego/Task Involvement. Other researchers have cast doubt on the generality of the "difficulty law of motivation." Nicholls (1984) and Dweck (1986) have proposed a differentiated view of effort mobilization under self-involving versus non-self-involving conditions, which is particularly important in the present context. Accordingly, the difficulty–effort relationship is only proportional when people *do not* try to demonstrate their abilities. The difficulty law of motivation is assumed to apply only to performance settings in which people want to learn about their abilities. This is supposed to be the case whenever people have a personal interest in performing a task (i.e., "task involvement" according to Nicholls, "learning goal" according to Dweck).

From this perspective, it is senseless to mobilize effort proportionally to the extent of subjective demand when people want to demonstrate their abilities (i.e., "ego involvement" according to Nicholls, "performance goal" according to Dweck). The reason is that abilities are best demonstrated by social comparison with others and not by mobilizing effort, according to Nicholls and Dweck. High-effort mobilization for a valuable or a difficult goal may even imply low ability in the eye of the beholder (Heider, 1958). Consequently, people may even strategically withdraw effort under this condition. There are, however, no data that directly refer to effort mobilization in support of this assumption. Rather, our studies on effort mobilization under conditions that correspond to ego involvement clearly speak against these predictions and suggest that Brehm's theory applies to all performance settings (Gendolla, 1999; Gendolla & Richter, 2002).

Risk-Taking Model. According to Atkinson (1957), people mobilize the highest effort to perform on intermediate task difficulty levels—if they cannot choose the preferred difficulty level on their own and if it is not possible "to leave the field." The reason is that people will try to attain the most positive affective reaction to their achievement when tasks are assigned rather than freely chosen. This is the case at intermediate difficulty levels because here the product of the probability of success (*P*s = .50) and incentive (1 – *P*s = .50) is maximal. However, if people can choose among tasks with different difficulty levels, only success-oriented individuals will prefer intermediate difficulty levels and mobilize the highest effort. Individuals who are oriented to the avoidance of failure will avoid such tasks in order to minimize negative affect.

Although the risk-taking model has instigated intensive research, most of the studies were concerned with task preferences in choice situations rather than with the intensity of motivation. Most relevant, there are no data that directly support the predictions about effort mobilization (Heckhausen, 1991), which differ from those of Brehm's model. The studies discussed here on self-involvement are hardly explicable in terms of the risk-taking model, because effort was most intense on high and unclear tasks rather than on intermediate difficulty levels.

Self-Concept of Ability. The effort-related predictions of this approach (Meyer, 1973, 1984) are similar to those of Kukla's (1972) model. Meyer assumed that effort is mobilized proportionally to the extent of subjective task difficulty and that subjective task difficulty is in turn determined by the discrepancy between objective task difficulty and people's beliefs about their actual ability. Like the motivation intensity model, this fits the "difficulty law of motivation." But Meyer made a substantial extension: Unlike other researchers (Dweck, 1986; Nicholls, 1984), he assumed that people *always* strive for reliable information about their actual abilities—a notion that has also been posited by other researchers (e.g.,

Festinger, 1954; Schneider, 1973; Trope, 1975; Weiner, 1986). This leads to the prediction that the effort function peaks at the subjectively intermediate level, because performance outcomes that are here attained under maximal effort expenditure are most diagnostic for an evaluation of one's actual ability.

Self-report data about the level of intended effort in face of demands have supported this reasoning (Meyer & Hallermann, 1977). As discussed earlier, such measures of effort have, however, their own problems. It is well conceivable that self-report measures of effort mobilization describe an inverted U-function, because effort is only ostensibly reduced on high difficulty levels. The reason could be a self-handicapping strategy: Reporting to withdraw effort on threatening high difficulty levels facilitates an attribution of potential failure to a lack of effort, rather than on a self-esteem threatening lack of ability (e.g., Pyszczynski & Greenberg, 1983; Rhodewalt & Fairfield, 1991). Likewise, success on high difficulty levels under the condition of ostensibly reduced effort facilitates an attribution to high ability (cf. Dweck, 1986; Nicholls, 1984), because the relationship between effort and ability is reciprocal (Heider, 1958). The studies discussed here on self-involvement as well as other studies on ability effects (Wright, 1998), have supported the motivation intensity model, rather than Meyer's predictions.

SUMMARY AND CONCLUSIONS

The present chapter highlights the question of what determines the intensity of motivation when people pursue goals that have direct implications for their self-esteem, their self-definition, or their personal interests. I argue that applying Brehm's motivation intensity theory (e.g., Brehm et al., 1983; Brehm & Self, 1989) to these self-involving performance conditions facilitates predictions, which differs from the most other approaches (e.g, Atkinson, 1957; Dweck, 1986; Meyer, 1984; Nicholls, 1984). Accordingly, the extent of self-involvement determines (only) the maximal amount of effort people are willing to mobilize in order to attain their goals, whereas the actual intensity of motivation is a direct function of the extent of subjective task difficulty as posited in the "difficulty law of motivation" (Ach, 1935; Hillgruber, 1912). The only condition under which effort is directly determined by the extent of self-involvement is when task difficulty is unclear. The preliminary experimental evidence discussed in this chapter clearly supports these predictions and suggests that effort mobilization takes place under a conservation principle according to which people do not mobilize more effort than is necessary for goal attainment. Thus, Brehm's model has proven its applicability to self-involving performance conditions and provides a general theoretical explanation for effort mobilization in all performance contexts; indeed a very practical theory.

ACKNOWLEDGMENTS

Preparation of the present chapter was supported by a research grant from the Deutsche Forschungsgemeinschaft (Ge 987/3–1). I would like to thank Andrea Abele, Michael Richter, Paul Silvia, and Rex Wright for valuable comments on a previous version of this chapter and I am indebted to Robert Wicklund for helpful advice on early stages of research presented here.

REFERENCES

Ach, N. (1910). *Über den Willensakt und das Temperament* [About the act of will and temperament]. Leipzig, Germany: Quelle und Meyer.

Ach, N. (1935). Analyse des Willens [Analysis of the will]. In E. Abderhalden (Ed.), *Handbuch der biologischen Arbeitsmethoden*. Berlin, Germany: Urban & Schwarzenberg.

Atkinson, J. W. (1957). Motivational determinants of risk-taking behavior. *Psychological Review, 64*, 359–372.

Bandura, A. (1986). *Social foundations of thought and action*. Englewood Cliffs, NJ: Prentice-Hall.

Baumeister, R. F. (1986). *Identity: Cultural change and the struggle for self.* New York: Oxford University Press.

Berntson, G. G., Cacioppo, J. T., & Quigley, K. S. (1993). Cardiac psychophysiology and autonomic space in humans: Empirical perspectives and conceptual implications. *Psychological Bulletin, 114*, 296–322.

Brehm, J. W., & Self, E. A. (1989). The intensity of motivation. *Annual Review of Psychology, 40*, 109–131.

Brehm, J. W., Wright, R. A., Solomon, S., Silka, L., & Greenberg, J. (1983). Perceived difficulty, energization, and the magnitude of goal valence. *Journal of Experimental Social Psychology, 19*, 21–48.

Carver, C. S., & Scheier, M. F. (1996). *On the self-regulation of behavior*. New York: Cambridge University Press.

Cottrell, N. B. (1968). Performance in the presence of other human beings: Mere presence, audience, and affiliation effects. In E. C. Simmel, R. A. Hoppe, & G. A. Milton (Eds.), *Social facilitation and imitative behavior* (pp. 91–110). Boston, MA: Allyn & Bacon.

Deci, E. L., & Ryan, R. M. (1985). *Intrinsic motivation and self-determination in human behavior*. New York: Plenum.

Dewey, J. (1897). The psychology of effort. *Psychological Review, 6*, 43–56.

Duval, T. S., & Wicklund, R. A. (1972). *A theory of objective self-awareness*. New York: Academic Press.

Dweck, C. S. (1986). Motivational processes affecting learning. *American Psychologist, 41*, 1040–1048.

Eisenberger, R. (1992). Learned industriousness. *Psychological Review, 99*, 248–267.

Feather, N. T. (1961). The relationship of persistence at a task to expectation of success and achievement related motives. *Journal of Abnormal and Social Psychology, 63*, 552–561.

Festinger, L. (1954). A theory of social comparison processes. *Human Relations, 7*, 114–140.

Fowles, D. C. (1983). Motivational effects on heart rate and electrodermal activity: Implications for research on personality and psychopathology. *Journal of Research in Personality, 17*, 48–71.

Geen, R. G. (1995). *Human motivation.* Belmont, CA: Brooks/Cole.

Geen, R. G., & Bushman, B. J. (1989). The arousing effects of social presence. In H. Wagner & A. Manstead (Eds.), *Handbook of social psychophysiology* (pp. 262–281). London, UK: Wiley.

Gendolla, G. H. E. (1998). Effort as assessed by motivational arousal in identity relevant tasks. *Basic and Applied Social Psychology, 20*, 111–121.

Gendolla, G. H. E. (1999). Self-relevance of performance, task difficulty, and task engagement assessed as cardiovascular response. *Motivation and Emotion, 23*, 45–66.

Gendolla, G. H. E., Abele, A. E., & Krüsken, J. (2001). The informational impact of mood on effort mobilization: A study of cardiovascular and electrodermal responses. *Emotion, 1*, 12–24.

Gendolla, G. H. E., & Krüsken, J. (2001). The joint impact of mood state and task difficulty on cardiovascular and electrodermal reactivity in active coping. *Psychophysiology, 38*, 548–556.

Gendolla, G. H. E., & Krüsken, J. (2002). The joint effect of informational mood impact and performance-contingent incentive on effort-related cardiovascular response. *Journal of Personality and Social Psychology, 83*, 271–285.

Gendolla, G. H. E., & Richter, M. (2002, March). *Ich-Involvierung und anstrengungsbezogene kardiovaskuläre Reaktivität.* [Ego-involvement and effort-related cardiovascular reactivity]. Talk at the 44th Tagung experimentell arbeitender Psychologen, Technical University Chemnitz, Germany.

Gollwitzer, P. (1993). Goal achievement: The role of intentions. In W. Stroebe & M. Hewstone (Eds.), *European review of social psychology* (Vol. 4, pp. 141–185). London: Wiley.

Greenwald, A. G. (1982). Ego task analysis: An integration of research in ego-involvement and self-awareness. In A. H. Hastorf & A. M. Isen (Eds.), *Cognitive social psychology* (pp. 109–147). New York: Elsevier/North-Holland.

Heckhausen, H. (1977). Achievement motivation and its constructs. *Motivation and Emotion, 1*, 283–329.

Heckhausen, H. (1991). *Motivation and action.* New York: Springer.

Heckhausen, H., & Strang, H. (1988). Efficiency under maximal performance demands: Exertion control, an individual difference variable? *Journal of Personality and Social Psychology, 55*, 489–498.

Heider, F. (1958). *The psychology of interpersonal relations.* New York: Wiley.

Hillgruber, A. (1912). *Fortlaufende Arbeit und Willensbetätigung* [Continuous work and will activity]. Leipzig: Quelle und Meyer.

Izard, C. E. (1977). *Human emotions.* New York: Plenum Press.

Klein, G. S., & Schoenfeld, N. (1941). The influence of ego-involvement on confidence. *Journal of Abnormal and Social Psychology, 36*, 249–258.

Kuhl, J. (1985). Volitional mediators of cognitive-behavior consistency: Self-regulatory processes and action versus state orientation. In J. Kuhl & J. Beckmann (Eds.), *Action control: From cognition to behavior* (pp. 101–128). Berlin, Germany: Springer.

Kukla, A. (1972). Foundations of an attributional theory of performance. *Psychological Review, 79*, 454–470.

Locke, E. A., & Latham, G. P. (1990). *A theory of goal setting and performance.* Englewood Cliffs, NJ: Prentice Hall.

McClelland, D. C. (1985). How motives, skills, and values determine what people do. *American Psychologist, 40*, 812–825.

Meyer, W.-U. (1973). Anstrengungsintention in Abhängigkeit von Begabungseinschätzung und Aufgabenschwierigkeit [Intended effort in dependence of estimated ability and task difficulty]. *Archiv für Psychologie, 125*, 245–262.

Meyer, W.-U. (1984). *Das Konzept von der eigenen Begabung* [The self-concept of ability]. Stuttgart: Huber.

Meyer, W.-U., & Hallermann, B. (1977). Intended effort and informational value of task outcome. *Archiv für Psychologie, 129*, 131–140.

Nicholls, J. G. (1984). Achievement motivation: Conceptions of ability, subjective experience, task choice, and performance. *Psychological Review, 91*, 328–346.

Nisbett, R. E., & Wilson, T. D. (1977). Telling more than we know: Verbal reports on mental processes. *Psychological Review, 84*, 231–259.

Obrist, P. A. (1976). The cardiovascular-behavioral interaction as it appears today. *Psychophysiology, 13*, 95–107.

Obrist, P. A. (1981). *Cardiovascular psychophysiology*. New York: Plenum.

Pyszczynski, T., & Greenberg, J. (1983). Determinants of reduction in intended effort as a strategy for coping with anticipated failure. *Journal of Research in Personality, 17*, 412–422.

Rhodewalt, F., & Fairfield, M. (1991). Claimed self-handicaps and the self-handicapper: The relation of reduction in intended effort to performance. *Journal of Research in Personality, 25*, 402–417.

Schneider, K. (1973). *Motivation unter Erfolgsrisiko* [Motivation under the risk of success]. Göttingen, Germany: Hogrefe.

Silvia, P. J. (2001). Interest and interests: The psychology of constructive capriciousness. *Review of General Psychology, 5*, 270–290.

Silvia, P. J., & Gendolla, G. H. E. (2001). On introspection and self-perception: Does self-focused attention enable accurate self-knowledge? *Review of General Psychology, 5*, 241–269.

Solomon, S., Greenberg, J., & Pyszczynski, T. (1990). A terror management theory of social behavior: The psychological functions of self-esteem and cultural worldviews. In L. Berkowitz (Ed.), *Advances in experimental social psychology* (Vol. 24, pp. 93–159). New York: Academic Press.

Smith, T. W., Baldwin, M., & Christensen, A. J. (1990). Interpersonal influence as active coping: Effects of task difficulty on cardiovascular reactivity. *Psychophysiology, 27*, 429–437.

Tesser, A. (1988). Toward a self-evaluation maintenance model of social behavior. In M. P. Zanna (Ed.), *Advances in experimental social psychology* (Vol. 21, pp. 181–228). New York: Academic Press.

Trope, Y. (1975). Seeking information about one's own ability. *Journal of Personality and Social Psychology, 32*, 1004–1013.

Weiner, B. (1986). *An attributional theory of motivation and emotion*. New York: Springer.

Wicklund, R. A., & Gollwitzer, P. M. (1982). *Symbolic self completion*. Hillsdale, NJ: Lawrence Erlbaum Associates.

White, R. W. (1959). Motivation reconsidered: The concept of competence. *Psychological Review, 66*, 297–333.

Wood, C. G., & Hokanson, J. E. (1965). Effects of induced muscular tension on performance and the inverted U function. *Journal of Personality and Social Psychology, 1*, 506–510.

Wright, R. A. (1996). Brehm's theory of motivation as a model of effort and cardiovascular response. In P. M. Gollwitzer & J. A. Bargh (Eds.), *The psychology of action: Linking cognition and motivation to behavior* (pp. 424–453). New York: Guilford.

Wright, R. A. (1998). Ability perception and cardiovascular response to behavioral challenge. In M. Kofta, G. Weary, & G. Sedek (Eds.), *Personal control in action: Cognitive and motivational mechanisms* (pp. 197–232). New York: Plenum.

Wright, R. A., & Brehm, J. W. (1989). Energization and goal attractiveness. In L. A. Pervin (Ed.), *Goal concepts in personality and social psychology* (pp. 169–210). Hillsdale, NJ: Lawrence Erlbaum Associates.

Wright, R. A., Dill, J. C., Geen, R. G., & Anderson, C. A. (1998). Social evaluation influence on cardiovascular response to a fixed behavioral challenge: Effects across a range of difficulty levels. *Annals of Behavioral Medicine, 20,* 277–285.

Wright, R. A., Killebrew, K., & Pimpalapure, D. (2002). Cardiovascular incentive effects where a challenge is unfixed: Demonstrations involving social evaluation, evaluator status, and monetary reward. *Psychophysiology, 39,* 188–197.

Wright, R. A., & Kirby, L. D. (2001). Effort determination of cardiovascular response: An integrative analysis with applications in social psychology. In M. P. Zanna (Ed.), *Advances in experimental social psychology* (Vol. 33, pp. 255–307). New York: Academic Press.

Wright, R. A., Tunstall, A. M., Williams, B. J., Goodwin, J. S., & Harmon-Jones, E. (1995). Social evaluation and cardiovascular response: An active coping approach. *Journal of Personality and Social Psychology, 69,* 530–543.

14

The Self-Regulation of Goal Pursuit

Gabriele Oettingen
Caterina Bulgarella
Marlone Henderson
Peter M. Gollwitzer
New York University

Goal pursuit starts with setting goals for oneself or with adopting goals assigned by others. Most theories of motivation (Ajzen, 1991; Atkinson, 1957; Bandura, 1997; Brehm & Self, 1989; Carver & Scheier, 1998; Gollwitzer, 1990; Locke & Latham, 1990; Sheeran, 2002; Vroom, 1964) suggest that people prefer to choose and adopt goals that are desirable and feasible. Desirability is determined by the estimated attractiveness of likely short-term and long-term consequences of goal attainment. Such consequences may pertain to anticipated self-evaluations, evaluations of significant others, progress toward some higher order goal, external rewards of having attained the goal, and the joy/pain associated with moving toward the goal (Heckhausen, 1977). Feasibility depends on people's judgments of their capabilities to perform relevant goal-directed behaviors (i.e., self-efficacy expectations; Bandura, 1997), their beliefs that these goal-directed behaviors will lead to the desired outcome (i.e., outcome expectations; Bandura, 1997; instrumentality beliefs, Vroom, 1964), the judged likelihood of attaining the desired outcome (i.e., general expectations; Oettingen, 1996) or desired outcomes in general (optimism; Scheier & Carver, 1987).

It is implicitly assumed that perceived feasibility and desirability not only affect goal setting, but also the intensity of subsequent goal striving, and a person's readiness to relinquish a set goal. More specifically, the intensity of goal striving is assumed to be higher the higher the respective feasibility and desirability beliefs. Finally, people are thought to give up on those goals that turn out to be much harder to achieve than originally anticipated (i.e., feasibility beliefs had to be corrected downward) or much less attractive than originally thought (i.e., desirability beliefs had to be corrected downward).

Recent research on goals has demonstrated that variables other than feasibility and desirability also affect goal setting and goal striving. For instance, people who hold incremental rather than entity theories of human capabilities set for themselves quite different types of goals (i.e., learning goals rather than performance goals; Dweck, 1999). Learning goals in turn lead to better achievements than performance goals as the former allow people to view setbacks as cues to acquire and use new strategies of goal attainment. People who construe their self as an ideal show a predilection for setting goals that focus on gain and achievement (i.e., promotion goals), whereas construing the self as an ought is associated with a predilection for setting goals that focus on safety and security (i.e., prevention goals; Higgins, 1997). These different types of goals in turn affect people's achievements. For instance, promotion goals lead to task performance that is strongest when both expectations of success and incentive value of success are high; if people have formed prevention goals, however, this effect is not observed.

But recent research has not only discovered that variables other than feasibility and desirability affect goal setting and goal striving, it has also ventured into exploring the psychological processes on which goal setting and goal striving are based (Oettingen & Gollwitzer, 2001). Process-focused research on goal setting discovered that the way people commit to goals (i.e., setting oneself binding goals) makes a difference. More specifically, whether a goal-setting determinant such as feasibility will take effect depends on the mode of self-regulatory thought with which the task of setting a goal is approached (Oettingen, 1996, 1999).

Process-focused research on goal implementation discovered that strong goal commitments formed on the basis of high feasibility and high desirability do not guarantee successful goal striving and goal attainment. A host of problems may be encountered on the way to the goal (e.g., failing to get started, becoming derailed by distractions) and thus thwart goal attainment. Whether these problems will be ameliorated depends on people's efforts to plan out goal pursuit ahead of time (Gollwitzer, 1999). Apparently, people's self-regulatory thoughts play an important role with respect to whether goal setting and goal implementation run off effectively.

Research on the self-regulation of relinquishing goals is still at its beginnings. We made first steps in this direction, and discovered that reflective and reflexive self-regulatory strategies can be used to facilitate the relinquishment of goal pursuits that have become unfeasible or unattractive. In this chapter, we first present our past research on the self-regulation of goal setting and goal striving, and then turn to recent research on goal relinquishment.

SELF-REGULATION OF GOAL SETTING

Oettingen (1996) analyzed goal setting by focusing on how expectations and fantasies about the future can be turned into binding goals. First, the differences between these two forms of thinking about the future were highlighted. Expectations were recognized as judgments of the likelihood that a certain future behavior or outcome will occur. Free fantasies about the future, in contrast, were understood as thoughts and images of future behaviors or outcomes in the mind's eyes, independent of the likelihood that these events will actually occur. For example, despite perceiving low chances of successfully resolving a conflict with another person, people can enjoy positive fantasies of harmony (Oettingen & Mayer, 2002).

Oettingen specified three routes to goal setting that result from how people deal with their fantasies about the future. One route is expectancy based, whereas the other two are independent of expectations. The expectancy-based route rests on mentally contrasting positive fantasies about the future with negative aspects of impeding reality. This mental contrast ties free fantasies about the future to the here and now, by making the future and reality simultaneously accessible, and by activating the relational construct of reality standing in the way of realizing the desired future (Oettingen, Pak, & Schnetter, 2001). Consequently, the desired future appears as something to be achieved and the present reality as something to be changed. The resulting necessity to act raises the question: Can reality be changed to match fantasy? The answer is derived from one's expectations of successfully implementing fantasy in reality. Accordingly, mentally contrasting positive fantasies about the future with negative aspects of impeding reality causes expectations of success (i.e., perceived feasibility) to become activated and used. If expectations are high, a person will commit herself to fantasy attainment; if expectations of success are low, the person should refrain from doing so.

The second route to goal setting relates to indulging in positive fantasies about the desired future, thereby disregarding impeding reality. This indulgence seduces the individual to mentally enjoy the desired future envisioned in the mind's eye, and thus fails to make reality appear as standing in the way of the desired future. Accordingly, no necessity to act emerges and relevant expectations of success are not activated and used. Goal commitment to act toward fantasy fulfillment solely reflects the pull of the desired events imagined in one's fantasies. It is moderate and independent of a person's expectations or perceived chances of success (i.e., feasibility).

The third route to goal setting relates to dwelling on the negative aspects of present reality, thereby disregarding positive fantasies about the future. Again, reality is not perceived as impeding the desired future and thus no necessity to act emerges. As expectations of success are not activated and used, goal commitment merely reflects the push of the negative events imagined in one's reflections on present reality. Similar to indulgence in positive fantasies about the future, dwelling on the negative reality leads to a moderate, expectancy-independent level of commitment.

This mental-contrasting theory is supported by various experimental studies (Oettingen, 2000; Oettingen et al., 2001; Oettingen, Hönig, & Gollwitzer, 2000, Study 1). In one such study, participants were confronted with an interpersonal opportunity: getting to know an attractive person. Female participants first judged the probability of successfully getting to know an attractive male doctoral student whose picture they saw. Participants then generated positive aspects of getting to know the attractive man (e.g., love, friendship) and negative aspects of impeding reality (e.g., being shy, his potential disinterest). Finally, they were divided into three groups for elaboration of these aspects.

In the fantasy–reality contrast or mental contrast group, participants mentally elaborated positive aspects of getting to know the man and negative aspects of reality standing in its way in alternating order beginning with a positive aspect. In the positive fantasy or indulging group, participants mentally elaborated only the positive aspects of getting to know this man; and in the negative reality or dwelling group, participants mentally elaborated only the negative aspects of impeding reality. When participants' commitment to the goal of getting to know the male doctoral student was assessed (in terms of eagerness to get to know him and anticipated frustration in case of failure), the strength of goal commitment was in line with perceived feasibility in the mental contrast group, whereas in the indulging and dwelling groups, feasibility was not related to strength of goal commitment. No matter whether perceived feasibility was low or high, goal commitment was at a medium level in the latter two groups. Apparently, mental contrasting makes people set binding goals for themselves if expectations of success are high, but refrain from setting binding goals if expectations of success are low, whereas indulging and dwelling cause people to be weakly pulled by the positive future or pushed by the negative reality, respectively.

A series of further experiments using various fantasy themes related to academic achievement, conflict resolution, emotional and financial independence, and occupational success replicated this pattern of results. For instance, in young adults, mental contrasting has been found to create expectancy-dependent goals to combine work and family life, to study abroad, and to stop smoking, whereas indulging and dwelling failed to do so. In school settings, mental contrasting facilitated the expectancy-dependent setting of goals to excel in mathematics and to learn a foreign language. In health care settings, mental contrasting led intensive care nurses to form expectancy-dependent goal commitment to better their relationships to patients' family members (Oettingen, Brinkmann, Mayer, Hagenah, Schmidt, & Bardong, 2003, Study 1). Moreover, health care professionals at the middle management level profited from being trained in mental contrasting in terms of increased decisiveness, better time management, and more effective delegating of authority to others (Oettingen et al., 2003, Study 2).

In all of these studies, cognitive, affective, and behavioral aspects of goal commitment were measured via self-report or observations by independent raters. Mental contrasting created expectancy-dependent goal commitments, no matter whether commitment was measured right after the experiment or weeks later, and no matter whether the desired future was self-set or assigned, and related to short-term or long-term projects. Mental contrasting turned out to be an easy-to-apply self-regulatory strategy, as described effects were obtained even when participants elaborated the desired future and current impeding reality only very briefly (i.e., were asked to imagine only one positive aspect of the desired future and just one respective obstacle; Oettingen et al., 2001, Study 1). In all of these studies, indulging in a positive future or dwelling on the negative reality only created goal commitments of a medium strength that were independent of perceived feasibility.

Taken together, these experimental findings suggest that whether people set themselves goals in a rational (i.e., feasibility based) or irrational (i.e., feasibility independent) manner depends on how people mentally deal with the desired future. Supporting this line of thought, recent laboratory experiments show that mental contrasting (as compared to indulging and dwelling) makes one's future and current reality affectively more distinct (i.e., the desired future is evaluated as positive and the current situation as negative; Scherer, 2001), and that feasibility-related information is processed more effectively as indicated in a superior cued recall performance (Pak, 2002). In other words, high perceived feasibility does not necessarily facilitate the setting of binding goals. Rather, it depends on a person's mode of self-regulatory thought whether the variable of perceived feasibility will play the pivotal role for determining goal commitments that is ascribed to it by most theories of motivation.

SELF-REGULATION OF GOAL STRIVING

From a self-regulatory perspective, forming a strong goal commitment is only a prerequisite for successful goal attainment as there are a host of subsequent implemental problems that need to be solved successfully

(Gollwitzer, 1996). For instance, after having set a goal, people may procrastinate acting on their intentions and thus fail to initiate goal-directed behavior. Moreover, in everyday life, people normally strive for multiple, often even rivalling goals, many of which are not simple short-term but long-term projects that require repeated efforts (e.g., starting a new business). Thus, goal pursuit may come to an early halt because competing projects have temporarily gained priority and the individual fails to successfully resume the original goal project. Getting started with or resuming an interrupted goal is only easy when the necessary steps are well practiced. Often, however, this fails to be the case as when the goal-directed behavior is not part of an everyday routine. Consequently, we have to seek viable opportunities to act on our goals, a task which becomes particularly difficult when attention is directed elsewhere (e.g., one is absorbed by competing goal pursuits, wrapped up in ruminations, or gripped by intense emotional experiences).

Gollwitzer (1993, 1999) suggested that forming a certain type of intention called an implementation intention is a powerful self-regulatory strategy that alleviates such problems and thus promotes the execution of goal-directed behaviors. Implementation intentions take the format of "If Situation X is encountered, then I will perform Behavior Y!" In an implementation intention, a mental link is created between a specified future situation and the anticipated goal-directed response. Holding an implementation intention commits the individual to perform a certain goal-directed behavior once the critical situation is encountered.

Implementation intentions are to be distinguished from goal intentions (goals). Goal intentions have the structure of "I intend to reach Z!" whereby Z may relate to a certain outcome or behavior to which the individual feels committed. Goal intentions are the type of intentions with which the majority of theories of motivation (as cited earlier) are concerned. Implementation intentions, on the other hand, are formed in the service of goal intentions and specify the when, where, and how of goal-directed responses. For instance, a possible implementation intention in the service of the goal intention to eat healthy food would link a suitable situational context (e.g., one's favorite restaurant) to an appropriate behavior (e.g., order a vegetarian meal). In other words, implementation intentions link anticipated opportunities with goal-directed responses and thus commit a person to respond to a certain critical situation in a stipulated manner.

Forming implementation intentions is expected to facilitate goal attainment on the basis of psychological processes that relate to both the anticipated situation and the specified behavior. Because forming implementation intentions implies the selection of a critical future situation (i.e., a viable opportunity), it is assumed that the mental representation of this situation becomes highly activated and thus more easily accessible (Gollwitzer, 1999). This heightened accessibility should in turn make it easier to detect the critical situation in the surrounding environment and readily attend to it even when one is busy with other things. Moreover, this heightened accessibility should facilitate the recall of the critical situation.

Forming implementation intentions involves first the selection of an effective goal-directed behavior, which is then linked to the selected critical situation. The mental act of linking a critical situation to an intended behavior in the form of an if–then plan leads to automatic action initiation in the sense that action initiation becomes swift, efficient, and does not require conscious intent once the critical situation is encountered. Thus, by forming implementation intentions, people can strategically switch from conscious and effortful action initiation (guided by goal intentions) to having their goal-directed actions directly elicited by the specified situational cues. This postulated automation of action initiation (also described as strategic "delegation of control to situational cues") has been supported by the results of various experiments that tested immediacy, efficiency, and the presence/absence of conscious intent (Brandstätter, Lengfelder, & Gollwitzer, 2001; Gollwitzer & Brandstätter, 1997, Study 1; Lengfelder & Gollwitzer, 2001).

Given that implementation intentions facilitate attending to, detecting, and recalling viable opportunities to act toward goal attainment, and in addition, automate action initiation in the presence of such opportunities, people who form implementation intentions should show higher goal attainment rates as compared to people who do not furnish their goal intentions with implementation intentions. This hypothesis is supported by the results of a host of studies examining the attainment of various different types of goal intentions.

As a general research strategy, goal intentions were selected for analysis that are not easily attained for various reasons (e.g., distractions, unpleasantness). Gollwitzer and Brandstätter (1997, Study 2) analyzed a goal intention that had to be performed at a bad time (e.g., writing a report about Christmas Eve during the subsequent Christmas holiday). Other studies have examined the effects of implementation intentions on goal attainment rates with goal intentions that are somewhat unpleasant to perform. For instance, the goal intentions to perform regular breast examinations (Orbell, Hodginks, & Sheeran, 1997), cervical cancer screenings (Sheeran & Orbell, 2000), resumption of functional activity after joint replacement surgery (Orbell & Sheeran, 2000), and engaging in physical exercise (Milne, Orbell, & Sheeran, 2002), were all more frequently acted on when people had furnished these goals with implementation intentions. Moreover, implementation intentions were found to facilitate the attainment of goal intentions where it is easy to forget to act on them (e.g., regular intake of vitamin pills, Sheeran & Orbell, 1999; the signing of work sheets with very old people, Chasteen, Park, & Schwarz, 2001). Furthermore, implementation intentions facilitated the attainment of goal intentions in patient populations that are known to have problems with the control of goal-directed behaviors (e.g., heroin addicts during withdrawal, Brandstätter et al., 2001, Study 1; schizophrenic patients, Brandstätter et al., 2001, Study 2; frontal lobe patients, Lengfelder & Gollwitzer, 2001).

The strength of the beneficial effects of implementation intentions depends on the presence or absence of several moderators. Implementation intentions were found to be more effective in completing difficult as compared to easy goals (Gollwitzer & Brandstätter, 1997, Study 1). Moreover, forming implementation intentions was more beneficial to frontal lobe patients, who typically have problems with executive control, than to college students (Lengfelder & Gollwitzer, 2001, Study 2). Also, the strength of commitment to the respective goal intention matters. Orbell et al. (1997) reported that the beneficial effects of implementation intentions on compliance in performing a breast examination were observed only in those women who strongly intended to perform this self-examination. This finding suggests that implementation intentions do not work when the respective goal intention is weak. Finally, Sheeran, Webb, and Gollwitzer (2002) conducted two experiments that tested whether implementation intention effects were dependent on the situational activation of the superordinate goal intention. Experiment 1 showed that assigning a goal and asking participants to form an implementation intention in tandem produced the greatest increase in study behavior, as compared to only assigning the goal or only asking to form an implementation intention, and a control condition. In Experiment 2, goals either related or unrelated to the implementation intention were primed, with the result that implementation intentions only affected the accessibility of a goal-directed behavior (in a lexical decision task) when the related superordinate goal had been activated. These findings suggest that implementation intention effects are moderated by the situational activation of the respective superordinate goal. In support of this hypothesis, a recent experiment (Bayer, Jaudas, & Gollwitzer, 2002) using the Rogers and Monsell (1995) task switch paradigm demonstrated that implementation intentions only affect a person's task performance if the task at hand is relevant to the superordinate goal in the service of which the implementation intention was formed.

Implementation intentions have been shown to be similarly effective for self-report and less subjective behavioral measures, for student and nonstudent samples, and for nonclinical and clinical samples (e.g., schizophrenic patients, drug addicts under withdrawal, frontal lobe patients).

Overall, more than 20 published studies have examined the effects of implementation intentions on the attainment of goals, with most of these studies in the health domain. All but one found statistically significant and meaningful differences in goal completion between participants who formed an implementation intention and control participants (Sheeran & Gollwitzer, 2002). However, these studies not only demonstrate that forming implementation intentions is an effective self-regulatory tool but also that forming implementation intentions qualifies as an easy-to-use technique, because it does not matter whether implementation intentions are assigned or self-set, are formed publicly or privately, are written down or not, or whether people imagined acting on their implementation intentions or not.

Whereas past research on implementation intentions focused almost exclusively on getting started with moving toward a desired goal, recent research analyzes how implementation intentions can be used to control unwanted derailing of an ongoing goal pursuit (summary by Gollwitzer, Bayer, & McCulloch, in press). The latter can be achieved in two different ways. As long as people are in a position to anticipate what could potentially make them stray off course (the relevant hindrances, barriers, distractions, and temptations), they can specify these critical situations in the if-part of an implementation intention and link them to responses that facilitate goal attainment. The response specified in the then-part of an implementation intention can be geared at either ignoring disruptive stimuli, suppressing the impeding responses to them, or blocking obstructions to goal pursuit by engaging in it all the more.

This way of using implementation intentions to protect goal pursuit from straying off course necessitates that people know what kind of obstacles and distractions need to be watched for. Moreover, people need to know what kind of unwanted responses are potentially triggered (so that people can attempt to suppress them), or what kind of goal-directed responses are particularly effective in blocking these unwanted responses (so that people can engage in these goal-directed activities). In other words, using such implementation intentions to control unwanted straying off course requires much cognitive, clinical, and social-psychological knowledge. Otherwise, no effective if-components and then-components can be specified.

However, an easier solution is also available. Instead of concentrating on potential obstacles and various ways of effectively dealing with them, people may exclusively concern themselves with the intricacies of implementing the goal pursuit at hand. People can plan out the goal pursuit by forming implementation intentions that determine how the various steps of goal attainment are to be executed. Such careful planning encapsulates goal pursuit, protecting it from the adverse influence of potential obstacles and distractions, whether internal or external. This use of implementation intentions allows the attainment of goals without having to change a noncooperative self or an unfavorable environment. Crucially, one does *not* need to possess any psychological knowledge on how to effectively deal with adverse self-states or situational contexts. It suffices if the person is aware of the demands of the current goal being pursued.

SELF-REGULATION OF GOAL RELINQUISHMENT

Goal relinquishment is commonly seen as preceded by a decrease in the perceived feasibility of goal attainment (Carver & Scheier, 1998), or by a decrease in perceived desirability (Klinger, 1977). According to Brehm's theory of energization (Brehm & Self, 1989; Wright & Brehm, 1989), however, things are more complicated as perceived feasibility and perceived desirability are said to work together in a complex way in determining when a goal-directed course of action is terminated. Based on energization theory, a person should terminate working on a task or goal if task demand requires such a high amount of effort that the task pursuit is no longer justified in view of the perceived desirability of task attainment (i.e., potential motivation that may stem from respective needs, instrumentality of the task at hand, or incentive value of task attainment). As long as the required amount of effort is still justified, people should not disengage from pursuing the task in the face of an increase in difficulty (i.e., a decrease in perceived feasibility). Rather, energization is predicted to increase linearly with increasing task demand.

The theory specifies a second reason for task or goal relinquishment. If the individual recognizes that the task or goal at hand can no longer be attained, no energization but disengagement is predicted, and this even in the face of high desirability. Various experiments manipulating the level of perceived desirability (e.g., via low/high need, low/high instrumentality, or low/high incentive value) and task demand (easy, difficult, impossible tasks) provide strong support for these predictions of energization theory (Wright, 1996).

On the basis of energization theory, the following self-regulatory problems of relinquishing tasks or goals can be identified: First, people may fail to see that the task or goal at hand is no longer attainable. As a consequence, they hang on to the goal even though disengagement from the goal and engagement to more feasible alternative goals is called for. Indeed, Pyszczynski and Greenberg (1987, 1992), in their self-regulatory perseveration theory of depression, have proposed that such disengagement failures can propel people into a downward spiral culminating in depression. We argue that reflective self-regulatory strategies such as mental contrasting can sensitize people to feasibilities and thus they can help people to relinquish the original unpromising goal and to commit to promising alternative goals.

Second, in situations where potential motivation (i.e., perceived desirability) is boosted momentarily (e.g., by self-defensive reasons), people may lose sight of the previously held level of potential motivation of the goal at hand. As a consequence, invigoration of effort induced by increased task demand may continue even though the original level of potential motivation has been surpassed. We argue that people can prepare themselves for such critical situations by advance planning that automatically refocuses them on the original potential motivation or purpose of performing the task or goal.

Relinquishing Goals by Reflective Self-Regulatory Strategies

Increasing Sensitivity to Feasibility: Mental Contrasting. Two experiments tested whether mental contrasting increases sensitivity to the feasibility of goal attainment (Oettingen, Mayer, & Losert, 2003, Studies 1 and 2). In the first study, we asked 7- to 12-year-old schoolchildren to name the most important goal that was presently occupying their minds. Participants named goals such as "getting better grades at school," "persuading dad to return home," and "to get violin lessons." They then reported on their expectations or perceived chances that their goal would be attained.

Thereafter, participants had to name two positive things of the future they associated with attaining their goal, and two negative things associated with their present situation lacking goal attainment. In the mental contrast group, participants then had to mentally elaborate the two positive things of a future associated with goal attainment and the two negative things associated with their present reality, in alternating order beginning with a positive thing associated with goal attainment. They had to start with a positive thing of goal attainment, because only then successful goal attainment is taken as a reference point to which the lack of goal attainment in the present situation becomes obvious, and thus only then a necessity to act should arise with subsequent activation of expectations. The experimental design had three further groups: In the positive-future-only or indulging group, participants had to elaborate only the two listed positive things associated with future goal attainment. In the negative-reality-only or dwelling group, participants had to elaborate only the two listed negative things associated with present lack of goal attainment. In a final group, participants mentally elaborated two negative things associated with a lack of goal attainment and two positive things associated with goal attainment in alternating order, this time starting with a negative thing associated with lack of goal attainment. Here the lack of goal attainment was taken as a reference point, and thus the gap to goal attainment should not become obvious and no necessity to act should arise with subsequent activation of expectations.

As a dependent variable, we measured participants' emotions related to energization and disengagement (Klinger, 1977). Participants answered questions assessing how they felt at the very moment. More specifically, questions pertained to depressive affect (e.g., sad, unhappy, lonely), frustration (e.g., angry, inert, shaky), and lack of energy (e.g., energized [reverse coded], bored, downcast). When perceived chances of attaining the goal were low, participants in the contrast group showed most depressive affect, frustration, and lack of energy as compared to all other groups. When perceived chances of attaining the goal were high, there were no group differences whatsoever. In other words, contrasting thoughts about attaining a goal with thoughts about the present reality lacking goal attainment leads to a heightened sensitivity for feasibility of goal attainment, which in turn makes people with low perceived feasibility emotionally relinquish their goals. Interestingly, low-expectancy participants who indulged in goal attainment, dwelled on the current situation, or reflected on the future and the present in reverse order, did not report emotions known to be associated with disengagement. Rather, they showed emotions of continued engagement at the level observed with contrasting participants entertaining high expectations of success. Because we also measured perceived chances of goal attainment (expectations) after the manipulation of the different modes of thought (i.e., contrasting, indulging, dwelling, and reverse elaborations), we could check whether these manipulations affected levels of perceived chances and whether such changes mediated the effects on the disengagement-related emotions. This was not the case. Therefore, we can assume that mental contrasting leads to relinquishing goals by heightening sensitivity to low feasibility, rather than by lowering the level of feasibility.

In the second experiment, we analyzed goal relinquishment in college students. Participants had to name a very important goal that they had thought to give up at least once. Goals such as "going to medical school," "becoming an actor," or "starting a business" were listed. They then had to indicate their expectations of successfully attaining their goal. Thereafter, we established three different groups. In the mental contrast group, participants named and mentally elaborated a positive aspect of goal attainment (e.g., being respected by my family), and right thereafter a negative aspect of their present situation that impeded goal attainment (e.g., having to pass the MCAT). In the positive future or indulging group, participants had to name and elaborate only positive aspects of goal attainment, and in the negative reality or dwelling group, participants had to name and elaborate only negative aspects of impeding reality.

To assess participants' readiness to relinquish goal pursuit, we asked them to indicate how disappointed they would feel if they failed to attain their goal. When expectations of success were low, participants in the mental contrast group reported least disappointment as compared to all other groups (i.e., they were the least committed to attain their goal). When expectations of success were high, participants in the mental contrast group reported much disappointment (i.e., their goal commitment was strong). Such expectancy-dependent goal commitment was not observed in the indulging group and the dwelling group. In both of these groups, participants with low and high expectations reported that they felt much disappointment (i.e., their goal commitment was uniformly strong).

The findings of the two studies reported suggest that mental contrasting makes goal-striving individuals sensitive to the feasibility of goal attainment. If feasibility is low, emotions and strength of goal commitment indicate a readiness to relinquish the goal at hand. Indulging and dwelling, on the other hand, makes goal-striving individuals insensitive to low feasibilities. No matter whether feasibility is perceived as low or high, emotions as well as levels of goal commitment show no indication of a readiness to disengage from goal pursuit. In the language of energization theory, mental contrasting increases the likelihood of motivation suppression when goal attainment is judged highly unlikely.

Increasing Sensitivity to Feasibility: Seeing the Goal on a Larger Scale. Oettingen, Mayer, and Losert (2002, Study 3) tested a further reflective self-regulatory strategy of goal relinquishment, this one based on the consideration that most goal pursuits are structured hierarchically (Carver & Scheier, 1998). In a correlational study with college students, Oettingen et al. (2003) analyzed whether making the higher order purpose of a goal salient helps to relinquish this goal, if alternative ways to reach the higher order purpose are perceived as highly feasible. Like in the previous study, college students had to name an important goal that they had thought to give up at least once (e.g., going to medical school). Then participants were to indicate the higher order purpose of this goal (e.g., to help people, to achieve high professional status) and to think up an alternative route or means to achieve this higher order purpose. Finally, they had to report on the perceived feasibility of this alternative route.

We assessed participants' commitment to attain the original, lower order goal by asking them how disappointed they would feel if they failed to reach this goal. Participants who perceived the feasibility of the alternative route to lead to the ultimate purpose as being high, felt less committed to the original goal than those who perceived this feasibility as being low. It appears, then, that there is a second reflective self-regulatory strategy that helps people to relinquish goals. This strategy entails the linking of the present goal to its higher order purpose, and the thinking up of an alternative route or means to achieve this purpose. If the alternative route is perceived as feasible, the original goal can easily be relinquished. The original goal is now no longer seen as an end in itself but as a substitutable means to reach the higher order purpose. Interestingly, Pyszczynski and Greenberg (1992) proposed this precise strategy as the pathway of recovery for depressed individuals; by considering their higher order goals, they can begin disengaging from the impossible goal upon which they were perseverating and can begin to reinvest in alternative pathways to their higher order goals, which will initiate an upward spiral out of depression.

In summary, people can use mental contrasting when they find it difficult to relinquish goals of low feasibility. Alternatively, they can search for the higher order purpose of the goal at hand and think of alternative ways (means) to attain this purpose. Still, both of these strategies are rather effortful, because they demand sophisticated mental elaborations of desired futures and impediments of present reality, or the generating of higher order purposes and alternative ways to achieve them. Often, however, the motivation to attain the goal at hand is so high that stepping back and engaging in reflective thought is precluded. In such cases, less reflective and more reflexive self-regulatory strategies are called for that stop goal pursuit without further mental ado. In the research described below, we explored whether forming implementation intentions qualifies as such a reflexive self-regulatory strategy.

Relinquishing Goals by Reflexive Self-Regulatory Strategies

We have analyzed two different, high motivation situations that make it hard for people to step back and ponder the relinquishment of an ongoing goal pursuit. The first one (Henderson, Gollwitzer, & Oettingen, 2003) is characterized by strong justification motives that lead to holding on to a failing course of action. The second situation (Bulgarella, Oettingen, & Gollwitzer, 2003) is characterized by strong competitive motives that redirect one's own goal pursuit to follow another person's goal pursuit.

Stopping a Failing Course of Action in the Face of an Activated Justification Motive. Using a modified version of a paradigm developed by Bobocel and Meyer (1994), we asked college students to perform well on a general knowledge test. All participants had to choose one out of four possible strategies on how to work on the test and then justify their choice. While being engaged in working on the test, participants were disrupted three times and given increasingly negative feedback. After each feedback, participants were asked whether they wanted to continue with the chosen strategy or switch to an alternative strategy. We measured to what extent participants relinquished the initially chosen and justified strategy as well as the overall number of times participants switched strategies.

Prior to working on the general knowledge test, in the goal intention condition, participants had to tell themselves: "I will always pursue the best strategy!" Participants in the implementation intention condition had to tell themselves in addition: "And if I receive disappointing feedback, then I'll switch to a different strategy!" Finally, participants in the control condition were provided with neither goals nor plans geared at facilitating the relinquishment of a chosen strategy.

We observed that a larger proportion of participants in the implementation intention condition relinquished their initially chosen and justified strategy than in the goal intention condition and in the control condition, whereas the proportion of participants in the goal intention condition and the control condition did not differ. A parallel pattern of results was observed for the overall number of times participants switched strategies. Implementation intention participants switched more often than did goal intention and control participants, whereas there was no difference between goal intention and control participants.

This pattern of data indicates that simply setting oneself the goal to always pursue the best strategy does not qualify as an effective self-regulatory tool of relinquishing a chosen strategy that produces negative results. Apparently, the motivation to stick to this strategy is so high that receiving negative feedback will not make people question their choice. Rather, it needs a stop rule that is adopted in advance in order to put a halt to the use of a chosen, but failing course of action.

A potential criticism of this study is that the implementation intention manipulation rather than instigating nonreflective disengagement led participants to experience a higher experimenter demand in the direction of switching strategies. That is, the wording of the implementation intention might have created the impression that the experimenter wanted participants to use alternative strategies to the chosen one. Therefore, we conducted a follow-up study comparing the demand effects of the various instructions. As in the previous study, we established a goal intention, an implementation intention, and a control condition. The cover story was the same as in the previous experiment, however instead of actually taking the general knowledge test, participants had to respond to the following items assessing experimenter demand: "During the test, how important do you think it is to stay with your chosen strategy?" and "The experimenter wants me to stay with my chosen strategy during the test!"

Participants' responses to these items did not support a demand effect explanation. First, importance ratings did not differ between groups and the same was true for participants' perceptions of whether the experimenter wanted them to stay with their chosen strategy during the test. Second, and most importantly, if a demand effect was responsible for the implementation intention effect in the previous study, then participants' responses to the items "The experimenter wants me to stay with my chosen strategy during the test!" and "During the test, how important do you think it is to stay with your chosen strategy?" should be positively correlated. For the control group and the goal intention group, we found such strong positive correlations, whereas for the implementation intention group, there was no relation between the responses to these two items. These observations speak against the possibility that a demand effect was at work in the previous study, and they support the claim that the assigned implementation intention provided an effective stop rule directly triggered by the specified cue (i.e., negative feedback).

Stopping a Goal Pursuit Derailed by an Activated Competition Motive. In a recent set of two experiments (Bulgarella et al., 2003), we developed a new experimental paradigm that allowed us to analyze the derailing of an ongoing goal pursuit by an activated competition motive. The paradigm demands participants to perform a speed–accuracy tradeoff task on the computer. The computer screen is divided horizontally. The upper portion of the screen displays numerous sets of parallel lines of different lengths and distances from each other and participants have to judge whether more or less than 10 lines are presented in a given set. As soon as the participants have given their judgment (more or less than 10 lines) by pressing a button, the lines disappear, and a new set of lines is presented.

Participants are informed that the lines appearing in the lower screen (i.e., the same sets of lines are presented at the same time) are those presented to another participant performing the same task in parallel in another experimental cubicle. In actuality, there is no other person, but only a preprogrammed response pattern adjusted around the reaction times of each participant. In the first block of 20 trials, the simulated other participant supposedly responds slower (i.e., the lines in the lower half of the screen disappear slower than those of the participant). In the second block of 20 trials, however, the simulated participant responds faster (i.e., the lines disappear faster than those of the participant). Moreover, when participants make mistakes in judging the number of lines presented as lower or higher than 10, the computer produces a noticeable beep. Participants are told that these beeps indicate having made a mistake.

In a first study using this paradigm, we tested whether entering the second block of judgments (in which the simulated person begins to make faster judgments than the participant) creates competitive behavior. Accordingly, we assigned participants to two different task conditions. In one condition, participants were given the task goal "be fast, but accurate." In the other condition, participants were given the task goal "be as accurate as possible."

Being confronted with comparatively faster judgments by the simulated other person in the second block of trials should lead to competitive behavior in the fast and accurate condition, but not in the accuracy-only condition. Only in the fast and accurate goal condition, being fast is part of the goal and thus a goal discrepancy with subsequent effort increase in terms of speeding up can be expected. No such discrepancy should be experienced in the being accurate-only condition, and thus no respective effort increase should occur. In the fast and accurate condition, the other person's being faster should thus derail the goal pursuit of being fast and accurate in the direction of being more fast than accurate, whereas no such effect should occur in the accurate-only condition. Indeed, when we assessed speed of judgments in block 2 as compared to block 1, we observed that speed and accuracy participants in the fast and accurate goal condition became faster, whereas the accurate-only participants did not. At the same time, participants in the fast and accurate condition made increasingly more mistakes from block 1 to block 2, whereas the accuracy-only participants did not differ in their mistakes from block 1 to block 2.

Having established a paradigm that produces the competitive derailing of a given goal pursuit, we wondered whether the self-regulatory strategy of forming implementation intentions can prevent such competitive derailing. Accordingly, we conducted an experiment containing two groups. The first condition was identical to the speed and accuracy goal condition in the previous study. In the second condition, participants were assigned the speed and accuracy goal, and in addition, were asked to form the following implementation intention: "If I hear a beep, then I think to myself: Be fast and accurate!" In the speed and accuracy goal condition, we replicated the speed-up effect triggered by the other person's comparatively faster judgments in the second block. In the implementation intention condition, however, no such speed-up effect was observed. Apparently, forming implementation intentions geared at sticking to the original goal prevents people from becoming derailed from the goal pursuit at hand simply due to a competitor who emphasizes only one select aspect of the goal. Such nonreflective running after one's competitor can effectively be stopped by making plans that refocus people on the content of their original goals.

CONCLUSION

Perceived desirability and perceived feasibility of a goal and variables related to the content of goals have a vast influence on goal setting, goal implementation, and goal relinquishment. However, over and above these determinants of goal pursuit, people can modulate in a self-regulatory effort whether goal setting, goal implementation, and goal relinquishment will take a more or less successful course. We have analyzed what people can do to make goal setting a more rational, feasibility-based endeavor, how people can promote the successful implementation of chosen goals even in the face of hindrances and barriers, and how people can assure that they will not cling to unpromising or unrewarding goals. As it turns out, effective self-regulatory strategies need to take a different form depending on whether goal setting, goal implementation, or goal attainment are at issue, and in addition, effective strategies can be either of a more reflective or reflexive nature.

REFERENCES

Ajzen, I. (1991). The theory of planned behavior. *Organizational Behavior and Human Decision Processes, 50,* 179–211.

Atkinson, J. W. (1957). Motivational determinants of risk taking behavior. *Psychological Review, 64,* 359–372.

Bandura, A. (1997). *Self-efficacy: The exercise of control.* New York: Freeman.

Bayer, U. C., Jaudas, A., & Gollwitzer, P. M. (2002, July). *Do implementation intentions facilitate switching between tasks?* Poster presented at the International Symposium on Executive Functions, Konstanz, Germany.

Bobocel, D. R., & Meyer, J. P. (1994). Escalating commitment to a failing course of action: Separating the roles of choice and justification. *Journal of Applied Psychology, 79,* 360–363.

Brandstätter, V., Lengfelder, A., & Gollwitzer, P. M. (2001). Implementation intentions and efficient action initiation. *Journal of Personality and Social Psychology, 81,* 946–960.

Brehm, J. W., & Self, E. (1989). The intensity of motivation. *Annual Review of Psychology, 40,* 109–131.

Bulgarella, C., Oettingen, G., & Gollwitzer, P. M. (2003). *Implementation intentions and the control of competitive urges.* Unpublished manuscript. New York University.

Carver, C. S., & Scheier, M. F. (1998). *On the self-regulation of behavior.* Cambridge, UK: Cambridge University Press.

Chasteen, A. L., Park, D. C., & Schwarz, N. (2001). Implementation intentions and facilitation of prospective memory. *Psychological Science, 12,* 457–461.

Dweck, C. S. (1999). *Self-theories: Their role in motivation, personality, and development.* Philadelphia, PA: Psychology Press.

Gollwitzer, P. M. (1990). Action phases and mind-sets. In E. T. Higgins & R. M. Sorrentino (Eds.), *Handbook of motivation and cognition: Foundations of social behavior* (Vol. 2, pp. 53–92). New York: Guilford.

Gollwitzer, P. M. (1993). Goal achievement: The role of intentions. *European Review of Social Psychology, 4,* 141–185.

Gollwitzer, P. M. (1996). The volitional benefits of planning. In P. M. Gollwitzer & J. A. Bargh (Eds.), *The psychology of action: Linking cognition and motivation to behavior* (pp. 287–312). New York: Guilford.

Gollwitzer, P. M. (1999). Implementation intentions: Strong effects of simple plans. *American Psychologist, 54,* 493–503.

Gollwitzer, P. M., Bayer, U. C., & McCulloch, K. C. (in press). The control of the unwanted. In J. A. Bargh, J. Uleman, & R. Hassin (Eds.), *Unintended thought* (Vol. 2). New York: Guilford.

Gollwitzer, P. M., & Brandstätter, V. (1997). Implementation intentions and effective goal pursuit. *Journal of Personality and Social Psychology, 73,* 186–199.

Heckhausen, H. (1977). Achievement motivation and its constructs: A cognitive model. *Motivation and Emotion, 1,* 283–329.

Henderson, M., Gollwitzer, P. M., & Oettingen, G. (2003). *Implementation intentions and relinquishing a failing course of action.* Unpublished manuscript, New York University.

Higgins, E. T. (1997). Beyond pleasure and pain. *American Psychologist, 52,* 1280–1300.

Klinger, E. (1977). *Meaning and void.* Minneapolis: University of Minnesota Press.

Lengfelder, A., & Gollwitzer, P. M. (2001). Reflective and reflexive action control in patients with frontal brain lesions. *Neuropsychology, 15,* 80–100.

Locke, E. A., & Latham, G. P. (1990). *A theory of goal setting and task performance.* Englewood Cliffs, NJ: Prentice Hall.

Milne, S., Orbell, S., & Sheeran, P. (2002). Combining motivational and volitional interventions to promote exercise participation: Protection motivation theory and implementation intentions. *British Journal of Health Psychology, 7,* 163–184.

Oettingen, G. (1996). Positive fantasy and motivation. In P. M. Gollwitzer & J. A. Bargh (Eds.), *The psychology of action: Linking cognition and motivation to behavior* (pp. 236–259). New York: Guilford.

Oettingen, G. (1999). Free fantasies about the future and the emergence of developmental goals. In J. Brandtstädter & R. M. Lerner (Eds.), *Action and self-development: Theory and research through the life span* (pp. 315–342). Thousand Oaks: Sage.

Oettingen, G. (2000). Expectancy effects on behavior depend on self-regulatory thought. *Social Cognition, 18,* 101–129.

Oettingen, G., Brinkmann, B., Mayer, D., Hagenah, M., Schmidt, L., & Bardong, C. (2003). *Self-regulation of goal setting in everyday life.* Unpublished manuscript, University of Hamburg.

Oettingen, G., & Gollwitzer, P. M. (2001). Goal setting and goal striving. In A. Tesser & N. Schwarz (Eds.), *Intraindividual processes: Blackwell handbook in social psychology* (Vol. 1, pp. 329–347). Oxford, UK: Blackwell.

Oettingen, G., Hönig, G., & Gollwitzer, P. M. (2000). Effective self-regulation of goal attainment. *International Journal of Educational Research, 33,* 705–732.

Oettingen, G., & Mayer, D. (2002). The motivating function of thinking about the future: Expectations versus fantasies. *Journal of Personality and Social Psychology, 83,* 1198–1212.

Oettingen, G., Mayer, D., & Losert, A. (2003). *Reflective self-regulation of goal relinquishment.* Unpublished manuscript, University of Hamburg.

Oettingen, G., Pak, H., & Schnetter, K. (2001). Self-regulation of goal setting: Turning free fantasies about the future into binding goals. *Journal of Personality and Social Psychology, 80,* 736–753.

Orbell, S., Hodgkins, S., & Sheeran, P. (1997). Implementation intentions and the theory of planned behavior. *Personality and Social Psychology Bulletin, 23,* 945–954.

Orbell, S., & Sheeran, P. (2000). Motivational and volitional processes in action initiation: A field study of the role of implementation intentions. *Journal of Applied Social Psychology, 30,* 780–797.

Pak, H. (2002). *Mentale Kontrastierung und die Verarbeitung erwartungsrelevanter Informationen* [Mental contrasting and the processing of expectancy-related information]. Unpublished doctoral dissertation, University of Konstanz.

Pyszczynski, T., & Greenberg, J. (1987). Self-regulatory perseveration and the depressive self-focusing style: A self-awareness theory of the development and maintenance of depression. *Psychological Bulletin, 102,* 122–138.

Pyszczynski, T., & Greenberg, J. (1992). *Hanging on and letting go: Understanding the onset, progression, and remission of depression.* New York: Springer-Verlag.

Rogers, D., & Monsell, S. (1995). Costs of a predictable switch between simple cognitive tasks. *Journal of Experimental Psychology: General, 124,* 207–231.

Scheier, M. F., & Carver, C. S. (1987). Dispositional optimism and physical well-being: The influence of generalized outcome expectancies on health. *Journal of Personality, 55,* 169–210.

Scherer, M. (2001). *Zukunftsdenken und Bewertungsreaktionen* [Modes of self-regulatory thought and automatic evaluations]. Unpublished doctoral dissertation, University of Konstanz.

Sheeran, P. (2002). Intention-behavior relations: A conceptual and empirical review. *European Review of Social Psychology, 12,* 1–30.

Sheeran, P., & Gollwitzer, P. M. (2002, June). *Meta-analysis of the impact of implementation intentions on behavioral performance.* Paper presented at the 13th General Meeting of the European Association of Experimental Social Psychology, San Sebastian, Spain.

Sheeran, P., & Orbell, S. (1999). Implementation intentions and repeated behavior: Augmenting the predictive validity of the theory of planned behavior. *European Journal of Social Psychology, 29,* 349–369.

Sheeran, P., & Orbell, S. (2000). Using implementation intentions to increase attendance for cervical cancer screening. *Health Psychology, 19,* 283–289.

Sheeran, P., Webb, T. L., & Gollwitzer, P. M. (2002). *The interplay between goals and implementation intentions.* Manuscript submitted for publication.

Vroom, V. H. (1964). *Work and motivation.* New York: Wiley.

Wright, R. A. (1996). Brehm's theory of motivation as a model of effort and cardiovascular response. In P. M. Gollwitzer & J. A. Bargh (Eds.), *The psychology of action: Linking cognition and motivation to behavior* (pp. 424–453). New York: Guilford.

Wright, R., & Brehm, J. W. (1989). Energization and goal attractiveness. In L. A. Pervin (Ed.), *Goal concepts in personality and social psychology* (pp. 169–210). Hillsdale, NJ: Lawrence Erlbaum Associates.

III

REFLECTIONS

15

Observations From Mount Oread

Jack W. Brehm
University of Kansas

Because I have already thanked my former and present associates—teachers, fellow graduate students, colleagues, graduate and undergraduate students, yes, and wives, mentioning names of many of them at the 1999 meeting of the Society for Experimental Social Psychology—I need only say here that my research has been a great adventure and it could not have been so without the help of all these people. Having thus made at least a downpayment on my debt, I would like here to move on to a few comments about the general field of study in which I have spent my time. Early on when I reluctantly agreed to write something for this book, I thought about doing a piece called "Fads and Fallacies in the Name of Social Psychology." And as I thought of one problem after another to complain about, it occurred to me that I was taking on the role of a crotchety old has-been who has nothing more of interest to say. So, although I have a few things to say about problems in the field of social psychology, I aim primarily at leaving you with a sketch of a new theory about social influence and the general direction in which our understanding of human behavior could move.

FADS AND FALLACIES

I have always thought it curious that people who study social influence tend toward fads in research paradigms. I suppose it is because each investigator has his or her own take on the newest paradigm, whatever it may be, and makes a contribution in that way. But when it came to cute titles for our publications, we needed the help of Senator Proxmire and a shortage of federal funds for research to mend our ways. And we have managed by and large to get through the scenario studies used to test hypotheses in attribution, and more generally, social cognition. In part, of course, scenario studies were more likely to be viable when the federal government was pressing for tighter reins on the use of deception in research, and much of our earlier and perhaps more meaningful research had sometimes used relatively strong deceptions, the need for which was more difficult for the lay person to understand. My perception is that we are slowly being allowed more latitude in what we do in our experimental research, as we have accumulated some wisdom about explaining to others what we are doing. For many years now, social psychology, and especially experimental social psychology, has been one of the more popular topics among undergraduates because it does deal with material that has ready meaning.

In contrast to the content of our research, perhaps, we have had disputes over fine points of methodology such as which (of the now many) kinds of comparisons of pairs of means are appropriate or what contrasts should be applied to complex designs. What we tend to forget is that all our experimental tests are only rough approximations of the world out there, and no single experimental (or statistical) test can provide the final word. Replication in one form or another is always the best insurance that X has an effect on Y.

For the same reason, it has seemed to some that one should combine studies that are ostensibly on the same hypotheses to determine not only the "truth" of an hypothesis but also to arrive at an effect size. I was glad to see this problem discussed in the literature over the last few years and trust by now that investigators realize it is no easy task to determine that two experiments in social psychology (let alone more than two) are sufficiently alike so that they can be combined. More important, of course, when it comes to estimating the magnitude of manipulations such as persuasive strength, attractiveness of the communicator, attraction to the group, and so forth, there is no common metric, nor is the purpose of most of our laboratory experiments to establish an effect size. The usual purpose is simply to see whether or not X has an effect on Y, and for that purpose, the published research in experimental social psychology passes the test.

From Alpha to Omega—The Psychology of Measuring Psychological Variables

Social psychologists are very sophisticated about problems of measurement. We know not only the differences between ordinal, interval, and ratio scales, we also know various methods of approximating the kinds of scales that permit the use of parametric statistical analyses. We have to know these things because we confront these problems daily. For example, a quick look at a current journal of social psychological research will reveal that most investigators routinely report the reliability of their measures (e.g., *Alpha*). And with this report of reliability, the author, editor, and readers may all rest assured that measurement has been properly treated.

Why is it that social psychologists frequently construct measures made up of multiple items? Why not use just one item? Some people might give the answer, amazingly enough, that if only one item is used, reliability of the measure is unknown. That, of course, is not the real reason for using multiple items. The real reason is that one does not know how to measure the variable one wishes to measure. If, for example, one wanted to measure anger but English contained no such word, one could ask people if they feel irritated, annoyed, peeved, disgusted, displeased, and so on. But if what one wants to know about is anger, then to whatever extent other items result in different responses is the extent to which the multiple measure has added error. This is not to say that there is no error if one simply asks about anger; it is to say that if it is anger one wants to know about, the other items can be misleading and may only increase error of measurement. My complaint is that many social psychologists, despite their sophistication in regard to measurement, have adopted the methods of personality and have routinely used multiple item measures instead of facing up to the tough question, "Do I know how to measure what I want to measure?" And in turn, is my theory—my understanding—sufficiently precise to permit a single measure of the dependent variable? It is, after all, validity, not reliability, that we should seek, and the use of multiple items is an admission that one does not know exactly how to measure the variable of interest. It is reasonable that when investigators are groping for understanding and the proper definition of conceptual variables, multiple items may help in the sharpening of appropriate measures. But it is revealing that when we check on the success of manipulations, we frequently use single items, presumably because we know in such cases exactly what the variable is.

Skepticism—A Healthy Attitude With Unhealthy Consequences

Graduate programs in social psychology give rigorous training, especially in regard to methodology. As a consequence, one practically never sees in our journals the kinds of errors that, at least until recently, have been found in, for example, medical journals. Furthermore, almost anyone who obtains a PhD degree in experimental social can competently judge the methodology of any behavioral research. And although we, like everyone else, are less able to see our own errors than those of others, we generally turn out methodologically sound work. But this competence, one might even call it perfectionism, in regard to methodology, has, I believe, a rather unfortunate consequence. For the stance learned by our students in social psychology is one of skepticism about the work of others in the field. We model skepticism and we use methodological perfectionism to defend our view of the work of others. In other words, if you don't like someone's idea about group influence, prejudice, or attitude change, you only have to point out a couple of flaws in their methodology in order to justify your skepticism. But note that the skepticism may not occur because of methodological flaws; it may occur because one doesn't like the idea or theory.

Just as people can learn how to make constructive responses to anger generated by a variety of injustices, so it may be possible for investigators to learn a response other than dismissal when they feel skeptical about an idea or claimed finding. Skepticism has at least two implications: (a) the idea or work is flawed, and (b) if the idea or work turned out to be true, it would be a real eye opener. One can guess which of these responses dominates in editorial quarters of journals as well as in panelists for research funding. The consequence, of course, is that the stranger the idea or research result, the more it deviates from extant models or findings, the less likely it is to be published or funded. We seem to have made it very easy for new, and especially fresh, ideas and findings to be squelched.

What we need, I believe, is to train students that the object of our science is to improve our understanding of (social) behavior. That is, the inspection of ideas and methods should be in the service of improving our understanding, not in the perfection of the idea or methods in question. Hence, the first judgments are not about perfection but rather about potential to tell us something we don't know. Is the idea interesting or surprising? Is the result surprising? If there is a yes to either question, then the subject of perfection in either theory or method is worthwhile.

However, there is yet another caution that will help us to avoid throwing the baby out with the bath water, and that is to apply a sometimes difficult judgment about plausibility. All imperfections in ideas and methods are not equal. Experiments on complex human behavior frequently require compromises that produce potential impurities in design—complex manipulations, complex cover stories, and complex measures. The presence of discernable covariables in cover stories, manipulations, and measures should not automatically disqualify a study from consideration as a contribution to our understanding. In short, the difficult judgment must sometimes be made that a study *plausibly* represents a test of a particular idea even when imperfections in methods are apparent.

SATISFACTIONS

There are doubtless many different motives that lead people to do research in social psychology. Although I have values that favor the downtrodden, it was not these values but rather the intrinsic interest of trying to understand social and individual behavior that has led me on and perhaps misled me at times. As other scientists have noted, getting a new insight, especially about a long-standing mystery concerning some aspect of psychology, is thrilling and at least as good as orgasm. No other reward is necessary to having spent weeks, months, or years, trying to account for some phenomenon. And when the theoretical implications of an insight take form, there is surely an esthetic experience not unlike that involved in the production of a painting, piece of music, or other original work. The experiences of insight and theoretical implication are sufficient not only to maintain one's pursuit of understanding behavior, but to justify protecting oneself from interfering pursuits such as editorial work, attendance at professional meetings, and so forth. It is not that these other activities are without value; it is simply a choice that one can make in order to do what seems most satisfying as long as satisfaction is consonant with increased understanding of human behavior.

I suppose professors are not looked upon as adventurers by most people, and especially by undergraduates, unless they are actually making field trips to the Amazon or the Antarctic. In truth, professors who are seriously interested in research live an adventurous life on the frontiers of knowledge. For any psychologist, there are many mysteries about human behavior, and trying to explain some particular aspect, such as a parent killing his own children, or understanding how behavior affects attitudes, or how emotions affect behavior are genuine adventures in the sense that one does not know what will be revealed. Is there a flaw in the structure of the human psyche, and if so, what is it? Are emotions beneficial, and if so, under what conditions? The reason we do research is because we don't know the answer, and because we don't know the answer, every research effort is an adventure. And if that were not exciting enough, one should remember that every adventure can turn out to be newsworthy to one's colleagues. That is, with skill and a little luck, one learns something that is worth communicating to one's colleagues, usually by way of a paper in a journal or a longer work such as a monograph or book. Finding something of interest to one's colleagues and students is a pleasure.

DANGLING ISSUES

The theory of cognitive dissonance, as proposed by Leon Festinger in 1957, was the major engine for research on attitudes and evaluations of choice alternatives for over a decade, and in a certain sense, the engine that gave rise first, to attribution theory, and second, to social cognition, as protest movements. The latter two movements have had their say and as we have begun to settle into a new age of social psychology in which the constrictions imposed by logical positivism have softened and become more fuzzy so that subjective events can be studied without apology, dissonance theory is still there although its proponents are trying to reshape it. Not to be left behind, Bob Wicklund and I (2002) have submitted for publication a paper on dissonance theory that takes issue with the major thrust of dissonance research, the work on forced compliance, in which individuals are induced to make a pronouncement in disagreement with some important prior attitude. This paper has been interpreted by some as a major attack on dissonance theory itself, and by others as ignoring current research and theoretical developments. Neither is true.

We have made a serious effort to understand exactly what Festinger said in his 1957 and 1964 publications on the theory. What distinguishes dissonance from other theories of cognitive balance is first, the statement that the magnitude of dissonance is a direct function of the proportion of all relevant cognitions that is dissonant, and second, the assumption that each cognition has some resistance to change. It is the latter assumption that makes possible the prediction of how dissonance will be reduced—cognitions that are dissonant with those most resistant to change will tend to be eliminated or reduced in importance. However, as Beauvois and Joule (1996) have made clear, and consistent with practically all "forced compliance" research, it is recent behavior that determines how dissonance is reduced—that is, attitudes tend to become more consistent with recent behavior. What Wicklund and I have pointed out is that the recent behavior does not often provide the cognition most resistant to change: If a strongly prochoice woman is induced to make a counterattitudinal statement, it simply does not make sense to assume that her cognition of her recent statement is more resistant to change than is her prior attitude. Thus, we suggest, there must be another explanation for at least some of the "forced compliance" experiments that have shown attitudes becoming more consistent with the recent behavior.

First, do the attitude shifts that are produced look like conversions? In the previous example, making a strong statement against the prochoice position should create a lot of dissonance, and that dissonance theoretically can be reduced or eliminated in either of two ways: by becoming completely antichoice or by reverting to completely prochoice. But typically, the attitudes produced by induced compliance tend to move toward the neutral point, between pro and anti. They are neither a conversion nor a bolstering of initial position, and so it does not look like dissonance reduction. Although these are always group data and may hide extreme positions on either side of the issue, sophisticated researchers have not reported that to be the case.

One problem is that taking only a summary measure of attitude may not permit participants to show how they are responding to the pro versus anti sides. The use of a summary measure assumes that dissonance will be resolved in favor of one side or the other. It does not permit a person to indicate, for example, agreement with arguments on both sides of the issue. A person who agreed with arguments on both sides might well take a neutral position on a summary measure that runs from pro through neutral to con. There would be no other way for the person to indicate that both sides have convincing arguments.

What Wicklund and I suggested was a "socialization" solution. Theories about how people acquire new roles and new attitudes suggest that they go through a process not unlike "forced compliance" in which they try out a new role, and such theories say nothing about limits on the number of roles or attitudes one may acquire in this way, nor anything about interference (dissonance) by virtue of holding logically or psychologically inconsistent attitudes. If asked about her attitude, a person who had learned both prolife attitudes from her parents and prochoice attitudes from her peers might well take a neutral position on a single scale because that would be the best reflection of her beliefs. But if she were given the opportunity to voice her opinion about arguments on both sides of the issue, she might well approve of both, and that is not a picture consistent with dissonance theory. Indeed, evidence of just this kind on the issue of smoking has been obtained by Pantaleo (1999). He found that nonsmokers who were induced to make a prosmoking pronouncement, when given a chance, tended to endorse arguments on both sides of the issue.

So it is not an attack on dissonance theory that we have written, it is an attack on the widespread assumption that the vast pool of evidence from induced compliance experiments unequivocally supports dissonance theory. It is our contention that investigators have not taken the theory seriously enough to have collected the kind of data that would make a case for dissonance theory as opposed to a socialization theory.

MOVING ON

If some readers have been entertained by the previous paragraphs on dissonance theory, then perhaps they will also be interested to see a different kind of explanation for at least some dissonance effects. Following several years of work on motivational arousal, the idea struck me that emotions may follow the same general rules. That is, the intensity of an emotion may be determined in part by whatever obstacles there are to the function of the emotion. Although one of the problems surrounding the understanding of emotion is to identify the function of each, and for some emotions such as sadness and happiness, those functions seem a bit obscure, emotions such as anger and fear, which have long been thought to have motivational properties, would seem to be obvious examples of motivational states. By motivational state, I mean, of course, an activated motivation—protective of rights in the case of anger, protective of safety in the case of fear.

Broadening motivational theory to include emotions mainly required broadening the definition of difficulty of goal attainment. Especially given that we are not sure what the purpose is of certain emotions—what function they are supposed to serve—it seemed appropriate to use a broader term, in this case, deterrence, and to define it as any factors that could inhibit or work against the function of the emotion. Given that emotions urge a person to behave in certain ways, it seems clear that deterrents would include any information that might replace the current emotion or that would impede the behavior the emotion urged.

Although the theory (Brehm, 1999) is somewhat more complicated, it is sufficient for our interests here to see that the forced compliance paradigm of dissonance theory can be seen in the terms outlined earlier. Figure 15.1 displays the relationship between the *affect* of an initial attitude and the magnitude of the inducing force to produce counterattitudinal behavior. The affect of the initial attitude, in the absence of any other force, is represented by the dashed line that runs horizontally across the figure. The magnitude of the inducing force varies along the horizontal axis from zero to some large amount. At zero, it has no effect on the affective component of the attitude, but at some small amount (slight) where it becomes noticeable as a deterrent, it reduces the affective component of the attitude, so that the attitude appears to become less strong. As the inducing force grows (moderate), its deterrent value begins to challenge the affective component and eventually it will become as strong as it is measured to be in the absence of any other forces—that is, equal to the dashed line in the graph. Beyond that point is where induced compliance begins. That is, the deterrent effect of the inducing force (strong) overcomes the resistance due to the affective component of the attitude, making it possible for the person to comply and make a counterattitudinal statement. Theoretically, when the inducing force makes compliance possible, it does so in part by eliminating the affect associated with the original attitude. *It is this loss of affect associated with the original attitude that is measured as dissonance reduction* in the forced compliance paradigm. Furthermore, any addition of the force to comply beyond a just-sufficient amount to produce compliance should have no further effect on the original attitude—its affect has already been squelched by the inducing force. However, as we know from

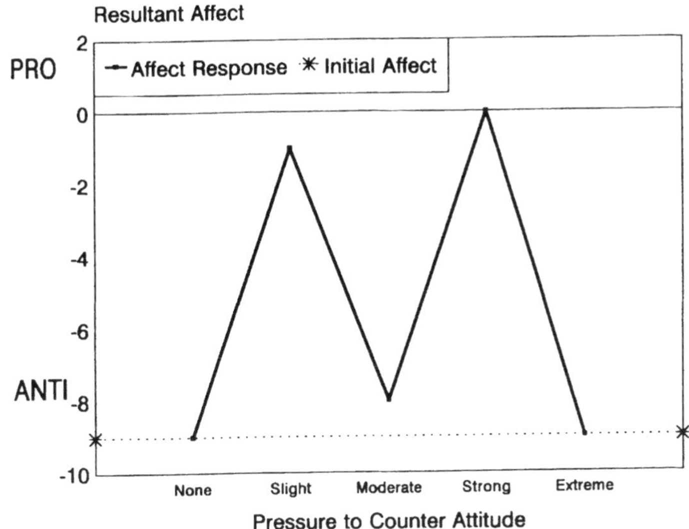

FIG. 15.1. Affective response to counterattitudinal pressure.

many forced-compliance experiments, a high force condition (extreme) tends to produce an attitude like that with which participants presumably start. What can plausibly produce such an effect is reactance, the urge to restore a threatened freedom, exactly what one would expect from people who are "forced" to do something they do not wish to do. Pressed too hard to comply, people may grimly maintain their initial attitude.

This explanation of forced compliance research seems a bit labored, but it predicts that the effect of a just-sufficient force to obtain compliance will result in a neutral attitude, which is exactly what most forced-compliance experiments have demonstrated.

What is more interesting is to consider the role of cognition in cognitive dissonance research. If an explanation of forced-compliance research can be based on affective rather than cognitive changes, then perhaps there is little or no cognitive activity involved in dissonance reduction. I hasten to add that I am suggesting no such thing. What I am suggesting is that the affective components of dissonance phenomena have been neglected (aside from the recent resurgence concerning the state of dissonance itself), and it is possibly time to look more carefully at the interplay of cognitive and affective factors. It is certainly possible to understand at least some dissonance reduction phenomena in terms of the affect, not cognition, associated with the attitude (e.g., Simon, Greenberg, & Brehm, 1995). Whether or not the cognition might follow change in affect is an interesting question.

More generally, I have the impression that the mix of cognitive and affective factors constitutes a fertile field for social psychological cultivation. I am pleased that recent trends in social psychological research have been in this direction, and I'm confident that contributors to the present volume as well as many other young investigators in the field will contribute to a better understanding of how affect and cognition intermingle to influence behavior.

REFERENCES

Brehm, J. W. (1999). The intensity of emotion. *Personality and Social Psychology Review, 3,* 2–22.

Beauvois, J.-L., & Joule, R.-V. (1996). *A radical dissonance theory.* London: Taylor & Francis, Inc.

Festinger, L. (1957). *A theory of cognitive dissonance.* Stanford, CA: Stanford University Press.

Festinger, L. (1964). *Conflict, decision and dissonance.* Stanford, CA: Stanford University Press.

Pantaleo, G. (1999). *Beyond dissonance reduction? Forced compliance and the internalization of multiple perspectives.* Poster presented at the 12th General Meeting of the European Association for Experimental Social Psychology, Oxford, England.

Simon, L., Greenberg, J., & Brehm, J. W. (1995). Trivialization: The forgotten mode of dissonance reduction. *Journal of Personality and Social Psychology, 68,* 247–260.

Wicklund, R. A., & Brehm, J. W. (2002). *Internalization of multiple perspectives or dissonance reduction.* Manuscript submitted for publication.

Jack Brehm's PhD Students

Duke University

Rick Archer
Lenore Behar
Tom Hammock
Bob Jones
Russell Jones
Gerald Leventhal
Matiur Rahman
John Sensenig
Larry Severance
David Smith
Judith Whatley
Bob Wicklund
Sharon Wolfe
Steve Worchel
Camille Wortman

University of Kansas

Paul Biner
Beverly Brummett
Silvana D'Anello
Luis Esqueda
Jeff Greenberg
Tom Hill
Becky Huselid
Laura Leviton
Tom Pyszczynski
Bruce Roberson
Elizabeth Self
Linda Silka
Paul Silvia
Stephanie Smith
Sheldon Solomon
Lynne Steinberg
Challenger Vought
Rex Wright

Author Index

A

B

C

D

E

F

G

H

I

J

K

L

M

N

O

P

Q

R

S

T

U

V

W

Y

Z

Subject Index

A

B

D

E

F

G

H

I

J

K

L

M

N

O

P

R

S